SERVANT OF EMPIRE

THOMAS WILSON BRACKEN:

SERVANT OF EMPIRE

Martin Gibson

HAYLOFT PUBLISHING

First published in 2009
by Hayloft Publishing Ltd, South Stainmore,
Kirkby Stephen, Cumbria, CA17 4DJ

tel: 017683 42300
email: books@hayloft.eu
web: www.hayloft.eu

ISBN 1 904524 71 0

CAP data for this title are available from the British Library

Designed, printed and bound in the EU

Papers used by Hayloft are natural, recyclable products made
from wood grown in sustainable forests.
The manufacturing processes conform to the environmental
regulations of the country of origin.

CONTENTS

LIST OF ILLUSTRATIONS

PREFACE

As I write this, Victorian England seems very far distant: a pre-eminently great and powerful nation, in possession of a vast Empire; sometimes swaggeringly self-confident, invariably disdainful of its rivals and firmly believing that its civilisation was the pinnacle of mankind's achievements.

But how do we define the Victorian period? Did it start at once on the Queen's accession in 1837 and end on the day of her death in 1901? Indeed can such a long and eventful period of time be characterised with a single title? Certainly most would agree that by the middle of the Queen's reign the era had got into its swing.

For the Queen herself the 1860s included the greatest watershed in the form of the death of Albert Prince Consort in December 1861 – an event that cast its shadow over the remaining 40 years of her reign. His death also illustrates that whatever the era's great achievements in commerce, manufacturing, engineering, transport, science and the arts, the field of medicine lagged far behind. Then as now it was unclear what had killed the Prince. Was it typhoid and the Windsor drains or some form of abdominal cancer? The doctors could not agree, let alone effectively treat or cure him; and the Queen would suffer many more bereavements among her children and grandchildren after 1861. Death was an omnipresent and visible feature of Victorian England for both the highest and the lowest in the land.

The Queen, on returning to Windsor's Blue Room to find her husband had just expired, exclaimed, "Oh, this is death. I know it. I have seen this before." Her attendant courtiers admired her initial, quiet submission to the Divine will. Perhaps this precariousness of life maintained the people's traditional religious devotion through what was otherwise a highly modernising era. The Queen constructed the Frogmore Mausoleum to house the Prince's mortal remains and over the door had inscribed in Latin, 'Farewell most beloved. Here at length, I shall rest with thee, with thee in Christ I shall rise again.' The Queen initially desired death, the after-life and the reunion of her spirit with Albert's and many of her subjects would have agreed with her that Heaven certainly involved a recognisable form of reunion with former loved ones.

The great majority still adhered to the doctrines of the Church of England and its clergy were immensely influential and significant figures across the country. Their churches were filled on Sundays, and their sermons and other theological writing often published. They dominated the country's education system at all levels and many of them were brilliant scholars and academics.

My great-grandfather, Thomas Wilson Bracken, was born into this world, in Westmorland in 1865. Westmorland would remain a source of loyalty and affection throughout his life. One of the Queen's 39 historic English counties, its name first appears in written documents in 966 as 'Westmoringaland' and its county status was formalised in 1226. Almost 650 years later, in 1974, it was swept away by a Conservative Government. Its sister county Cumberland also went and the area of the two, plus parts of Lancashire and Yorkshire, were merged to form Cumbria.

Both Queen Victoria and Thomas Wilson would have had something to say about that reform. In 1897 the Queen rapidly dismissed the idea of even temporarily moving the statue of Queen Anne from outside St. Paul's Cathedral, so as to make more room for her outdoor Diamond Jubilee service. She conveyed her objection to her Conservative Prime Minister with the words, "It might some day be suggested that my statue should be moved, which I would much dislike!" The proposed removal was hastily dropped.

Westmorland was a county of mountains, moorland and fells and included the major part of the Lake District. The Industrial Revolution had largely bypassed the county and it was without a manufacturing base. Its parishes were predominantly agricultural as they had been since their creation. As the nineteenth century progressed the county was increasingly traversed by railways, enabling its stunning natural landscape to be accessible to and admired by the rest of the population. Its combined possession of some of the finest upland shooting in England and a large number of great landed estates, such as Lowther, in the north and Underley, in the south, ensured it was visited annually by royalty and by the country's political and social elites.

Steam, based on the country's great mineral wealth, powered the era's infrastructure. Steam-driven trains performed a variety of duties ranging from transport at the coal mines to conveying the fashionable on holiday to Westmorland. Equally, the railway carried many of the rural poor to the wharves of Liverpool and Glasgow, from where steam ships took them to new lives in the colonies of Canada, Australia, New Zealand and elsewhere. Many of these emigrants would help create a greater England across the world.

The last great unexplored continent was Africa and to this the Victorians increasingly turned. Their interest was not merely about sourcing raw materials to feed their hungry factories. Explorers and missionaries who entered the continent's interior for the first time brought back alarming stories of superstition, paganism, slavery and even human sacrifice. These could not be overlooked by a largely Protestant and evangelical population or their like-minded governments.

As a result Africa was seen as presenting the best remaining opportunity for Empire-building. Colonial officers were despatched to export a Victorian model of civil government while the Church of England through the Church Missionary Society exported the Victorian model of Christianity. Following on their heels were the traders and merchants who pressed for yet greater involvement to secure their emerging markets. Increasingly they called for railways to be built to transport them, their goods and exports.

Certain of their moral purpose, all of these Empire-building groups suffered disease and even death with equanimity. Many did so in the sure and certain hope of resurrection. If, regrettably, the Empire-building agents of Victorian England encountered African resistance or internal strife, the Queen's soldiers and sailors would be used because Victorian England sincerely believed it knew what was best.

England had achieved far greater prosperity than any other European nation and its aims, values and governance were far more civilized than theirs. So when serious competition in Africa emerged from other European nations, Victorian England resented their presence on the African continent – almost as an impertinence. Eventually these rivalries and tensions between European nations in Africa would become part of the origins of the First World War, which in many ways marks the end of the Victorian era.

As an engineer, a railway-builder, and a soldier, Thomas Wilson's life was at the epicentre of all this. Although he outlived Queen Victoria by over 30 years he was in spirit a Victorian to the day he died.

How very different Victorian England was.

Martin Gibson
London, 2008

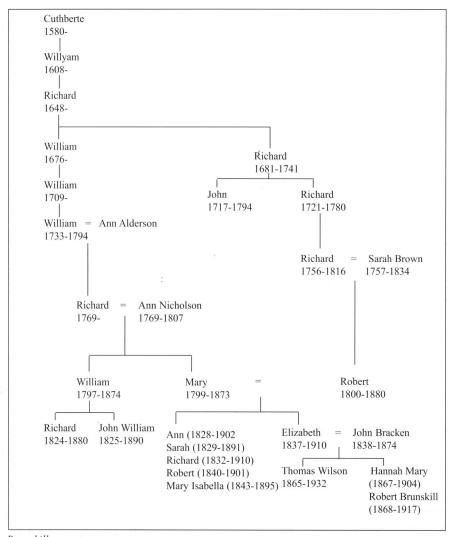

Brunskill ancestry.

1 – THE BRUNSKILLS OF STAINMORE

The Romans took until 75AD to complete their occupation of Britain, and in very short order established a road network that is still with us. Britannia, like their home land, has a spine of hills running north-south down its middle – in modern Italy, the Appenines; in England, the Pennines. Finding easy routes across this mountain range was always a challenge. Among a very small number of cross-routes was the Stainmore pass, which had been in use since the Bronze Age, and remains with us as the A66. Here they established a camp, Verterae, which became a significant trading post on this east-west route. The Saxons named it Burgh, a corruption of the word borough, and in modern times it is one of several Broughs in the British Isles.

From Roman Britain to the eighteenth century the physical state of the road through Brough was probably pretty atrocious until Parliament autho-rised the construction of turnpike roads in the old county of Westmorland. In 1774 the turnpike road from Bowes over Stainmore to Brough and Appleby was opened and at the same time the 'Fly' stage coach commenced running over Stainmore between London and Glasgow.[1] By 1791 when *The Universal British Directory* was published Brough was a significant coaching town:

> *Its being situated on the great road from London to Glasgow and the southern parts of Scotland and North of Ireland (crossing at Port Patrick) occasions the town to be much frequented by travellers. It has two very good inns, viz. the Swan… and the New Inn… to the latter of which inns arrives, every morning about nine o'clock, the Glasgow mail-coach from the South; and another arrives every day, at the same inn, from the North, about two o'clock in the afternoon.*

In the 1850s when the railways arrived in the area Brough was by-passed and like many other towns left off the rail network, it declined as a result. The station serving Brough was at Barras, three and a half miles away to the south-east. Barras was not a village or even a hamlet but before the railway is variously referred to as a house or farm, sometimes both and sometimes neither. Since the mid-1830s it had been the family home of Robert Brunskill (1800-1880) his wife Mary (1799-1873) and their six children. When Robert and Mary married at Brough in June 1827 they already shared the same surname. Robert's great-great-grandfather was Mary's great-great-great-grandfather. Their common ancestor was baptised in Brough church on 11 March 1648. From the mid-seventeenth century to the late eighteenth century these two branches of the Brunskill family moved nowhere but remained near neighbours and yeoman[2] farmers at Oxenthwaite and Upmanhow respectively. Robert's and Mary's parents are both listed by the Parish Constable in the surviving Stainmore return for the December 1787 census of Westmorland. From this return it appears that Robert's parents at Upmanhow were the more affluent in that they employed two servants, whereas Mary's grandparents at Oxenthwaite had none and this may explain why her father left the area and farming in his early twenties to become an officer of the Excise. Confusingly each of their fathers was named Richard – something of a favourite Brunskill name.

The Excise, not be confused with the Customs, had been established to collect a duty on home produced goods by Parliament in 1643 as a temporary expedient to pay for the parliamentary army. Like so many 'temporary taxes' the duty is effectively still with us. Initially it covered beer, spirits, cider and soap but by 1794 it had been extended to cover such necessities as bricks, candles, glass, paper and a variety of other basic goods. Its impact was highly regressive and its collectors were highly unpopular but nonetheless a career in the Excise was still a most attractive one with far more applicants than vacancies.

Dr Johnson's definition of 'Excise' in his dictionary of 1755 as 'a hateful tax levied upon commodities and adjudged not by the common judges of property, but by wretches hired by those to whom the excise is paid' illustrates the unpopularity of the tax and its collectors. As both the rates and coverage of the tax grew to pay for the almost continuous war against Revolutionary, and then Napoleonic, France, evasion and smuggling became rife.

It was into this Excise environment that Richard Brunskill made his entry in the 1790s. He first appears in the minutes of the Board of the Excise in January 1794 aged 24 when on the dismissal of his predecessor he was, on an annual salary of £50, made a temporary assistant to cover the winter candle making season in Kirkham, Lancashire. With spring and the longer days he was in Excise speak 'dropd' but he evidently had passed through this probationary period to the satisfaction of his superiors for in June 1794 he was given his commission as a full excise officer with a salary of £60 a year. That he was commissioned as an officer suggests that his job was similar to that of an army officer and the Librarian and Archivist of H. M. Customs and Excise[3] has compared the eighteenth century excise officer favourably with their contemporary officers in the army. Their pay and prospects were good and uniquely the Excise ran a pension scheme for retired and invalided officers. Also, like the army, the career was not without danger and Richard would have carried both a sword and a pistol to protect himself and the revenue he was assessing and recording.

Prior to 1794 he would have trained under an existing excise officer and been certified to the Board of the Excise as being 'healthy, free from debt and likely to make a good officer.' This certificate would have been provided by at least one Collector who was responsible for the collection in his administrative area. Each Collection was loosely based on the county boundaries. There were 39 Collectors outside London in England and Wales and each Collection was divided into districts headed by a supervisor. The districts consisted of divisions within towns and cities and rides for the rural areas outside. Division officers made their rounds on foot whereas ride officers as the name suggests, rode around their designated area of the countryside. Richard Brunskill was a ride officer throughout his Excise career as was his contemporary the poet Robert Burns, who was an Excise officer in Dumfries from 1789 to his death in 1796. Burns wrote of the arduous duties of the excise ride officer, "Five days in the week, or four at least I must be on horseback and very frequently ride thirty or forty miles ere I return; besides four different kinds of book-keeping to post every day."[4]

As Burns indicates the task was not simply one of collecting money but of effectively continuously auditing the manufacturers by measuring the contents of moulds, vats and barrels so as to ensure that all the end product was recorded and taxed without being secretly squirrelled away.

Another feature of work in the Excise was the frequent changes or 'removes' of station both within the same Collection and even to other Collections far distant. Richard Brunskill moved 'rides' six times within the Lancaster Collection between 1794 and 1811 taking him from Burnley in the south to Kendal in the north. His movements were more frequent than some but all officers were subject to a maximum of five years in any one station. This was in part for the officers' own protection but also because the Board in London were anxious to minimise opportunities for bribery and corruption by ensuring that officers and local brewers and manufacturers did not become too well acquainted. Similarly if an officer married within his ride he would automatically be moved to a new ride area.

As a result Richard Brunskill was never to serve in the Brough area of his birth and upbringing and was only to return there for his marriage to Ann Nicholson, a weaver's daughter and Stainmore neighbour, in Brough church on 8 February 1796. After the marriage she left the area with him for Ingleton, Yorkshire and thereafter as the baptisms of their four children in a variety of parishes testify she and they followed him from post to post. She died, almost certainly during childbirth, in 1807 aged 37. Her music book dated 1783 containing the words and tunes of various hymns and psalms has survived – doubtless treasured by her eldest daughter Mary who was eight years old when her mother died and who later wrote her mother's Nicholson ancestry in its back cover.

According to the Board minutes on Tuesday 22 January 1811, the Commissioners of the Excise in Broad Street, London spent a good part of their meeting discussing Richard Brunskill's misconduct as reported to them by his supervisor and the Lancaster Collector. The long list of complaints over two months includes loitering, misrecording, absenteeism and even absconding with his books. The language used seems highly intemperate and includes the Collector's accusation that:

> the said Brunskill has so wholly given himself up to drinking and idleness and a disregard to business that the revenue is by no means secure in his hands.

Given such a damning report it is scarcely surprising that the Commissioners dismissed him. However feeling the loss of pay which the Treasury had increased by £15 a year in 1800 and which rose again to £100 per annum just after his dismissal, he successfully petitioned for reinstatement after four months without work. Not all petitioners were reinstated but his was a first offence and there had been no allegation of fraud or dishonesty. Given their frequent contact with brewers and distillers, drunkenness and its consequences were common in the Excise and were not regarded too seriously. His reinstatement though was not immediate and depended upon him accepting the next vacancy irrespective of its location. Such a vacancy arose in December 1811 in the Northwich, Cheshire Collection at Tarporley and Richard spent five years there before being transferred to Knutsford. In May 1817 he was moved to the Shropshire collection where he served in Wenlock, Wellington and Newport before being retired with a pension aged 60 in September 1829. He had served the Excise for almost 35 years enduring the difficulties caused by the long war with France and the economic dislocation which followed 1815.

Before the railways most people in England rarely travelled more than a few miles from the town or village of their birth but those employed by the Excise and their families were a notable exception. Therefore when Mary Brunskill left Shropshire for Westmorland and her marriage to her distant cousin at Brough she was a very well travelled 28 year old. By comparison to her future husband Robert who had spent all of his 26 years on the same Stainmore farm at Gillses she was cosmopolitan. Their marriage was almost certainly effectively an arranged one for they can have had few opportunities

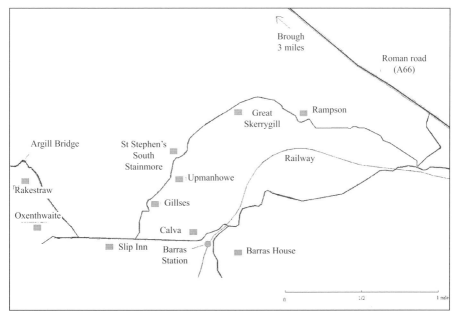

Sketch map of Stainmore.

to meet and any local marriage by her in Shropshire may not have found favour with her father's Collector boss.

Although Robert Brunskill and his parents accorded with the usual contemporary parochial standards, his father's uncle John Brunskill (1717-1794), was even more well-travelled than his excise officer cousin. In October 1737 he had left his father's farm at Upmanhow for admission to Pembroke College, Cambridge.[5] He acquired his BA in the summer of 1742. In the December following he was ordained a deacon by the Bishop of Lincoln in St. Margaret's, Westminster, and then a year later the Bishop of Rochester ordained him a priest in the Henry VII Chapel of Westminster Abbey. Two days afterwards he was licensed as curate of Overton Waterville in Huntingdonshire.[6] Overton Waterville is now known as Orton Waterville and is a south-western suburb of Peterborough. The Rev. John Brunskill remained the incumbent there for six years but after 1749 it is unclear where his later parishes were but it is clear that after a long life of service to the Church he was buried at Brough aged 76 in 1794.

In even earlier records the Brunskill family's presence in the parish of Brough-under-Stainmore is readily confirmed by numerous sources although before the eighteenth century their name is often written 'Brunskell'. They are shown as having paid the Hearth Tax for Westmorland there in 1674. Earlier still in 1661 'Willyam Brunskell' was one of the church wardens who along with their decidedly non-puritan vicar reinstituted bell ringing and other pre-Interregnum church ceremonies as soon as they were free to.[7] About 150 years earlier the four bells had been presented by Willyam's ancestor John Brunskill, yeoman of Stainmore. The church tower at Brough was built in 1513 by Thomas Blenkinsop of Helbeck and the story behind John Brunskill's presentation of the bells, shortly after the tower was built, is described in Nicolson & Burn's *History and Antiquities of the Counties of Westmorland and Cumberland* published in London in 1777:

> *Concerning these bells at Brough, there is a tradition, that they were given by one Brunskill, who lived upon Stainmore, in the remotest part of the parish, and had a great many cattle. One time it happened that his bull fell a bellowing, which in the dialect of the country is called cruning (this being the genuine Saxon word to denote that vociferation). Whereupon he said to one of his neighbours, Hearest thou how loud this*

bull crunes? If these cattle should all crune together, might they not be heard from Brough hither? He answered, yea. Well then, says Brunskill, I'll make them all crune together. And he sold them all; and with the price thereof he bought the said bells. There is a monument in the body of the church, in the fourth wall, between the highest and second windows; under which it is said the said Brunskill was the last that was interred.

Aside from the monument in Brough Church, John Brunskill's gift is commemorated in Robert Southey's[8] 1828 poem *Brough Bells*. Southey, who had been made Poet Laureate in 1813, wrote the poem at Greta Hall, Keswick, his home for 40 years. He was a friend of both Coleridge and Wordsworth: the trio came to be known as 'the Lake School'. He based his Brough Bells poem on Nicolson and Burn's account and he plainly knew that the Brunskills remained a local family when composing it. Southey's version opens with a conversation between the poet and his companion while walking in the fells surrounding Brough:

> *One day to Helbeck I had stroll'd*
> *Among the Crossfell hills,*
> *And resting on its rocky grove*
> *Sat listening to the rills;*
>
> *The while to their sweet undersong*
> *The birds sang blithe around,*
> *And the soft west wind awoke the wood*
> *To an intermitting sound.*
>
> *Louder or fainter as it rose,*
> *Or died away, was borne*
> *The harmony of merry bells,*
> *From Brough that pleasant morn.*
>
> *'Why are the merry bells of Brough,*
> *My friend, so few?' said I,*
> *'They disappoint the expectant ear,*
> *Which they should gratify.*

'One, two, three, four; one, two, three, four;
'Tis still one, two, three, four.
Mellow and silvery are the tones;
But I wish the bells were more!'

'What! Art thou critical?' quoth he;
'Eschew that heart's disease
That seeketh for displeasure where
The intent hath been to please.

'By those four bells there hangs a tale,
Which being told, I guess,
Will make thee hear their scanty peal
With proper thankfulness.

'Not by the Cliffords were they give,
Nor by the Tuftons line;
Thou hearest in that peel the crune
Of old John Brunskill's kine.

Southey then proceeds to recount Brunskill's conversation with his Stainmore neighbour about his noisy bull and his resolution to sell the cattle to endow the church with bells, before continuing:

'So while the merry Bells of Brough
For many an age ring on,
John Brunskill will remember'd be,
When he is dead and gone;

'As one who in his latter years,
Contented with enough,
Gave freely what he well could spare
To buy the Bells of Brough.

'Thus it hath proved: three hundred years
Since then have passed away,
And Brunskill's is a living name
Among us to this day.

'More pleasure,' I replied, 'shall I
From this time forth partake,
When I remember Helbeck woods,
For old John Brunskill's sake.

'He knew how wholesome it would be,
Among those wild wide fells,
And upland vales, to catch, at times,
The sound of Christian bells;

'What feelings and what impulses
Their cadence might convey,
To herdsman or to shepherd boy,
Whiling in indolent employ
The solitary day;

'That when his brethren were convened
To meet for social prayer,
He, too, admonish'd by the call,
In spirit might be there.

'Or when a glad thanksgiving sound,
Upon the winds of Heaven,
Was sent to speak a Nation's joy,
For some great blessing given –

'For victory by sea or land,
And happy peace at length;
Peace by his country's valour won,
And 'stablish'd by her strength;

'When such exultant peals were borne
Upon the mountain air,
The sound should stir his blood, and give
An English impulse there.'

Such thoughts were in the old man's mind,
When he that eve look'd down
From Stainmore's side on Borrodale,
And on the distant town.

And had I store of wealth, methinks,
Another herd of kine,
John Brunskill, I would freely give,
That they might crune with thine.

John Brunskill's association with Thomas Blenkinsop was not limited to the belfry of the impressive church tower. Seven years earlier in 1506 they co-operated to found an oratory or chantry chapel at Market Brough.[9] Blenkinsop supplied the ground at Gilgarth upon which the chapel was to be built by John Brunskill at a nominal annual rent of tuppence payable at Pentecost. As well as the chapel dedicated to St. Mary and St. Gabriel by the terms of Brunskill's agreement with Blenkinsop, a hospital was built alongside containing two beds for travellers and other poor people.

Brunskill's foundation was approved by both the Bishop of Carlisle and the Archbishop of York and two priests were engaged to sing and pray in the chapel for evermore, for the souls of all benefactors of the chapel and for the welfare of the living. In addition the priests were to teach the local children grammar and singing free of charge. A man and his wife were appointed to be the keepers of the ornaments of the chapel, the books of the school and the beds of the hospital.

The foundation of chantry schools was a common feature of fifteenth and early sixteenth century England. For example Roger Lupton, who was born in the parish of Sedbergh in 1456 the son of a tenant farmer, rose on the Church's back in the manner of Cardinal Wolsey, to be elected Provost of Eton in 1504. That ascent gave him the means to found a chantry school just like John Brunskill's in Sedbergh, in 1525.[10]

In Brough's case, the town's strategic location made it a significant trading centre as well as an important resting place for travellers who had either made or were about to make the long and arduous climb over Stainmore Pass between Westmorland and Yorkshire. As early as 1331 Brough gained its royal charter from Edward III[11] to hold a weekly market and an annual fair to commence two days before the Feast of St Matthew.[12] Almost 200 years later

Brough was a busy and thriving market town and the new chapel, to the consternation of the incumbent of Brough's earlier and main church, attracted considerable support. Soon the chapel was said to be the scene of miracles which were attested to by both the Abbot of Shap, who served as governor of the chapel, and the Bishop of Carlisle. In response pilgrims flocked to Market Brough and the chapel was further endowed with land in Westmorland, Cumberland, Yorkshire and Durham. The vicar of Brough's response to being deprived of both congregation and revenue is described in *Nicolson and Burn*:

> *the vicar of Brough... conceived himself much prejudiced thereby, and particularly in respect of the oblations which were given from him to the said chapel. Whereupon he set up the cross, and lighted up candles in the church at mid-time of the day, caused the bells to be rung, and cursed with bell, book and candle all those that should receive any oblation of them that resorted to the said chapel, or should give any encouragement unto the same. Brunskill the founder complained to the archbishop's court at York against the vicar... and obtained a sharp citation against him, censuring him as an abandoned wretch and inflated with diabolical venom for opposing so good a work. Notwithstanding which, the vicar appealed to the pope; and an agreement was made between the founder and him, by a composition of 20 shillings yearly to be paid to him and his successor vicars of Brough.*

Upon this basis the chapel continued until the dissolution of chantries under King Edward VI. The visiting Commissioners dismissed the singing priest but the other was retained to continue teaching grammar in the role of first master of the Free School with a Royal endowment of seven guineas eleven shillings and four pence out of the chapel's confiscated lands and revenues. The Crown continued to pay this endowment until 1874 when the old Free School was reorganised as a Board School under the Elementary Education Act of 1870.

Eleven years before the dissolution of chantries, Henry VIII's dissolution of the monasteries, together with the severance of the English Church from Rome, led to a serious popular uprising across the north of England. It was variously known as the 'Pilgrimage of Grace' or 'Northern Rebellion,' and Brough and its vicar Robert Thompson, played a significant part in it during 1536-1537. One of his crimes, for which he was arrested early in 1537, was praying for the Bishop of Rome and he was judged by the Duke of Norfolk as significant enough to be sent to the King in London. Other Westmerian rebels were dealt with more locally at Carlisle and among Norfolk's list of those condemned to die there is 'Christopher Blenkensoppe of Brough' and two others of 'Staynemore'. The name Brunskill or Brunskell does not appear in Norfolk's list[13] suggesting they wisely adapted their piety to the changed circumstances. The Vicar of Brough was spared but was imprisoned and interrogated in the Tower. Under interrogation he implicated Blenkinsop and told his interrogators, who included Cromwell, that he only prayed for the Pope under compulsion and while fearing for his life. On conviction he was sent to the King's Bench prison from where, late in 1537, he wrote to Cromwell begging him to intercede with the King, with the required fawning, that only his regard for Cromwell had kept him alive in the cold and hunger of prison.[14]

Almost 300 years later, in the *History, Directory and Gazetteer of Cumberland and Westmorland* of 1829 Robert Brunskill, now two years married, is listed as a farmer at Oxenthwaite. His elder brother John is listed as a yeoman farmer at Gillses where Robert was born in 1800 and where his father died in 1816. Another older brother is listed as farming at neighbouring Calva and his third older brother Edward is in occupation of their grandfather's farm at Upmanhow. All three of his elder brothers married but unlike his own, their marriages were to be either infecund or plagued with infant deaths and as a result the scale of the Brunskills' presence in the area declined markedly as the nineteenth century progressed.

In the same Directory the occupant of Barras is described as John Winskill but Robert Brunskill had moved there by 10 May 1837 when his third daughter Elizabeth was born there. The three older children Ann born 1828, Sarah 1829 and Richard 1832 were each noted in the baptism register as being 'of Oxenthwaite' where their mother's grandfather had been farming up to his death in 1794. Without a will or deeds it is not possible to say how the young married couple gained occupation of this farm after their marriage in 1827 or why they left it for Barras in the mid-1830s. Robert and Mary were to remain at Barras for the rest of their lives and their youngest two children Robert and Mary Isabella were also born there.

The initial size of Robert Brunskill's farm at Barras is hard to ascertain, as the 1841 census does not record this information, but by 1851 he is listed as having 100 acres and by 1861 this had grown to 119. For Westmorland, before mechanisation, this was a sizeable acreage for a mid-nineteenth century farmer. Even by 1870 only eighteen per cent of Westmorland land holdings were above 100 acres.[15] More locally the Stainmore parish agricultural return for 1870 contained 79 farms of which fifteen were above 100 acres with the commonest size being between 20 and 50 acres.[16]

Barras's principal claim to fame must be the view from there down the wide Eden valley towards Carlisle and the Solway Firth, framed on one side by the Lake District fells and by the peaks of the Pennines on the other. This view was allegedly immortalised in John Martin's[17] painting *The Plains of Heaven* which now hangs in Tate Britain. Certainly the similarity of Martin's sylvan landscape and the view from Barras is undeniable but the evidence that Martin conceived the painting there is anecdotal rather than documentary.[18]

Martin began the canvas measuring two by three metres in 1851 and took two years to complete it. In the event, it was to be his last work. Martin died while on a visit to the Isle of Man in 1854. The following year *The Plains of Heaven* along with *The Day of Judgment* and *The Great Day of his Wrath* caused a sensation when they were exhibited in London and across England on a regional tour. The text for the painting was Revelations 21:1 'And I saw a new heaven and a new earth' and it shows a celestial landscape where paradise is in the form of a wide and lush river valley filled with lakes and waterfalls and surrounded by mountains. A company of angels assembled on a rocky platform in the foreground look down upon paradise regained. If true that Martin conducted the preliminary sketches for the painting at Barras in 1851 it is easy to imagine the artist to have been the object of considerable fascination to the youngest three Brunskill children, Elizabeth aged thirteen, Robert ten and Mary Isabella seven, who were each described as 'scholars' on the 1851 census.

Not long after *The Plains of Heaven* was completed the paradise of the Vale of Eden was disturbed, not by the serpent's hiss but by the noise and smoke of the steam engine. In 1857 the South Durham and Lancashire Union Railway was formed with the object of building a trans-Pennine route over 50 miles from Bishop Auckland in Durham to Tebay in Westmorland. From the Stockton and Darlington Railway's existing line near Evenwood, the route of the new line passed through Barnard Castle and the junction of the existing line to Darlington, before passing over Stainmore summit at 1,370 feet, then descending to Barras,[19] where a station was built just below the Brunskill farm, and on to Kirkby Stephen and Tebay where it joined the existing Lancaster and Carlisle Railway.

The impact of the railway on the hitherto isolated farm at Barras cannot be exaggerated. Barras House is 1,250 feet above sea level and it was akin to building a railway adjacent to *Wuthering Heights*. Emily Bronte's novel spans the late eighteenth and early nineteenth centuries but both the Yorkshire and Westmorland moors and the lives their occupants lived were little changed fifty years later. The arrival of the railways was to change them forever. The Brunskills now had a train service on their doorstep to ferry them and their farm produce both east and west. Kirkby Stephen was now within minutes and Appleby and Barnard Castle were both easily accessible. Even Darlington and Durham were a day trip away. The proximity of the new railway to Robert Brunskill's farm at Barras is demonstrated by the list of owners and occupiers of the land through which the new railway was to pass which was submitted to Parliament in 1859. From this list four of Robert Brunskill's pastures or what the list referred to as 'Grass Fields' were affected along with an orchard or in Parliamentary speech a 'Plantation'. Interestingly between the 1861 and 1871 censuses Robert Brunskill's land acreage fell from 121 to 119 acres and this small diminution is probably accounted for by the building of the railway across his land.

On 25 August 1857 the first sod of the Stainmore section of the railway was cut by the 2nd Duke of Cleveland[20] at Kirkby Stephen. Ironically his father the 1st Duke (1766-1842), a famous sportsman, had successfully opposed the first proposal for a Stockton to Darlington railway in 1820 because its proposed course would interfere with a favourite fox cover.[21]

For the next four years until the line was opened on 7 August 1861 Stainmore and Barras would have been crowded by hundreds of peripatetic railway workers attracted by the high rates of pay on offer. Predictably, in such a remote rural area, high wages led to drunkenness, disorder, fights and petty theft. The Railway Company's grudging response was to pay for a single constable to try to keep order. In these conditions Robert Brunskill's four unmarried daughters probably had their movements from the house severely curtailed. Ranging in age from 33 to 17 it seems remarkable that none of them were married and with one exception, all were still living at home on census night 1861. However the general disinclination to marry also seems to have applied to Robert Brunskill's two sons aged 28 and 20 who were similarly single and still tied to their parents' farm and home.

Why they did not marry, and what Robert and Mary Brunskill, now in their 60s, made of it, is hard to guess. It may well have been a symptom of a declining parish population or social changes which had caused a diminution in the size of the yeoman class of small owner-occupiers of land. Despite these changes the 1860s were something of a 'golden age' for English agriculture and the price of the meat and dairy produce which Barras Farm produced rose significantly between the mid-century and the late 1870s. The parish's agricultural statistics for 1870 illustrate the wealth of Stainmore's meat, wool and to a lesser extent milk production. There were recorded 7,057 sheep, 4,468 lambs, 740 beef cattle including calves, 499 cows and heifers in milk or calf and 79 pigs of all kinds. In addition there is evidence of significant horse breeding - other than for agricultural use - and this was probably associated with the annual late September Brough Hill Fair.

The Fair had existed since the 1330s. In the 1790s it was described as being "well known through the kingdom... where immense numbers of cattle, horses and all sorts of goods are exposed for sale."[22] From the description of it in the *Post Office Directory of 1873* it was evidently still thriving then:

> *the annual fair, held on Brough hill, two miles north-by-west from the town has become justly celebrated and prosperous: it is kept on the 30th of September and on the 1st of October when that extensive common is crowded with people and booths, and stalls for woolen cloth and other merchandise, and numbers of horses, sheep and other cattle.*

As well as the annual fair a weekly market was held at Brough on a Thursday and in February 1926 Thomas Wilson wrote an account of this to the *Penrith Observer* based upon an old handbill dated 1858 which he had acquired from his uncle Richard Brunskill together with his recollection of the market during 'the seventies':

> *This ancient weekly market, held on Thursdays, was established Toll Free for ever, in the year 1331, and has, since that time, been kept more or less in existence.*

The increase in farm prosperity fuelled by the railway's ability speedily to transport agricultural produce and, in Brough's case, its remarkably long-lived medieval weekly market and annual fair probably explains how the profits of the farm were sufficient to keep all eight Brunskills at Barras. With regard to space, it was evidently not a problem, for in addition to Robert, his wife and children, Robert's widowed sister-in-law Betty Brunskill aged 64, together with a schoolmaster lodger are recorded as being present on the 1861 census form.

The apparent aversion to marriage at Barras was to last until 24 September 1864 when their third daughter Elizabeth was married at the age of 27 in Brough Church. Her younger sister Mary Isabella now aged twenty acted as her chief bridesmaid and witnessed her signature on the marriage certificate. The man she married was John Bracken, a 25-year-old tenant farmer's son from Firbank in Westmorland. Firbank is on the west side of the river Lune west of Sedbergh and approximately twenty miles away from Barras to the north-east.

The Brunskills of Barras were obviously pleased enough by the marriage to announce it in their local newspaper, the *Penrith Observer and Appleby and Kirkby Stephen News* and in the 4 October 1864 edition the following marriage announcement appeared:

At Brough, on the 24th ult., by the Rev. S. Inman, John Bracken, Fair Bank (sic), Sedbergh to Elizabeth third daughter of Robert Brunskill, Barras.

2 – A DOUBTFUL PATERNITY

The Bracken family farm in Firbank was Newfield, where John Bracken had been born on Christmas Eve 1838 to Thomas and Hannah Bracken. At his birth Newfield was the farm of his grandfather John Bracken who died there aged 76 in June 1840. Thomas was the youngest of seven children but nonetheless in John's will proved before the Bishop of Chester's surrogate three weeks later he left Thomas "all my farming stock, such as cows, heifers, and heath going sheep, with all my husbandry gear such as carts, wheels, plows (sic) and harrows with every other article belonging to husbandry." In return for this bequest Thomas was obliged to pay his mother Elizabeth an annuity of £5 until her death aged 80 in 1849. As was common at the time their landlord was quite content to transfer the tenancy of the farm from father to son.

It is unclear when Thomas's parents had first become tenants of Newfield farm. The baptism of their children in the neighbouring parish of Sedbergh may suggest that they only moved there after 1807 when their youngest son was born. In 1833 Thomas married Hannah Wilson in Firbank Church. She was a neighbouring tenant farmer's daughter who had been born in the parish in 1813.

On the 1851 census return Thomas Bracken's farm is described as being a farm of 77 acres and his eldest son John aged twelve is still in school. By 1861 the farm had expanded to 94 acres and by now both John, now 22, and his younger brother Edmund aged 20 are working on it.

The town of Sedbergh is three miles away from Newfield farm and this proximity almost certainly explains Elizabeth Brunskill's meeting of her future husband. Her maternal uncle William Brunskill (1797-1874) had, helped by the connections of his excise officer father, served an apprenticeship as a glazier and established a successful glazing business in Sedbergh by 1820. By glazing local churches, chapels and the homes of the local gentry and tradesmen his business expanded sufficiently by 1834 to merit two entries in Pigot's Directory for the town where as well as being described as 'painter, glazier and plumber' he is also described as 'druggist & glass, earthenware and toy dealer' and by the 1841 census he was living in Main Street, Sedbergh. His two sons Richard and John William joined his business and its combination of glass and chemicals awakened an early interest in photography in them.

In 1851 Frederick Scott Archer (1813-1857) had invented the use of glass for photographic negatives which allowed for a much finer definition than the earlier paper Daguerreotype images. Within seven years the Brunskill brothers

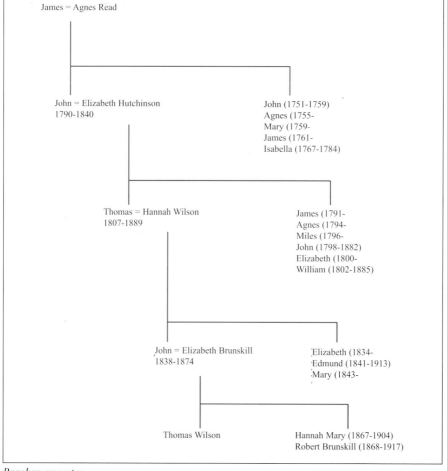

Bracken ancestry

Richard and John William or 'R & J W Brunskill' as they were to trade, were taking street scenes of Sedbergh. By the early 1860s they opened a photographic studio there and photographed their first cousin Elizabeth Brunskill and at least one of her sisters on a visit to Sedbergh. Two of these glass ambrotypes in their leather cases with a black velvet background which makes the silver nitrate on the glass appear positive[23] have survived. This coincidence of her Sedbergh photographer cousins who by 1864 were already local celebrities and the Bracken farm at Newfield almost certainly explains Elizabeth's marriage to John Bracken in September 1864.

Five months and a day after the marriage, Elizabeth gave birth to a boy. He was born at Barras and on the day of his birth, 25 February 1865, he was baptised Thomas Wilson in St. Stephen's, Stainmore. Throughout his life he was to use both his forenames and his signature contained both of his initials. Therefore, henceforth I shall refer to him as Thomas Wilson.

His swift baptism may have been because he was sickly but even if he was not, given the contemporary rate of infant mortality, it was almost certainly done to avoid the much feared possibility of death before baptism. Premature live births were not uncommon in mid-Victorian England. Famously the Princess of Wales gave birth two months prematurely to Prince Albert Victor on 8 January 1864. He was a likely future king weighing just three pounds and Queen Victoria was horrified by such an inauspicious royal start. However there was a world of difference between seven and five months and it is almost certain that Elizabeth and John Bracken's son had been conceived before their marriage.

Was this the reason that his mother chose to leave Newfield and return to her family home for the birth? Would it have been an event worthy of serious concealment in a rural farming community like Firbank? And after two months or so away, would returning with a young baby really have fooled anyone? The third question posed does not fall to be answered because, although Elizabeth Bracken did eventually return to the area, Thomas Wilson did not accompany her and remained a stranger to Firbank until he was old enough and independent enough to decide his movements for himself.

The journey from Firbank to Barras was approximately twenty miles but even when travelling along the newly laid railway tracks it was not an entirely easy one. The nearest station to Firbank was just outside Sedbergh, a mile and a half away to the south-east, and from there the northbound line joined what remains the West Coast main line at Lowgill and ran through the spectacular Lune gorge to Tebay. At Tebay a change of trains was required for Kirkby Stephen and Barras. Evidently for some reason Elizabeth Bracken felt the need to leave the Bracken farm and make this journey in advance of her confinement. The hostility of her husband's parents to her early pregnancy seems the most likely explanation. Aside from their own censoriousness their next door neighbour was the vicar of Firbank and there was probably a strong desire to conceal the birth from him.

At the time Firbank was a poor curacy carved out of the ancient rectory of Kirkby Lonsdale. The Vicarage House or Ivy Cottage as it is variously described in the censuses in no way resembles the classic Victorian vicarage and is so close to Newfield farm as to be almost touching. The cry of a young baby in 1865 would most certainly have been audible to the incumbent the Rev. William Clarke and his teenage son Henry[24] who in 1905 would become the first Archbishop of Melbourne.

How long Elizabeth remained at Barras after the birth is unclear but when she travelled to Kirkby Stephen just under a fortnight later to register the birth she gave her address to the registrar as Barras, Stainmore, rather than the Bracken farm in Firbank. By 1867 she had certainly been re-united with her husband as they were both photographed that year by her photographer cousins. Perhaps tellingly there is no image of the infant Thomas Wilson.

In June 1867 Elizabeth gave birth to a second child, a daughter Hannah Mary and then in November 1868 a second son named Robert Brunskill Bracken was born. Hannah and Robert were not born at Barras or at Newfield but at a Bracken cousin's farm, Grassrigg. Grassrigg farmhouse still consists of two semi-detached cottages a mile away from Newfield but in the parish of Killington where Hannah and Robert were baptised. The indications are that following her return from Barras Elizabeth and John lived in one of these cottages and John farmed with his cousin until they acquired their own farm at Moss Foot, Firbank in 1869. They did so from John Bracken's maternal grandparents Edmund and Mary Wilson. His mother Hannah was their only child and in March 1869 when Mary Wilson died there aged 80, her widower husband Edmund aged 82 moved the short distance to Newfield to live with his daughter and son-in-law. Thereby Moss Foot and its accompanying 50 acres was vacated for his eldest grandson, his wife and young family.

Moss Foot is a most attractive and well built farmhouse set back from the road, facing south and with stunning views down the upper Lune valley. Like Grassrigg in 1869 it was part of the Ingmire Hall estate which had been acquired through marriage by the Cornish family of Upton in the seventeenth century. Since then the wealth and status of the Upton family and their estate of Ingmire had grown considerably. John Upton had been MP for Westmorland from 1761-1768.[25] His son, also John, established significant cotton mills in Sedbergh before making two socially advantageous marriages. The wealth generated by his cotton interests made a significant contribution to the fortunes of William Brunskill's Sedbergh business and the expansion of the Ingmire estate. In 1858 his grand-daughter Florence Anne had married Clement Cottrell-Dormer of Rousham, Oxfordshire, leading to the union of two large estates when in 1876 his wife inherited the Ingmire estate. As a mark of the importance of this inheritance to them they changed their name by Royal Licence to Upton-Cottrell-Dormer. Thereafter they continued to expand the Ingmire estate by buying up farms in the area. They were easily the largest local landowner and were to fill one of the few gaps in the estate

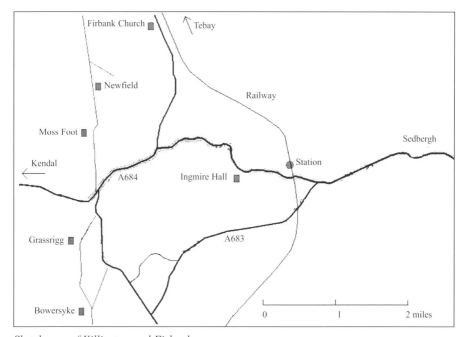

Sketch map of Killington and Firbank.

when in 1878 Mrs Upton-Cottrell-Dormer bought Newfield farm for £2,000 and thereby acquired Thomas Bracken as a tenant.

The acquisition by his parents of Moss Foot farm in 1869 had no obvious effect on Thomas Wilson (now four years old) who remained at Barras with his Brunskill grandparents. This was just one, if to us rather fundamental, distinction between his upbringing and those of his younger siblings. They each attended the village school at Firbank up to the maximum permitted age of thirteen. The Firbank School records survive and contain references to them both between 1874 and 1879. Their father was seemingly somehow involved in the school's governance, in that he is recorded as visiting the school to meet the school's external inspectors in October 1871. Nowhere in the records is there any reference to his eldest son being in the school. After Firbank School, Hannah and Robert were to marry into local farming families and remained in the Sedbergh area for the rest of their lives. Conversely their elder brother Thomas Wilson was educated to the age of seventeen and as such seems to have been pushed to higher and better things than a career in farming. He was to achieve far greater wealth and success, and spent all of his professional life outside Westmorland. Absent any other evidence this distinction might be referable to the eldest son's bounty but there is other evidence which may provide a far more fundamental explanation of the different lives they were to lead.

At the beginning of my research I had been told that Thomas Wilson was born and brought up on Stainmore but not until examining the census records for 1871 did it become clear that this meant he spent his boyhood away from his parents and siblings. The 1871 census entry for Barras lists Robert and Mary Brunskill, now in their 70s, together with their five adult and still unmarried children, a farm servant and their six-year-old Bracken grandson Thomas Wilson. The corresponding entry for the Bracken family, now living at Moss Foot farm in Firbank lists John and Elizabeth Bracken, their two children aged three and two respectively and two servants. Might an unaccompanied school holiday visit to his grandparents be the explanation for this separation? The answer is no because school terms were then based around the four quarters of the year and census night 1871 did not coincide with 25 March.

Ten years later in 1881 Thomas Wilson was similarly absent from Firbank and again listed with his Brunskill relatives and in that instance Easter fell two weeks after census night. The inference from the two census returns was confirmed by the contents of his obituary in the *Penrith Observer* of Tuesday, 13 December 1932 which stated: "He was a nephew of the late Mr Richard Brunskill, Barras, with whom he was in close association during the early part of his life." The remainder of the obituary makes no reference to either Firbank or John Bracken.

What was the reason for this family separation? The only immediate explanation relates to his pre-marital conception but for his parents effectively to give up their eldest son just because he was conceived outside wedlock seems an incredibly extreme reaction even for the 1860s. He did not bear the disadvantage of illegitimacy: his parents were married at his birth and his legal father John Bracken appears on his birth and marriage certificates and doubtless all other official forms he completed throughout his life. But was the problem that John Bracken was not his natural father? John Bracken either knew on his wedding day or very soon thereafter that his wife was pregnant and he also knew whether or not he was the father. If he was not, did he make it a condition of the marriage that his wife's child was born away from Firbank and raised by her family at Barras? This seems by far the most likely explanation. Exactly who knew what and when, will of course never now be established but the announcement of the wedding in the newspaper certainly suggests that the wedding was not a clandestine affair, by reason of the bride's condition. It may well indicate that Elizabeth's parents were ignorant of her situation until the reaction of her new husband and parents-in-law compelled Elizabeth to confide in them. In contrast, her parents' reaction was plainly both sympathetic and tolerant and they may have felt, in their childless world, that any grandchild was welcome, whatever the circumstances.

After 144 years it is quite impossible to speculate who his natural father was. By 1864 Barras was no longer an isolated farmhouse perched on the hillside overlooking the town of Brough and the old turnpike road from London to Glasgow. Barras railway station, which served Brough, was right next to the Brunskill farm and railway passengers and workers maintaining the line would have been a permanent if still novel feature of the area in the summer of 1864. In such an environment the encounter which led to his conception might have been anonymous and even non-consensual. Alternatively he may have been conceived in similar circumstances during his mother's visit to her Sedbergh relatives. Of course in a Victorian age which valued the appearance of respectability far more than anything approaching unpalatable reality, the names he was given could not have tied him more firmly to the Bracken family. Thomas was the name of his paternal grandfather and Wilson the maiden name of his paternal grandmother. However it would never have occurred to anyone to have chosen non-family names and left clues to a doubtful paternity and the reality was that he appears to have had little childhood or adolescent contact with anyone else named Bracken. Each of his Bracken grandparents died aged 83[26] and this meant that the average age at death of his four grandparents was almost 80. For people born either at the end of the eighteenth century or at the beginning of the nineteenth, this is a most impressive average. Seemingly the clean if often bracing Westmorland air was a great spur to longevity.

Whatever the full truth of his paternity and his strange upbringing away from his parents, it was not without its advantages. As well as his grandparents, he had two uncles and three aunts to help occupy him and, being the focus of so much attention, it is easy to imagine him as a precocious and slightly spoilt child. The advantages extended outside Barras House in that Stainmore School was of a higher order than the village school at Firbank. It had been founded by a local man made good: Sir Cuthbert Buckle, a vintner and Lord Mayor of London 1593-94 when he was knighted by Queen Elizabeth I.[27] The son of Christopher Buckle of Brough, he was born on Stainmore and walked 261 miles to London to make his fortune. Having done so he did not forget his roots and left a bequest to found a grammar school on Stainmore. The school was built by 1607 and in the following year was consecrated by the Bishop of Carlisle as a chapel of ease to the parish church at Brough. The chapel, eventually dedicated to St. Stephen, had the dual purpose of school and chapel and the incumbent was both curate and schoolmaster.

In 1699 it was further endowed by the Earl of Thanet[28] who settled land to augment the curate/schoolmaster's income, repaired the chapel and built a separate adjoining school. After this rebuilding the curate-cum-schoolmaster was one John Bracken who left £30 in his will of 1754, the interest on which to be used to buy books for the chapel, school books for use by poor children and to make payments to the poor of Stainmore[29] with "regard being had to those who have been most constant at Prayers and Sacrament." It seems unlikely that this Bracken was an ancestor of the Brackens of Firbank but Thomas Wilson certainly knew of his existence and would later joke that his was an 'honoured name' on Stainmore.[30]

In the early 1800s it became the practice of the curate to employ a school-master out of his stipend to do the teaching for him but the salary was generally insufficient to attract good teachers and when John Wharton M.A. arrived as Priest in Charge of St. Stephen's, Stainmore in 1866 he reverted to teaching the school himself.[31] He was if anything over-qualified to do so. A vicar's son, he was born in Appleby in 1834. He was educated at Appleby Grammar School where his father was the Latin Master and Queen's College, Oxford where, as Hastings Exhitioner, he took a first in classics in his Mods[32] in 1856. Two years later he obtained his B.A. and following his ordination he, by strange coincidence, became headmaster of another Appleby School, Appleby, Leicestershire, where he taught from 1861-1864.[33] After being widowed with two young sons he arrived in the Stainmore vicarage along with them and his spinster sister in 1866. He was to remain vicar of Stainmore for 37 years until he became vicar of Milburn three years before his death in 1906. As such he would have been a very significant figure in the lives of the Brunskills of Barras and of the young Thomas Wilson, who not only attended his school but, inspired by Wharton's church services, became and remained a devout practising Anglican throughout his life. According to Wharton's *Penrith Observer* obituary, while in 1850s Oxford he "took a deep interest in what might be called the after-effects of the Oxford Movement" and as a result "was distinctly High Church."

In an article written for the *Penrith Observer* in June 1922 Thomas Wilson rather obliquely referred to the Stainmore part of his education as follows:

> *Sir Cuthbert Buckle, Brough, a Lord Mayor (of London), in the later part of the reign of Queen Elizabeth, and who by his will dated June 28th 1594, left funds toward providing a school in his native parish… from this and the school house which the inhabitants built originated St. Stephen's Stainmore and the old Free Grammar School where the vicar taught as late as the seventies.*

Wharton, the vicar to whom he refers, was not alone in being a scholarly clergyman. For an area that now we would think of as isolated if not obscure, all of the local clergy were, from their entries in *Crockford's*, in modern terms highly educated. At around the same time the vicar of Brough, William Lyde, was a graduate of Queens' College, Cambridge where he had won a University Maths prize in 1851. After Cambridge he had gone to Bath where he had taught maths at King Edward's School until 1855. His curate Thomas Watson Anderson was another Queen's, Oxford, graduate as was the curate of Kirkby Stephen, Joseph Chapelhow. The vicar of Kirkby Stephen, James Simpson, had been a Scholar of University College, Durham, where he had won university prizes in Hebrew, Hellenistic Greek and Greek Theology before becoming a university lecturer at Durham. Nine years after his arrival at Kirkby Stephen he was made a D.C.L.[34] by the Archbishop of Canterbury in 1872 and two years later a Canon of Carlisle.

The profession of educator in the period prior to the 1870s was dominated by the schoolmaster-parson and the don-parson[35] but such a scholarly concentration in a remote part of Westmorland seems remarkable. The explanation behind this high calibre of clergy ministering to a largely rural and unfashionable population was in part the general improvement in the educational standard of the clergy which was one feature of the great Victorian religious revival and more specifically in Westmorland's case was obviously aided by the ancient connection the county had with Queen's College, Oxford.[36]

3 – THY WILL BE DONE

On Saturday 21 March 1874 a 35-year-old married man fell from a railway carriage between Lowgill and Tebay on the London and North Western Railway. He suffered severe head injuries, from which he died six days later. The man was John Bracken and the accident, his death and the subsequent inquest was extensively reported over three weeks in the *Westmorland Gazette*. On the day of the accident John Bracken had travelled by train to Kendal for market day[37] and in the early evening he took the train to Oxenholme accompanied by his gamekeeper friend James Mason. At Oxenholme they had some time before the train for Tebay arrived and they had a drink in the refreshment room.

The reports indicate how the Victorians were quite content to make long and time-consuming journeys by rail just to travel between neighbouring towns. Sedbergh is almost due east of Kendal and is now an easy, if steep journey by road but in order to travel between them by rail, it was necessary to proceed ten miles north to Tebay before changing to a south bound train destined for Ingleton which would leave the main line at Lowgill junction and proceed to Sedbergh, Kirkby Lonsdale and Ingleton.

Mason told the inquest jury that he had a glass of beer and his friend a squib[38] of something and when their train came in, the off-side of the carriage was facing the refreshment room. Mason's evidence to the inquest was that the station master, who he knew, unlocked the door and put them into their compartment on the wrong side, even though they had offered to go round to the next platform and board, as was conventional, on the near-side. At Grayrigg station, Mason got out and left his friend alone in the compartment. When the train arrived at Tebay at 6.50pm a carriage door was found to be open on the off-side. Down the line between Borrow Bridge[39] and Tebay the wife of the local signalman found John Bracken lying unconscious by the northbound offside rail. A goods train was following the passenger train along the up line and this was stopped to carry him to Tebay. From there he was taken south to Sedbergh station, where his head wound and dislocated shoulder were treated by Dr Robert Inman. Just before 10pm he was brought home to his wife at Moss Foot.

On the following day he regained consciousness and over the next two days, according to Elizabeth Bracken's evidence, he knew her and was able to speak but all that he could say about the accident was that he could remember nothing after Mason left the train at Grayrigg. In the second half of the week his condition deteriorated and he died in the afternoon of Friday 27 March 1874. On the following day the inquest was opened by the coroner for Westmorland with a jury, who initially sat at Moss Foot to view the body and take Elizabeth Bracken's evidence before resuming in Kendal on 7 April 1874. Sadly none of the three newspaper reports refer to John Bracken's children and it is impossible to say whether the nine-year-old Thomas Wilson was brought from Barras to see his injured father before his death. The younger children Hannah aged six and Robert aged five must have been aware of the traumatic accident and its tragic outcome in the farmhouse.

At the resumed inquest evidence was given by the gamekeeper James Mason, Dr Inman, George Hodgson the station master at Oxenholme, Mrs Benson who found the injured John Bracken, and two other railway workers. Elizabeth Bracken was represented by a Sedbergh solicitor and the London and North Western Railway Company also had legal representation. Much of the evidence and the lawyers' questions related to the issue of whether Bracken and Mason had entered the carriage from the wrong side and whether if they did, in breach of the railway's rules, the off-side door was not locked after they were let in.

The jury's verdict was accidental death but they also made a point of finding that Bracken and Mason had (despite the evidence given to them by the station master) been put into the carriage on the wrong side and that greater care should have been taken to ensure that the railway's rules concerning locking the off-side carriage door was kept to. Of course the rule existed to prevent the opening of doors and falls into the path of an oncoming train.

What the jury did not decide, because there was no evidence as to what happened in the railway carriage after Grayrigg, was why John Bracken went up to the off-side carriage door between stations? The *Westmorland Gazette* of 28 March 1878, unaware of his death the day before publication, had speculated on the point:

Mr Bracken... can therefore give no account of how the accident happened. There can be no doubt however from the fact of the carriage door being open and the wound upon the skull that the unfortunate man was leaning out of the window and the door being unfastened it by his weight burst open and he was precipitated head foremost from the train to the ground.

Mason's evidence was that his friend was neither drunk nor unwell and that he had talked rationally and sensibly in the train. Further surely if he had been leaning out of the carriage door window either for air or to vomit when the door unexpectedly opened, he would have fallen feet first, whereas his injuries indicated head first. As such, contrary to the opinion of the *Westmorland Gazette,* the most likely explanation must be that the door opened while the train was moving and while leaning out to grab the door and close it he fell head first between the up and down tracks. However, why should the door open at the point it did? If the stationmaster at Oxenholme had not closed it properly, surely it would have been noticed sooner or come open lower down the line? Maybe he did get up from his seat to open the window and in doing so caught the door catch and it then fell open.

The Accident Report Book for this date and section of the London and North Western Railway's line has not survived and therefore it cannot be said whether Elizabeth Bracken received any compensation for the accident, although from the contents of other accident report books it is clear that compensation for railway accidents was quite regularly paid. Certainly the jury's verdict and the presence of her own and the railway's lawyer at the inquest would have helped her to mount a successful claim.

John Bracken did not leave a will – which is unfortunate because the contents might have indicated his feelings for his eldest son. His widow Elizabeth obtained an Order for the Administration of his estate at Carlisle in April 1874. Thereafter, helped by her farm servants and in due course her younger son, she continued to farm at Moss Foot into her 60s. She was never to remarry.

Although John Bracken left no will his father Thomas when he died aged 83 in November 1889 did do so. Interestingly he made it at his solicitors in Kendal on 21 November 1874 within eight months of his eldest son's death. In it he divided his residuary estate equally between his four surviving children and made the common proviso that in the event of their predeceasing him their children would receive their parent's share. The three children of his recently deceased eldest son he treated quite differently. He left them a legacy of a

pound each. It is hard to interpret his motives charitably for although he treated Thomas Wilson no worse than his siblings he plainly had very little sympathy for his fatherless grandchildren, still less their widowed mother. Did
this dislike stem back to his son's marrying a pregnant woman ten years earlier? Of course it can only be speculation but perhaps he felt his son had been
fooled into the marriage as a result of the Brunskill's greater wealth and social
status and their prominent Sedbergh relations. The indications are that
Thomas was not initially unhappy with his eldest son's marriage and soon
after it both Thomas and Hannah put them themselves through the novel and
seemingly disconcerting experience of being photographed by their daughter-
in-law's relations. Another explanation might be that, now his eldest son was
dead, he wanted Moss Foot farm for another of his sons and resented his
daughter-in-law's stubborn possession of it.

It is not clear whether Thomas Wilson ever discovered the contents of his
Bracken grandfather's will. By 1889 he was already a successful civil engineer and he probably greeted receipt of his one pound with a large shrug. The
Probate records show the amount of his grandfather's residuary estate was far
less than that of his own father fifteen years earlier. This illustrates both the
expense of longevity and the declining fortunes of agriculture over the intervening years.

1874 did not witness the only family funeral. Three weeks before John
Bracken's death Thomas Wilson's great uncle William Brunskill, the now
retired glazier, died at Matsons Cottage, Windermere, aged 77. In the late
1860s he and his two sons had moved from Sedbergh to take advantage of the
greater commercial opportunities Windermere with its tourist season offered
to professional photographers. In the newspaper obituary notice they had published they paid tribute to, "the respected father of R & J W Brunskill photographers, Windermere." Given the evident closeness of the family it seems
likely that the Brunskills of Barras travelled to Windermere for this funeral
and Thomas Wilson may have had a rare meeting with his mother at it. His
grandmother Mary Brunskill would not have been with them at her brother's
funeral. She had died at Barras aged 74 the previous summer and this event
probably also briefly united mother and son. There is firm evidence that they
were united for Thomas Wilson's sixth birthday in February 1871 when she
visited him at Barras. At the conclusion of her visit her mother presented her
with a large brown leather bound Bible with the inscribed words: *"To*

Elizabeth Bracken with the kind Christian love and sincere prayers of her affectionate Mother, Mary Brunskill, February 28th 1871, Barras House, Stainmore, Westmorland." Both her expression and handwriting reveal that Mary was an educated woman and that her faculties were still undimmed in her 72nd year.

Since census night 1871 there had been several other changes to the occupants of Barras House. In the summer of 1871 Thomas Wilson's uncle Robert Brunskill married a local farmer's daughter Isabella Ion and moved to her father's farm at Oxenthwaite. In 1873 Ann, one of Thomas Wilson's three spinster aunts, was married aged 46 to Thomas Simpson a farmer from Winton near Kirkby Stephen – unsurprisingly, given her age, there were to be no children of the marriage.

None of these changes or the death of John Bracken in Firbank appears to have caused any significant change to Thomas Wilson's life at Barras where he continued to live with his grandfather, uncle and two spinster aunts. Perhaps all of them felt that his father's death was no reason to disturb his education, which was of a higher quality than was available at Firbank. On his mother's part she may have been glad that they were keeping him and anxious to avoid aggravating her seemingly difficult relationship with her late husband's father by moving her eldest child to Firbank.

Proof of his advancing education is found in the New Year's Day 1876 gift by his aunt Mary Isabella of 'The Villa of Claudius'.[40] Before giving it she inscribed her name, his, the date and their address, Barras House, Stainmore in the front cover. Published by the Society for the Promotion of Christian Knowledge in 1861, it is a fictional tale of the Roman British Church in AD383. It is full of Latin tags and Roman history and would be heavy going for a modern theology undergraduate. It seems an extraordinary book to give a ten-year-old and suggests Thomas Wilson's precocious intelligence. Mary Isabella, like her elder sister Sarah, was never to marry and her devoutness is evidenced by two bibles presented to her in her childhood by the Stainmore Sabbath school – the first in 1851 for her ability in bible reading and the second in 1852 for her knowledge in religious instruction. She was respectively seven and eight years old when these prizes were awarded. Thomas Wilson was himself given a large leather-bound bible by his Brunskill grandmother on his eighth birthday in 1873 again suggesting an impressive level of literacy.

At around this time, the earliest known photograph of Thomas Wilson was taken. In this and all later pictures he is shown as having a distinctive raised right eyebrow: unlike his younger brother Robert, he shows no obvious resemblance to his father.

He was highly fortunate in having his intellect nurtured by the Reverend John Wharton M.A. at Stainmore Grammar school. Usually at the age of thirteen Victorian children who had lasted that long in school went on, generally only if they were male and always only if their families could afford the fees, to Public or Grammar school. For the rest their formal education ended. However in the case of Stainmore with its generous benefactors the school served both an elementary and secondary function and, notwithstanding its name, the fees charged by the Free Grammar School were modest.

However in the late 1870s the advantages this arrangement gave him were threatened by a petition from the parishioners of Stainmore to the Local School Board to take over the school. They were supported by Her Majesty's Inspector who found that, "not more than 20 per cent of the children of school age are in attendance."[41]

Their petition was made possible by the Elementary Education Act passed by Gladstone's first government in 1870. It is often known as Forster's Act after the minister in charge of it, W. E. Forster. It was designed to cater for the large number of children of elementary school age (five-thirteen) who were not receiving an education. Prior to its passage elementary schools only existed where they had been established by local churches or benefactors and in the growing urban and industrial centres the provision was either inadequate or non-existent. Where a satisfactory denominational school already existed the new Act did not seek to disturb it and its philosophy was that such a school could be a suitable place of education for children of all other denominations.[42] What Forster's Act established was Local Education Boards across the country to build and administer schools for the estimated two million children who fell outside any educational provision in 1870.[43]

Like so often this piece of government legislation had unintended consequences. In the case of Brough and Stainmore, Board Schools were established under Forster's Act in 1874 and 1879 respectively. Gladstone, a very devout Anglican, would not have been happy that this brought to an end both John Wharton's clerical teaching career on Stainmore and the sixteenth century school at Brough which had evolved from John Brunskill's 1506 oratory. In Brough's case the original endowment had become insufficient but in

Stainmore's case the complaint was non-attendance seemingly because the locals did not like what was on offer.

It is not hard to imagine why the local farmers failed to send their children to be taught John Wharton's specialisms of Latin, Greek and ecclesiastical history. Such subjects were of no use for a life in farming, and given elementary schools continued to charge modest fees their parents probably considered that their children were of greater use at home. These children were not destined to make the step up to secondary school where the education John Wharton provided was of far greater use. What they wanted was a rudimentary elementary education suitable for all, which the non-denominational Board Schools provided and which John Wharton evidently failed to.

That Thomas Wilson fell within the minority twenty per cent who did attend John Wharton's school is scarcely surprising. He was the sole focus of two generations of Brunskills at Barras House. Other Stainmore farmers, particularly tenants with smaller holdings and a large number of children, could not entertain such aspirations for their offspring who were needed at home as farm labour.

In this environment the majority were to win the argument. John Wharton stepped aside in 1880 and accepted a pension[44] and in 1879 two new Board Schools were erected on Stainmore.[45] Another unintended consequence of Forster's Act would be that for the remainder of the nineteenth century the ablest minority in Board schools would struggle to satisfy the entrance requirements of Grammar and Public Schools. Although some schooling was plainly better than no schooling, the reorganisation of elementary education undoubtedly meant for some a reduction in the opportunity for secondary education. Gladstone in his guise of meritocrat and anti-elitist should have been troubled.

As a further consequence of Forster's Education Act, Sir Cuthbert Buckle's Free Grammar School at Stainmore was no more and its senior scholars, if they were to continue their education, had to find places elsewhere. Thomas Wilson certainly did. He is described as a scholar, aged sixteen, on the 1881 census; and without a Grammar or Public School education beyond the age of sixteen he would not have been accepted for training for his chosen profession in 1882.

The question of which school he attended from 1880 is rather harder to answer because he omitted to tell the Institution of Civil Engineers where he was schooled when he applied for membership in 1897 and no inscribed school books or prizes remain. So far as the admission records for the local grammar schools are concerned; those for Appleby have survived (and he does not feature), whereas those for Kirkby Stephen have not. As there is not any indication that he was sent away to Public School, Kirkby Stephen seems the most likely.

Kirkby Stephen grammar school was founded in 1566 as a Free Grammar School by Thomas, Lord Wharton.[46] By this point in the nineteenth century it was a school in transition. Since 1845 its freehold headmaster was George Rowland who despite the damning complaints of the Inspectors was, because he held the freehold, unremovable by the school Governors. On 1 May 1876 after 31 years in post, this impediment to reform was removed when according to the *Kendal Mercury* for Saturday 6 May 1876, Mr Rowland fell down dead outside his house.

The Governors, chaired by the Vicar of Kirkby Stephen, the Rev. Dr James Simpson JP, seized the opportunity to obtain the consent of the Charity Commissioners, who were ultimately responsible under the 1869 Endowed Schools Act, to completely reorganise and rebuild an enlarged school. According to the history of *Kirkby Stephen Grammar School 1566-1966* published in celebration of its 400th anniversary, the result was the school was without a headmaster until January 1879 and before this "the School was closed for about two years and its scholars dispersed to other schools in the neighbourhood." In January 1879 just as the upheaval in education on Stainmore was occurring the school re-opened under a new headmaster James Davis. John Wharton was appointed in the same year as an inspector of the school, at a fee of £2 per visit.

Without the school admission records it is uncertain precisely when Thomas Wilson entered the school or whether he took the train from Barras daily to attend. However the 1881 census entry suggests that by then Thomas Wilson had moved closer to Kirkby Stephen to the farm of his eldest Brunskill aunt Ann and her husband Thomas Simpson. Their farm, Lady Ing, was just to the north of Winton and just over a mile from Kirkby Stephen. Census night 1881 was Sunday 3 April, two weeks before Easter and two weeks after Lady Day, the first of the quarter days of the year which then divided the school year into four terms. The following day, Monday 4 April, would have been a school day at the Grammar School.

Interestingly a 30-year-old visitor Elizabeth Ann Brunskill was also present at Lady Ing on census night. Her father, Richard, the elder of the photographer brothers, had died the previous December: his brother John William continued to trade as R & J W Brunskill until his own death in March 1890. His *Lakes Chronicle* obituary indicates that he was not in the ordinary class of contemporary photographer; describing him as "a photographic artist… whose works have been exhibited at exhibitions and his portrait productions are spread throughout the world." The fact that Elizabeth was at Lady Ing on a visit from Windermere is further proof of the continued closeness of these two branches of the Brunskill family.

Simpson's farm was a large one at 155 acres and as well as three live in servants, Simpson employed an additional local farm worker. Without any children of their own, his aunt and uncle may well have paid or contributed towards payment of the Grammar School's fees of one and half guineas per quarter or £6/6/0 per year.[47] These fees were almost certainly higher than those formerly paid at Stainmore and the other likely payor or contributor to these school fees was Thomas Wilson's grandfather, Robert Brunskill, at least up until his death from what Dr Allen called 'natural decay' at Barras, aged 79 in May 1880. Barras then passed to the eldest son Richard who along with his two unmarried sisters and a young female servant continues to live there. Richard, who was childless, might well have also paid or contributed to the school fees, although it seems less likely that his widowed mother, with a far smaller farm at Moss Foot, did so.

By the 1880s England was in the grip of a great agricultural depression which was to last well into the twentieth century and eventually leave its mark on his family of farmers. Its effects were most severe in the grain producing areas of eastern England which finally suffered from a long-delayed reaction to the free traders' repeal of the Corn Laws in 1846. The Corn Laws had imposed protective tariffs on the import of foreign grain and other agricultural produce and their repeal left domestic agriculture in open competition with foreign farmers. For 30 years the full effect of repeal was avoided by a lack of internal peace in the United States, limited shipping and railway capacity to move grain, and in particular wheat, cheaply between the great prairies of America and Russia and the English market.[48]

In Westmorland and in particular Stainmore the Corn Laws[49] controversy sparked less interest because very few cereals were grown there in the 100 years between Waterloo and the Great War.[50] The staple agricultural produce of Stainmore was meat and dairy and the profits of each boomed between the late forties and late seventies as an increasingly affluent and growing urban population consumed less bread and more railway-transported meat, butter and milk. Of course, just as now, there were bad years caused by the weather and outbreaks of animal disease but overall meat and dairy prices rose by as much as 50 per cent[51] over these 30 years, whereas wheat prices were broadly static.

By the end of the 1870s this indian summer for this category of domestic agriculture was over as falling prices caused by growing foreign imports of wool, meat, cheese, bacon and butter started to hit the areas of pasture as it had earlier and more severely effected the grain producing areas. Falling agricultural prices eventually caused a massive reduction in the rural population and land in cultivation across Britain.[52] Thomas Wilson in the form of his education and expense of his professional training was one of the beneficiaries of this boom in farm profits. In this economic climate, Thomas Wilson was fortunate to have been educated sufficiently to avoid a career based on his agricultural background and to be able to choose instead the far more lucrative one of civil engineer. It seems unlikely that his decision was based on an informed view of the prospects of agriculture for there was no consensus as to how long the agricultural downturn would last and some commentators were even advising that the early 1880s was a good time to buy farms.[53]

4 – INSPIRATION

The railway at Barras was one of Thomas Wilson's early enthusiasms and seemingly not one dimmed by the cause of his father's death. The station was just over 100 feet below the farmhouse and if he could not actually see the trains clearly from the house, the station was minutes away and the engines' smoke and steam would have left a trail across his view. Also his grandparents, aunts and uncles occupied him with stories of the line's construction and in particular the 1,000 feet long Belah Viaduct, just to the west of the farm which, when completed in 1859 at a cost of £31,630, was the highest railway viaduct in England.[54] His enthusiasm for the railway would not though have been merely as an onlooker. With so many aunts, uncles and his grandparents to occupy him he was taken on regular trips by train to the shops and markets of Kirkby Stephen, Appleby and Barnard Castle. During school holidays, he was taken on longer day trips to Darlington, Carlisle and Durham.

As well as seeing and experiencing rail travel, in the 1870s Thomas Wilson had the opportunity to witness first hand the progress of construction of one of the greatest feats of Victorian railway engineering in the form of the Midland Railway's 72 mile Settle-Carlisle line. The line was conceived by the ambitious railway company to give it an independent third route to Scotland. This was considered necessary because without a Railtrack or Network Rail the separate railway companies owned and controlled their own track. Whether they permitted their rival's trains to run on their track, and if they did, on what terms, was purely a matter of commercial agreement. In such an environment, the Midland, the youngest of the great railway companies, was at a considerable commercial disadvantage and its passengers were particularly prone to inconvenience on its north-south routes. The situation was at its worst at the small town of Ingleton on the Yorkshire-Lancashire border where the Midland Railway and its greatest rival the London and North Western Railway[55] each had a station. The Greta Viaduct separated the two stations but it was little more than ornamental, for passengers arriving at Ingleton wishing to continue north had to leave the Midland train and walk beneath the viaduct to Thornton Station where the London and North Western was then in charge of them. The inconvenience did not end there, as the General Manager of the Midland Railway was to record in a letter in 1862, "I have been by fast train from Derby to Ingleton and then been attached to 6 or 8 coal trucks to be carried on to Tebay."[56]

The railway companies at this time were enormously rich and powerful and their directors were very proud men determined that their company would achieve pre-eminence over their rivals. Not by accident does the Midland Railway's St. Pancras station tower over and eclipse its rival London termini of King's Cross[57] and Euston.[58] The desire to end the perceived humiliation of not having its own route from London to Scotland was at least an equal motive as that of the potential profit. This hubris was to cost Midland dear.

Parliament first authorised construction of the Settle-Carlisle line in July 1866 but the London and North Western, fearing the new line's capacity to damage their own, moved to improve relations between the two companies and Midland applied again to Parliament, this time to abandon construction of the line. Parliament refused and effectively forced them to build a line which nearly ruined them.

Construction began near Settle, Yorkshire in November 1869. It was estimated to last four years and the approved budget was £2.2 million. In fact the line took six-and-a-half years to complete[59] and cost £3,467,000[60] or £47,500 per mile.[61] The line was dug by hand with only the aid of dynamite and thousands of contractors, who descended on the area attracted by wages as high as ten shillings per day.[62] They came from all over Britain and Ireland and many were Crimea veterans who named the shanty towns where they lived Inkerman and Sebastopol. Many of them were to die in accidents and of diseases and the Midland paid for memorials and graveyard extensions in several local churches. Their best memorial must surely be the line itself with its fourteen tunnels,[63] seventeen major viaducts,[64] and a summit of 1,169 feet above sea level.

Thomas Wilson would have followed the slow and difficult construction of the line in the local newspapers and probably knew best the eleven mile central section of the line between Kirkby Stephen and Appleby. Amazing as it seems now, once the line opened this small if ancient market town had two stations, Kirkby Stephen East and Kirkby Stephen West.

Surrounded as he was by great feats of Victorian civil engineers who had designed and executed railways over, through and under the Pennines, it is scarcely surprising that Thomas Wilson was to choose civil engineering as his profession. But a particular event in late December 1879 may have specifically shoved him in that direction. The event was the collapse of the Tay Bridge in Scotland on 28 December when, in a violent storm and just as a train was crossing, the central span of the bridge collapsed. There were no survivors and 75 lives were lost in what was the worst bridge disaster in history. Just six months earlier the bridge's engineer Thomas Bouch[65] had been knighted by Queen Victoria after the royal train had passed over what, at just under two miles, was easily the longest bridge in the world.

Following Bouch's seeming great success in bridging the Tay, construction began on a Bouch-designed suspension bridge over the other great unbridged Scottish estuary, the Forth, and by the date of the Tay collapse, one pier in the estuary had been built. Work on the rest was stopped and Bouch was removed from his post. He died a broken man in October 1880 before the inquiry into the disaster was concluded. When those conclusions were published, inadequate bracing of the ironwork was blamed and Bouch's wind calculations were also criticised.[66] His unexecuted design for the Forth Bridge remained just that.

News of this Scottish disaster would have been read with especial interest by Thomas Wilson and by everyone at Barras, because twenty years earlier Bouch had been the civil engineer responsible for the railway there and in particular the design of the Belah Viaduct between Barras and Kirkby Stephen. Belah with its sixteen spans of 60 feet each was built of lattice girders on iron piers and was to last over 100 years until demolished as a consequence of the 1960s rail closures.[67] However, even though of an entirely different design, in the national hysteria which followed the Tay disaster, Belah was scrutinised. Thomas Wilson who had known and doubtless admired this viaduct throughout his fifteen years of life, was surely gripped by the post-Tay story and the vilification of Bouch in the newspapers. His grandfather Robert Brunskill and his uncle Richard Brunskill would have recalled Bouch, from the visits he had made to Stainmore in connection with the construction of the viaduct twenty years earlier.

The *Westmorland Gazette* of 3 January 1880 referred to the collapse of the Tay bridge as an 'appalling catastrophe'; three days later the *Cumberland and Westmorland Advertiser,* anticipating a gathering storm, thundered, "seldom has such an accident as this occurred in the annals of the railways… the grim facts as they now appear are sufficiently appalling to enlist the public sympathy and to demand that a searching inquiry should be made into the causes of so deplorable a calamity."

Five years later when the *History, Topography & Directory of Westmorland* was published its authors, while admiring Bouch's more successful Belah Viaduct, still felt the need to reassure their readers:

> *The Belah Viaduct, over which the N. E. Railway is conveyed, is one of the most imposing triumphs of engineering skill in the British Isles. It rests upon what appear to be very light, and yet are very strong, though graceful groups of open columnar iron work, planted on solid stone foundations of an almost Cyclopean character. No adequate idea of the wonderful height of the viaduct can be formed unless a person walks underneath it and then views it at a short distance. The design was furnished by the late Mr Bouch. No accident of any kind occurred during its erection or has occurred since.*

Not only railway construction and disaster aroused his interest in the newspapers of the 1870s. Just one of several local papers for the area was the *Penrith Observer and Appleby and Kirkby Stephen News*. Delivered to Barras by rail it aroused in the young Thomas Wilson a life-long interest in the paper. In 1904 in one of many contributions he made to the letters column, he confessed that while at school he had learned "the Imperial lessons taught the country by Lord Beaconsfield" from reports in the columns of this newspaper. As Disraeli went to the Lords in August 1876 and resigned as Prime Minister for the final time in April 1880 it is easy to date these 'lessons' to these final four years of Disraelian Imperialism. This was the high point of regional newspapers and the *Observer*'s vast and impressively informative pages covered national and international events as well as more mundane local matters. In its pages he would have read of the Prime Minister's triumphal return from the Congress of Berlin and his subsequent 1879 Guildhall speech in which he proclaimed his political creed as 'Imperium et Libertas' and applauded "the noblest of human sentiments, now decried by philosophers – the sentiment of patriotism." In the same newspaper he would have followed the progress of the 1878 Second Afghan War and the Zulu War of 1879, and Gladstone's resultant denunciation of the evils of Beaconsfieldism and its imperial adventures. Thomas Wilson was perhaps already not enamoured by personal experience of the effect of Mr Gladstone's education reforms. Disraeli's appeal to patriotism would fix his party political loyalty forever and eventually lead him to active membership of the Conservative party.

Thomas Wilson's final year in school was that of 1881-1882 and his final term would have ended on the March quarter day of 1882, following his seventeenth birthday. Prior to his leaving, the headmaster would have provided a reference in support of his application for pupillage with a civil engineer. At this time the secondary school year ended around mid-summer day and the school year commenced in early August. An annual examination was held just before the school year ended in June and prizes were awarded on the last day of term. In Kirkby Stephen's case the external examiner was the vicar of Stainmore, John Wharton, who having known Thomas Wilson almost since birth, may well have also provided a reference in support of his application for professional training. If he did and it contained his latest examination results these would have been those for June 1881. A report of this examination was given in the *Cumberland and Westmorland Advertiser* for Tuesday 28 June 1881; it leaves the reader in no doubt of the breadth and length of the exam:

Kirkby Stephen Grammar School. Headmaster Mr Davis. The half yearly examination took place in the past week and the Rev. J. Wharton M.A. put the pupils to a very severe test in the various subjects. The examination was brought to a close on Friday when the School broke for the mid-Summer holidays. The subjects examined were history (scripture and english), grammar, geography, arithmetic, chronology, Latin, Greek, Algebra, Euclid, French and other branches, such as drawing (freehand and perspective) and mapping in which the scholars have exhibited marked proficiency.

The newspaper did not publish the names of the subject prize winners but John Wharton's annual report to the governors was published in full. It applauded the results and ends:

To judge from the good behaviour of the pupils themselves during the long hours of the examination I feel convinced that they appreciate the privileges which they enjoy.

5 – DARLINGTON

Throughout the nineteenth century significant numbers of people left the countryside to seek employment and higher wages in the ceaselessly expanding towns and cities of Britain and from the 1880s the agricultural depression accelerated this urbanisation. In May 1882 at the age of seventeen Thomas Wilson followed this trend when he left Westmorland for Darlington and the urban north-east. However unlike so many others who made the same or a similar migration, in his case it seems that his heart remained in Westmorland and there is ample evidence that he returned there for weekends and holidays as often as he could, particularly once he had completed his professional training.

Just like the humblest factory worker who had abandoned village life to find more lucrative employment Thomas Wilson's motives were financially driven. From the contemporary directories it is clear that there were virtually no civil engineers practising in the county and the opportunities the rural area had once offered for railway work had been exhausted not only by what had already been done but also by the growth of a significant movement to protect the Lake District from incursion by the railways, industry and manufacturing. As early as 1876 the Cambridge University Union passed the motion, "the house sympathises with the agitators against the proposed railway from Windermere to Keswick."[68] One of those agitators was John Ruskin and his young disciple the Reverend H. D. Rawnsley[69] who in 1883 was to form the Lake District Defence Society with the object of preventing "the introduction of unnecessary railways into the Lake District, and to all other speculative schemes which may appear likely to impair its beauty or destroy its present character." Eventually Canon Rawnsley was to co-found the National Trust: Thomas Wilson would meet him in 1904.

In later life Thomas Wilson both spoke and wrote of his pride in the unspoilt natural beauty of his native Westmorland but whether he felt the same as a seventeen-year-old aspirant engineer is doubtful. There is though no evidence that he ever resented his relocation at so young an age. In a letter he wrote to the *Penrith Observer* published in December 1929 principally in relation to his hero the huntsman John Peel, he dilated on the subject of the nineteenth century rural diaspora:

> *Peel was a type of a race bred for generations in the dales of whose descendants the greater part have had to scatter far and wide and still do. We seldom remember that from Cumberland and Westmorland for the last 150 years or perhaps more the whole natural increase of population born outside the few industrial towns, in numbers several times the present population, have perforce gone forth to find their livings in towns elsewhere, in the Colonies, or in foreign lands. A glance at the census returns since 1801 shews in nearly every dale a population less today than it was 130 years ago.*

Denied a career within the county he loved it is not hard to see why Darlington in the industrial north-east was chosen as the next best thing. It was the eastern terminus of the railway from Kirkby Stephen and Barras, and would make travel back to his family relatively easy. The contemporary timetable shows the journey from Kirby Stephen to Darlington's North Road Station of 36 miles with seven intermediate stops, took an hour and twenty minutes; or fifteen minutes less from Barras.

Aside from the stunning natural scenery and the slow climb up to Stainmore Summit and the rapid descent to Bowes, the most noteworthy view from the carriage windows was the Bowes Museum, more worthy of the Loire valley than Teesdale, which had been under construction since 1869. The Brunskills of Stainmore would have known all about the scandalous relationship between the tenth Earl of Strathmore and Mary Milner which produced the Museum's founder. In 1809 when Milner first became the Earl's mistress, she was no more than one of his more attractive young servants, who had been born on his Streatlam Castle estate, just outside Barnard Castle. Two years later John Bowes was born and shortly after, Lord Strathmore married Mary Milner as he lay dying, in an attempt to legitimize his son under Scots law. After years of court proceedings, in 1821 Bowes' claim to the title and the family's Scottish estates was finally rejected but he did succeed to the English estates and upon the basis of that wealth, created the museum bearing his name.

The chief attraction of Darlington especially for someone with a youthful enthusiasm for the railways and railway engineering was that, having given birth to passenger railways in 1825, it remained a significant railway centre

60 years later with lines out of it in all four directions. Following the initial line to Stockton, Darlington was linked with York in 1841 and Gateshead in 1844. In 1856 the old Stockton-Darlington line was extended eastwards to Barnard Castle and eventually to Tebay. As a result of this gradual development, organised by a plethora of different railway companies, Darlington had acquired two stations, North Road serving the east-west routes and Bank Top those north-south.

With his early interest in railways, Thomas Wilson would have been well aware of Darlington's railway pedigree resulting from the combination of the Pease family finances[70] and George Stephenson's engineering genius. Coming together in what was an unexceptional market town they launched a great railway age which would transform not just the economy of Britain and its empire but eventually the entire world.

On a plinth outside the North Road Station since its retirement in 1857 was 'Locomotion', the original 1825 steam engine. As North Road Darlington was where the line from Barras terminated Thomas Wilson had almost certainly

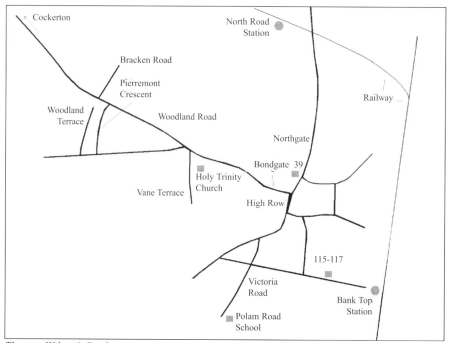

Thomas Wilson's Darlington.

marvelled at the prototype steam engine on trips to the town ever since his early boyhood.

Within the substantial Darlington engineer community of the 1880s, Edward Whyte Lyall was to be his pupil master, responsible for his four year professional training. In the 1881 census taken just over a year before Thomas Wilson moved to Darlington, Lyall is described as a 'civil engineer and surveyor'. He is living, along with his wife and six children, at 13 Woodlands Terrace, Darlington. He had been born in Edinburgh in 1840 and from the ages and birth places of his children it appears that he moved from Edinburgh to Darlington around 1868. In the Scottish 1861 census he is unmarried and living in the house of his parents in Edinburgh at 5 Heriot Mount and is then described as a 'land surveyor'.

Thomas Wilson would have had to pay a significant fee to Lyall for taking him as his pupil. Just how much, and how he did so, is unclear although it seems likely that his Brunskill relatives paid it. In addition he would have had to find lodgings in the town for given the number of Lyall's children it seems unlikely that he lodged with his principal.

In Kelly's 1885 directory of Darlington Lyall describes himself as a 'civil engineer, surveyor, land agent and mining engineer.' Lyall plainly had a broad practice. His office was in the very centre of the town at 39 Northgate. Just a few doors away on the same side of the street at the junction with Union Street were the first purpose built offices of the Stockton & Darlington Railway, dating from 1830. Since 1863 they had been occupied by its absorber the North Eastern Railway Company (NER). Northgate then formed part of the Great North Road and the view from Lyall's offices would have been crowded with people and horses and beyond them, the numerous inns and hotels which had been providing for travellers for centuries.

With a population of over 35,000 Darlington must have seemed a noisy, bustling and exciting place to the teenage Thomas Wilson who had only experience of the bucolic charm of Westmorland. The poet John Horsley in his 1886 poem *Darlington – 50 years ago* gives a flavour of the bustling industrial town:

> *Now tall smoking chimneys stand up everywhere,*
> *With cloud-curling smoke high up in the air,*
> *And the sparks from the Works, and the hum from the Mills,*
> *With pleasure and joy the workman's heart fills.*

The 1885 Directory also gives a flavour of what was a thriving manufacturing town:

The principal manufactures of Darlington are iron and worsted. Here are the extensive worsted mills of Messrs. H. Pease & Co; the extensive rolling mills of the Darlington Iron and Steel Company; the Darlington Forge Company; and Messrs. Fry, Ianson and Co. besides two other iron and brass foundries, and some extensive tanneries, maltings and breweries. Four banks, exclusive of the Savings Bank are established at Darlington... there are five weekly papers published every Saturday.

Although the Directory omits to mention them, Horsley's 'Works' were the NER Locomotive Works, opened in North Road in 1863 and the town's largest employer. Another very significant employer was the Cleveland Bridge and Engineering Company, which since its opening in 1878 had built iron and steel bridges which were subsequently shipped for installation to India, Africa and South America. As Sunderland in his 1972 *History of Darlington* summarised it: "Coal, iron and the steam engine were the foundations of the first Industrial Revolution and upon these the fortunes of Darlington were built."

Without surviving records relating to Lyall's practice, the best indication of what work Thomas Wilson actually engaged in during the period of his traineeship and later as Lyall's assistant is contained in the information he supplied to the Institution of Civil Engineers (ICE) when he applied for membership in March 1897, and to the North of England Institute of Mining and Mechanical Engineers (IMME) when he sought membership there in June 1899. From these two descriptions it is clear that Lyall's practice included mining, civic and utility work, as well as the more glamorous railway work.

From Thomas Wilson's own account of his career it is clear that the first significant project he was involved in was the construction of the Darlington tramways from 1882 to 1883 at a total cost of £38,000. Three lines were built from the statue of Joseph Pease[71] in High Row, Darlington's principal street with the Town Hall and Market Hall: from there the trams ran to North Road, Cockerton and Bank Top.

The trams were drawn by a single horse except the line to Bank Top where the gradient of Victoria Road needed a second trace horse.[72] A tram depot was constructed in Woodland Road, with the stables in Four Riggs.[73] The rules governing urban tramway construction were first laid down by the Tramways Act of 1870 and specific government authority for the construction of a tram system in Darlington was given by the Darlington Tramways Order of 1880. A total rail length of four miles was sanctioned and the approved construction drawings remain at Kew. These drawings show that the design engineer was a Mr T. F. Mackay of Westminster, leaving Lyall and the trainee Thomas Wilson in charge of the on-site engineering. It is evident from the file that construction delays occurred and as the Order sanctioning construction limited it to two years The Stockton & Darlington Steam[74] Tramways Co Ltd had to seek an extension of the construction period from the Board of Trade. This was granted despite the objection of the town council to "the long continued obstruction in the streets to the general traffic; and the great inconvenience to the public"; in addition it was the Town Clerk's view that "the work has been unnecessarily prolonged." By October 1882 three of the six tramways were ready for inspection by Major-General Hutchinson of the Royal Engineers on behalf of the Board of Trade.

Hutchinson has the rather dubious claim to fame of having inspected and approved the Tay Bridge for public use in 1878 and following the disaster he was sent by the Board of Trade to inspect the wreckage in January 1880. None of that seems to have affected his career as a Government inspector. Probably the great public respect for the British Army and its officers saved him from attack in the newspapers and the treatment meted out to the civilian engineer Sir Thomas Bouch.

From General Hutchinson's report it is clear that each of the tramways were single lines with passing places. The tramcar he observed in operation was in Victoria Road and so was pulled by two horses. *The Northern Echo* of Friday 6 October 1882 announced their approval for public use and described the approved lines as "possessing comfortable seats and are easy to ride in. The fare from Bank Top to the Joseph Pease Statue will be a penny and also a penny from the Statue to North Road and the Statue to Cockerton."

After the tramways Thomas Wilson was involved in several railway construction projects, some for the NER with its conveniently neighbouring office further up Northgate. Others were private colliery or factory lines as the great period of English railway construction was now over. Aside from actual railway construction he was engaged in the design and parliamentary approval stages of several railway extensions. These included the Forcett

Railway Extension on the Durham/Yorkshire border in 1883, Passage West and Carrigaline Light Railway near the city of Cork, Ireland 1883-1884, and the Wear Valley Extension Railway where he was involved in the selection of the route, surveys and estimates in 1886-1887.

This extension of the railway into the upper reaches of the Wear valley and into the wild and remote upland landscape separating the counties of Durham and Cumberland seems pretty incomprehensible today and even at the time there are indications that many wise heads thought it financially very hazardous. The scheme was initially promoted by the residents of the valley who enlisted the support of their MP Sir Joseph Pease.[75] Using his own money he asked Lyall to conduct a survey of the route which Thomas Wilson carried out. Travelling, by horse after Stanhope, to conduct the survey through the wild and remote Weardale landscape, he must have felt like one of the earlier pioneer surveyors of the route from Barras to Bowes.

When the survey was submitted to the NER they gave it a very unenthusiastic response, on account of the estimated cost, and it lay in abeyance for the next five years. What revived it was the raising of a rival scheme promoted by a local vicar the Reverend R. Shepherd to build a railway all the way up the valley and into Alston, Cumberland.

Alston is the highest town in England and the expense and difficulty of taking the railway there from Weardale had been considered and dismissed on the basis of Thomas Wilson's survey in 1886. The NER, with existing lines to the east and west of the proposed extension, did not wish to see their dominant position weakened by the building of a rival railway on what was effectively their territory. As a result, in a situation reminiscent of the railway mania of the 1850s, the two competing schemes in the form of Bills to Parliament went before a select committee of the House of Lords in May 1892.

The heated debate of the merits of the rival schemes was enthusiastically reported by the local press. On 23 February 1892 the *Northern Echo* reported the speech of Thomas Wilson's old master Edward Lyall, "Sir Joseph Pease when he took up this question in 1886 was anxious that the railway should be made through to Alston, but when it was found on a survey being made that the cost would not be less than £260,000 it was dropped in favour of the line to Wearhead, which it is believed will serve all of the requirements of the valley at a cost of £51,000."

A week later the same newspaper reported a speech on the subject by Sir

Joseph Pease in which he referred to the survey that Thomas Wilson had conducted as "a practical survey of the valley, and in that connection he must say
his friend Mr Lyall had put him to as little expense as possible. (Cheers). Well,
they went to the North East Railway Board and were courteously received,
but the directors did not see their way to give the deputation much encourage-
ment and there were reasons for that." Parliament eventually decided in
favour of the NER scheme and the line was built and opened in 1895 on the
basis of Thomas Wilson's survey from Stanhope to Wearhead.

Other than his railway work, Thomas Wilson's principal category of work
concerned coal mining and he worked on colliery projects in Durham,
Cleveland and Lancashire. In his application for membership of the Mining
Institute he described this work as "including output and general development, drainage schemes, geological surveys, etc."

In his earlier application to join the ICE he referred to the design and construction of embankments on the river Tees, the Douglas Viaduct and the
Redcar Water Works. The rather bland reference to work on the Douglas
Viaduct in 1886 is interesting in that Douglas is in Lanarkshire, Scotland: the
viaduct Thomas Wilson worked on is situated on the railway between Lanark
and Douglas at the point where it crossed the Douglas Water. However the
reference may help explain the longstanding family anecdote of his having
worked on the Forth Rail Bridge – easily the greatest bridging project of the
last quarter of the nineteenth century. Although the dates of construction from
1883-1890[76] almost exactly tally with the period of his traineeship and early
practice, there is no firm indication that he worked on the great Edinburgh to
Dunfermline rail crossing and perhaps Lanark has been confused with the
Forth. A further problem in establishing a link between Thomas Wilson and
the Forth Bridge is the opinion of Dr Scott Arthur of the Forth Bridges Visitor
Centre Trust, that given the rail crossing was the contemporary equivalent of
the moon landing, it would be staggering if he had failed to mention it to the
ICE when applying for membership in 1897.

Both of its designers Sir John Fowler[77] and Sir Benjamin Baker[78] were former ICE Presidents and any significant involvement in its design or with the
on-site engineer team would have been irresistible to the ICE membership
committee. At the time of its opening the bridge was regarded as the eighth
wonder of the world. It was easily the largest nineteenth century engineering
structure and it held the record for the longest cantilever bridge until 1917.

Baedeker's Great Britain of 1890 gushingly describes it before quoting Monsieur Eiffel's statement that it was "the greatest construction of the world." Its statistics remain dizzying today: its total length is 8,000 feet, trains cross at a height of 158 feet over the Firth, the steel towers from which the three double cantilevers spring are 360 feet high, 54,000 tons of steel was used and 6.5 million rivets hold it together. It cost a phenomenal £3,200,000 and this sum was raised by the four railway companies with a commercial interest in its construction. Once completed the task of painting it as a never ending or Sisyphean one led to the phrase 'like painting the Forth Bridge' entering the language: the bridge still features on our coinage.

There is no surviving list of the 4,000 labour force who worked on the bridge's construction. Most of them were employed by the contractors Tancred Arrol and Co. The engineer component of the workforce would have been relatively small. Under Fowler and Baker the resident engineer from 1883-1886 was Patrick Meik and from 1886-1890 F. E. Cooper. Patrick Meik was born in County Durham while his engineer father Thomas Meik[79] was working on railway and port construction in the Sunderland area. The Meik family consisting of Thomas and his two sons Patrick and Charles were a significant civil engineering family. From the nineteenth century business they founded the business has grown into the modern engineering giant Halcrow with 6,000 employees and a turnover of £250 million.

The younger of the two brothers Charles had acted as Sir Thomas Bouch's assistant on his discredited design for a suspension bridge across the Forth between 1878 and 1880. Given the public outcry it was scarcely surprising that after Bouch's death he quietly entered the Edinburgh office of his father and thereby avoided all involvement with construction of the new cantilever design which until 1886 was under the care of his brother. Their father was born in Edinburgh and his office in the city was in York Place. Given Edward Lyall's own Edinburgh roots and his participation in the close knit northern engineering community it is not unlikely that the Meiks were known to him. Is it therefore possible that Lyall sent Thomas Wilson from Douglas up to the Forth with a letter of introduction addressed to Patrick Meik in South Queensferry? Possibly he even spent some weeks or even months on secondment under Meik and has this given rise to the family legend?

As to his failure to include any reference to it on his curriculum vitae when he applied for membership of the ICE in 1897, he may have felt that the period he spent there, and what he actually did there, were not independently verifiable as supporting his application for membership. Also given both Fowler and Baker's prominence in the ICE[80] any exaggeration of his involvement with the great bridging project might have amounted to professional suicide and certainly rejection by the ICE membership committee.

Also not mentioned in either his ICE or IMME applications, doubtless because he considered it irrelevant, was Lyall's significant domestic development surveying practice. Lyall is chiefly remembered today as the surveyor and designer of parts of Darlington's Victorian suburbs.

Lyall's work in this respect was principally focussed on Woodland Road which formed the western approach to the town from Cockerton and this may explain the frequent changes in Lyall's residential address within a very small distance. Within ten years he moved from Woodlands Terrace to Pierremont Crescent to Vane Terrace all of them offshoots of Woodland Road. The development of this area between Darlington and the village of Cockerton had begun in the 1830s when several large fashionable houses and the new church of Holy Trinity was consecrated in December 1838. In testament of the area's wealth the architect of Holy Trinity was the highly fashionable London-based Anthony Salvin.[81]

From the 1860s middle class terraces and villas were constructed. By the 1880s these had filled the area and contemporary photographs show Woodland Road as a wide tree-lined avenue lit by gas lamps, with high walls hiding the larger villas from view. Intriguingly one of the streets running north off Woodland Road is named Bracken Road although it is unclear whether by coincidence, or if Thomas Wilson played a part in its construction.

He certainly did design a pair of substantial four storey terraced houses at 115-117 Victoria Road, Darlington. Both the application and the accompanying coloured plans drawn and signed by Thomas Wilson survive in Durham. They are of interest in that they represent the only concrete evidence of Thomas Wilson's building design work. However, as he drew them in July 1891 after he had left Darlington and seemingly only as a favour to a friend, they cannot be the only instance of his design work in the town. He submitted them and a planning application on behalf of Mr William Wood. The plans show a large basement dining room which is explicable by Wood's listing in Kelly's *Durham Directory* of 1890 as the proprietor of a temperance and commercial hotel at 119 Victoria Road. As such the application obviously related to an hotel extension. Just a week later the Streets Committee of the Darlington Board of Health passed the plans. Both the submission and the speed of the result suggest that he was not unfamiliar with the process and members of the committee.

Victoria Road was a new road of the 1880s, built as an approach to Bank Top Station which was completed in 1887 to the design of the NER's architect William Bell. Both the town and the NER's directors had been stung by Queen Victoria's criticism of Bank Top's 1841 predecessor as being unworthy of the birthplace of railways.[82] Victoria Road gently rises and frames Bell's central Victoria Tower and the large new houses which were built to line it at the lower end were first occupied by the professional classes, with temperance hotels at the upper end, adjacent to the station.[83]

Just before the new station was opened John Horsley had eulogised in verse the pre-railway view from Bank Top:

> *I stood on Bank Top when meadows were green,*
> *Where little but Cuthbert's tall spire was seen,*
> *Where far in the distance, an old-fashioned shop*
> *And the old Town Hall with its cupola top,*
> *Where magnates arraign, and condemn those who sup*
> *To regions below, - or rather lock up.*
> *No North-Eastern then had its trains to annoy*
> *The dairyman's horse, or the passive ploughboy,*
> *He would whistle away ne'er troubling his brain*
> *About whistles that scream from the passenger train;*
> *Victoria Road, and the streets that stand round,*
> *In his path from the plough could never be found.*
> *No Station, replete, with an Engineer's skill*
> *Will e'er surpass that on Victoria Hill.*[84]

In 1886 as he came of age at 21 he completed his almost four years of professional training. Evidently Lyall was happy with his work because he retained him as his assistant. Shortly thereafter and as a result of his increased salary he took out a with-profits life insurance policy with the United Kingdom Temperance & General Provident Institution and started to pay annual premiums of £2/12s/4d. At roughly the same time he opened a savings account with the York City and County Bank conveniently located in

The Plains of Heaven by John Martin (1789-1854), allegedly inspired by the celestial landscape he viewed from Barras, Stainmore, in 1851.

Ambrotype of Elizabeth Brunskill before her marriage in 1864, taken by R & J W Brunskill in Sedbergh.

Thomas and Hannah Bracken of Newfield Farm, Firbank, in 1865 at the Sedbergh studio of R & J W Brunskill.

Newfield Farm, Firbank (right) and the former vicarage (left) 2007.

Moss Foot Farm, Firbank, 2007.

*Elizabeth Bracken, née Brunskill, in 1867 at
the Sedbergh studio of R & J W Brunskill.*

67

The view from Moss Foot Farm, Firbank, 2007.

John Bracken in 1867 at the Sedbergh studio of R & J W Brunskill.

Elizabeth Bracken in 1872 at the Windermere studio of R & J W Brunskill.

John Bracken in 1872 at the Windermere studio of R & J W Brunskill.

Thomas Wilson's Simpson aunt and uncle on a visit to the Windermere studio of R & J W Brunskill in 1875.

Thomas Wilson Bracken, aged about eleven, photograph by R & J W Brunskill, Windermere, 1876.

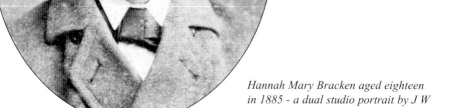

Hannah Mary Bracken aged eighteen in 1885 - a dual studio portrait by J W Brunskill, Windermere.

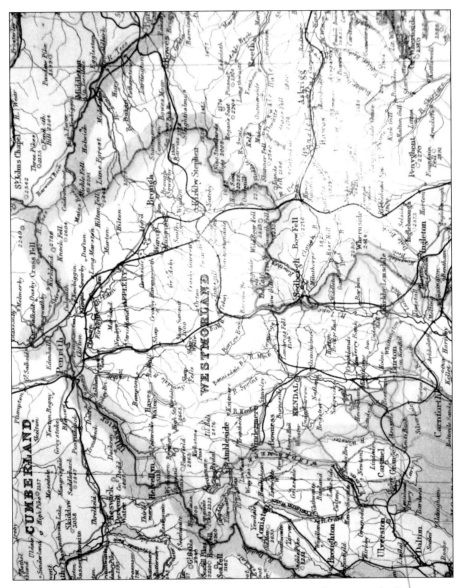

Nineteenth century map of Westmorland showing its extensive railway network. Barras Station right centre.

Two views of the Belah Viaduct, South Stainmore.

Joseph Pease (1799-1872) who, together with his father Edward (1767-1858) transformed the fortunes of nineteenth century Darlington.

The 1825 engine Locomotion prior to its retirement and mounting on a plinth outside North Road station, Darlington. Photograph circa 1857.

Victoria Road, Darlington, constructed in the 1880s as an approach to the new Bank Top station of 1887. 115-117 Victoria Road, built to Thomas Wilson's 1891 design, is shown on the left side (bay fronted) in this circa 1906 photograph.

W G Law's now disused 1876 railway bridge at Wylam, Northumberland, precursor of both Sydney Harbour and Tyne Bridges.

Thomas Wilson aged about 25 following his arrival on Tyneside and a very clear illustration of his unusual raised right eyebrow; photograph by James Bacon & Sons, Newcastle, 1890.

Dora Oliver's watch presented by the men of Spen Colliery, April 1892.

Brass medallion on the revolver case presented to Thomas Wilson on his departure for Africa, 20 May 1897.

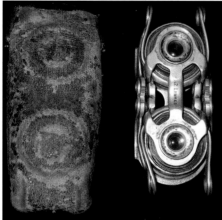

Thomas Wilson's 1897 field glasses and case.

Original staff quarters, Ebute Metta, Lagos, 1897.

'Native village' adjacent to the Lagos Government Railway, photographed by 'The Engineer', 1898.

77

Extending the staff quarters, Ebute Metta, Lagos, 1898

A section of the Lagos Government Railway running through the jungle north of Lagos 1897.

Construction train, Lagos Government Railway, 1896-7.

The bridge over the Ogun at Onibuku (93 miles from Lagos) 1899.

Bridge works on the Lagos Government Railway, 1898.

Construction of the line crossing marshy ground south of Itori, 21 September 1898.

Northgate close to his office. Evidently as soon as he had a surplus income he invested with institutions which still survive with the rather more manageable names of Friends Provident and HSBC. It is not unlikely that he also subscribed to the life fund's temperance philosophy but the policy certainly illustrates his youthful concern with savings and investment and the welfare of his post-death future dependants. His was to be no mis-spent youth or Rake's Progress as his early membership of the YMCA in Darlington also indicates.

The YMCA had been first established in London in 1844 to save young men from the urban attractions of liquor, prostitution, gambling and other vice. It was particularly aimed at those young men who had gone to the industrialising towns and cities to find better employment and as a result were living away from their families and birth communities, so leaving them open to temptation without supervision.[85] Almost 40 years later Thomas Wilson aged seventeen and living away from his family, was a textbook candidate for the evangelizing movement.

Although his working week was long and hard by modern standards and certainly would have included Saturday morning, during his limited leisure time he was susceptible to 'vice' and this free time was what the YMCA of the 1880s largely took care of. The Darlington YMCA was conveniently located in Bondgate and included both a reading room and library. Lectures and foreign language classes were also provided and the recreation room had games of chess, dominoes and draughts. Devotional meetings were usually held on Saturday evenings. On Sundays, in addition to regular Sunday morning church attendance, members participated in afternoon outreach work in Sunday schools, as well as mission work and holding open-air services. The mission work was often carried out some distance away and sometimes meant staying overnight on Saturdays as guests of sympathetic evangelical clergymen. These visits usually targeted "spiritually neglected localities… to bring the inhabitants of such neighbourhoods under the influence of the Gospel."[86]

The annual subscription was four shillings if under 21 (five, if over) and under the 1880s' rules members pledged themselves "to discourage all drinking habits" and "to unite continually in prayer for the world's conversion." In testament of his YMCA activism the local committee of the YMCA gave him an inscribed copy of John Ruskin's book of lectures *The Crown of Wild Olive*[87] in the summer of 1890 when he left the town. Given his career and place of residence he may have had mixed feelings about Ruskin's eloquent epistle on the moral and aesthetic objections to uncontrolled industrial development. However Ruskin's status as an honorary Lakelander and his passion for his native County of Westmorland seemingly ensured the book's survival.

6 – COAL AND IRON

Thomas Wilson left Darlington in July 1890 because he had accepted an appointment as surveyor to the Consett Iron Company in north-west Durham. The records of the once great iron and steel manufacturer survive in Durham. They show that the Chairman of the Board of Directors, David Dale[88] was a Darlington resident living in the Woodland Road enclave where Lyall, many of his associates and possibly Thomas Wilson himself lived. His house West Lodge was the principal 1830s' mansion on Woodland Road and it matched his status as a very significant local entrepreneur. In addition to his Consett chairmanship he was a director of the NER and an active member of the Durham Coal Owners' Association and the Cleveland Mine Owners Association.

Dale's name also appears in the newspaper reports of the Wear Valley Extension Railway where he is listed as both a promoter and investor. As such, it is highly likely that he met Thomas Wilson and certain that he knew Lyall very well. His connection with Sir Joseph Pease is referred to in his entry in the DNB – he was managing partner of J. W. Pease & Co (later Pease and Partners Ltd) throughout the period. From the remaining entry it is clear that David Dale was almost as prominent in the Darlington entrepreneurial community as the Pease family. We know that Edward Lyall and Thomas Wilson under him were regular advisers to the Pease family and it therefore seems just as likely that their paths crossed also with David Dale. Given the double connection of geography and business interests it seems likely that Dale advised Thomas Wilson of the vacancy at Consett and suggested that he apply.

For him the attraction was doubtless partly financial but also his travels from Darlington had taught him that there was a tier of civil engineers above Lyall who were nationally recognised and members of the London based ICE which Lyall would never join. He had also most probably been advised that in order to progress into this higher stratum he needed more exposure to its members.

The position he obtained as surveyor and engineer did not take him to

Consett itself but to the area to the north-east centred on the village of High Spen, a valuable coal mining area between the rivers Derwent and Tyne. This area had been purchased by the Consett Iron Company Ltd (CIC) from the third Marquess of Bute[89] in July 1889[90] with a view to CIC entering the coal retail market. For the substantial sum of £120,000, the existing colliery and associated railway at Garesfield, High Spen and the Chopwell Estate to the south-west were acquired: a further £20,000 was paid for plant, stock and the relevant way-leaves.

The Butes' experience of Durham mining had a significant effect on the development of their greater mineral wealth in South Wales and by the 1880s these had made the third Marquess the largest individual receiver of mineral royalties in Britain. He lavished those royalties on redecorating Cardiff Castle and rebuilding Mountstuart House on the Isle of Bute. In 1848 when as an infant Lord Bute inherited his father's estates in Ayrshire, Glamorgan, Durham and the Isle of Bute (in total over 100,000 acres) he became one of the richest heirs in Britain. He was to be used by Disraeli as the model for the hero of his eponymous novel *Lothair*.[91] By 1889 his South Wales collieries had exceeded the production of those of his in Durham and this justified Lord Bute's decision to sell his Durham estate to CIC.[92]

Following their significant investment in the area, Dale and his fellow directors planned to improve operations at Garesfield and open a new mine at Chopwell with a railway linking the two mines, and it was with this expansion in mind that Thomas Wilson was recruited. Doubtless his combined mining and railway experience made him attractive to the directors, while on Thomas Wilson's part the increasingly rare opportunity for railway building was probably a factor. Others were probably the secure salary and potential promotion opportunities which employment by a venture the size of CIC presented. Ambitious and aged 25 Thomas Wilson may well have felt that after eight years his opportunities for promotion in Darlington were exhausted and he was ready for exposure to the far more significant Tyneside engineering community.

His first encounter with a significant figure from that community was with Hubert Laws,[93] who had been selected by the board as consulting engineer for the new railway from Garesfield to Chopwell. According to the company records in Durham, Laws attended a meeting of the CIC board of directors on 7 April 1891 and presented his plans of the route, along with sections and specifications. Although Thomas Wilson does not feature in the board minutes at this stage, in his application to the ICE he states that he laid out this railway in the later part of 1890 and in 1891 acted as resident engineer under Hubert Laws.

The railway line as far as Garesfield had been built as early as 1837 by the second Marquess of Bute[94] to carry coal from the mine to the staithe wharf on the Tyne at Derwenthaugh.[95] From there the coal was carried downstream to the coal markets in Newcastle. Almost 60 years later the directors of CIC now planned to extend the line to carry coal and coke from their new Chopwell pit to the Tyne. This expansion of coal production for sale was a significant expansion of CIC's emphasis, as hitherto their coal production had largely been used to feed its great iron works. The result was to make it one of the largest coal producers in the north-east.

The rate of growth is illustrated by the five-year average outputs:[96]

	Coal (tons)	Coke (tons)
1886-1890	882,452	418,044
1891-1895	1,026,561	401,604
1896-1900	1,424,017	522,141
1901-1905	1,568,017	491,814

In large part the expansion in the second half of the 1890s was achieved by the new pit at Chopwell and improvement to the existing pit at Garesfield, both sites where Thomas Wilson was to work between 1890 and 1897. Again his ICE submission refers to both earthworks and road works at Garesfield and drainage work on the new Chopwell pit but he places most emphasis on his railway work in the area. Thomas Wilson's ultimate boss at Garesfield from 1890 was the CIC director and chief company mining engineer W. H. Hedley. Between Hedley and Thomas Wilson came William Logan, also a company director and mining engineer responsible for Langley Park and Garesfield collieries.

The progress of that railway work is fully recorded in the surviving board minutes. By May 1891 the tender of the railway construction contractor was accepted and by June the main contractor Mr John Jackson was in possession of most of the ground. At the meeting of 22 June 1891 the board were in possession of a letter from Hubert Laws which is quoted in full in the minutes. It states, "A sharp return of my recent attack of acute rheumatism prevents me waiting upon you at your meeting as I had hoped to do." It is signed on Hubert Laws' behalf by his son of the same name. Within eight days Hubert Laws senior was dead. His obituary published by the ICE explains the medical background, "His health was never very good; in his school days at Christ's Hospital he suffered from severe rheumatic fever which left pronounced heart disease. He died from an attack at Ryton on the 30th of June, 1891, after a week's illness."

In consequence of his death at the next board meeting in July his elder brother William George Laws[97] was appointed in his place. Of the two Laws brothers, who were in practice together from 1860-1878, George (as he was known) was the more influential in engineering terms and he would become a very important contact in Thomas Wilson's career. He had a significant railway engineering practice throughout the 1860s and 1870s before becoming the city engineer in Newcastle-upon-Tyne, a post he held for twenty years. His greatest monument is the 1876 railway bridge over the Tyne at Wylam[98] which connected the railways on the north and south sides of the river. The iron bridge consists of a single span as, owing to the coal-workings near the surface, it was not possible to put piers in the river. Pevsner's *Northumberland* states that such a design for a railway bridge was unprecedented and credits it as a design forerunner for Newcastle's famous Tyne Bridge.

The address Thomas Wilson gives on the July 1891 application to the Darlington Board of Health for the Victoria Road houses is Garesfield Colliery, Lintz Green,[99] via Newcastle on Tyne. *The History and Directory of the County Palatine of Durham* published in 1894 regards Garesfield Colliery and High Spen as synonymous and describes it as "a village pleasantly situated about two miles above the river Derwent at Lintz Green railway station and three miles south west of Winlaton... At the Garesfield Colliery which was opened early this century the seams at present being worked are of very high class quality."

This is as precise as can be established where Thomas Wilson lived at Garesfield during the period 1890 to 1893 as on the census night of 1891[100] by quirk of fate he is listed as staying at his mother's farm of Moss Foot, Firbank, where his profession is described as 'Civil Engineer & Surveyor'; also listed there are his sister Hannah and his brother Robert. This is the first definite date in his life when it can be demonstrated that he was at Firbank and on census night 1891 he was 26-years-old. Both later indicators and family anecdote suggest that he was close to his mother and siblings and that family along with religion was one of the bedrocks of his life. Certainly there is no evidence of any estrangement on account of his odd upbringing by his maternal grandparents at Barras. Whether he ever asked his mother for an explanation of the reason for it cannot be said. Certainly from the 1880s when his Bracken grandfather was no longer a near, if hostile neighbour at New Field, and he had the income and independence to travel between Westmorland and Tyneside, there is some suggestion that he was making up for lost time spent with them. His mother is not listed as this time it is she that appears on Stainmore, as a visitor to her Brunskill siblings. Therefore in all three nineteenth century censuses in which Thomas Wilson appears he is shown at a separate address to his mother but while the reasons for their separateness may be more complex in 1871 and 1881, within three years of the 1891 census he is listed along with his mother as co-proprietor of Moss Foot farm in Kelly's *Directory* of 1894. Of course in reality he was no farmer and the entry indicates merely a sleeping partnership, in which his finances cushioned his mother and younger brother from the worst effects of the by now established agricultural depression.

Returning to the minutes of the CIC Board, on 3 November 1891 the manager of the Garesfield colliery Mr Robert Oliver submits his resignation which is accepted. Within six months of this resignation Robert Oliver became Thomas Wilson's father-in-law when he married Dorothy Jane,

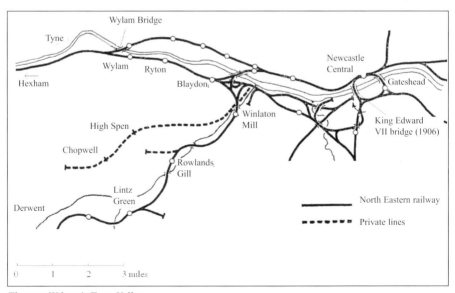

Thomas Wilson's Tyne Valley.

known to the family as Dora. Dora was three years younger than Thomas Wilson and was born[101] at Witton Gilbert just to the north-west of the city of Durham. On her birth certificate her father is described as an 'Overman at a Colliery'. On the 1891 census he is described as a widower and mining engineer aged 49. His eldest daughter Dora appears next followed by her younger sister Jessie and then an eighteen-year-old servant Jane Hope. Their address is given as 91 Cardiff Square, High Spen, and this house would have been provided with his job at the mine. Cardiff Square had been laid out by Lord Bute in 1838 when the mine shaft at Garesfield was sunk, in what was then just a field.[102] Whether Thomas Wilson was also provided with a house in Cardiff Square I cannot say but he would certainly have lived nearby and have had a great deal of working and possibly social contact with Dora's father in the sixteen months when they were both employed at High Spen. Family anecdote suggests that Dora worked in the colliery office at Garesfield under her father's management and this was how Thomas Wilson met her.

After Robert Oliver's resignation from Garesfield, he and his daughters moved to Bewis Hills House, Blaydon, just three miles to the north-east and Robert became the manager of the Lilley Colliery.[103] Lilley was owned by Priestman Collieries Ltd of Newcastle on Tyne[104] and was located just a couple of miles away from High Spen further down the Derwent valley near Rowlands Gill where there was a station on the Newcastle to Consett line. From an inscription on a gold watch which remains in the family, it seems Dora continued to work in the mine office at Garesfield after her father resigned and up until she married Thomas Wilson. The inscription reads 'To Miss Dora Oliver from the workmen of Spen Colliery April 1892.'

In the previous month the 75,000 Durham miners had gone on strike, stopping all coal production across the county and leading to the partial closure of the Consett Iron Works. The strike commenced on 12 March 1892 and was provoked by a reduction in wages of 13.5% by the owners. Once the miners struck they were locked out of the pits and presumably the money to buy Dora's watch had already been collected when the dispute arose.

The labour and industrial relations of the 1890s were in another world from those of today, where the unilateral imposition of any cut in pay seems unimaginable. However miners' wages were among the highest of nineteenth century manual workers and very much higher than those working in agriculture. From the CIC letter and minute books covering the strike period it is plain that its directors took a purely commercial view of the imposition of a pay cut. They obviously had no sympathy for the striking miners and considered the wage reduction a quite reasonable reflection of the contemporary coal market; while they obviously did feel sympathy for the miner's suffering dependants, this was tempered by a belief that the cause of their suffering was needlessly self-inflicted. Where Thomas Wilson stood in that debate I cannot say but the strike was a threat to his own employment and the directors' investment strategy upon which it was based and if he felt differently, as a senior employee, he would have kept any view adverse to his employers to himself.

When the wedding took place on Thursday 12 May 1892 the strike was two months old and there would have been great poverty and distress among the miners' families across the Durham coalfield. This may be why the Church of the Holy Cross in Ryton was chosen as the venue for the wedding. Ryton is on the Tyne to the west of Blaydon and was further from the Durham mines than the other parish churches of Winlaton (High Spen) and Stella (Blaydon) where Thomas Wilson and Dora were eligible to marry without the need for a licence. Winlaton was then a curacy under the ancient parish church of Ryton and the theory that it was chosen for being outside the strike-dominated area is given credence by the Curate of Winlaton performing the marriage service. Kelly's *Directory of Durham* of 1890 describes Ryton as "a pretty village on the south bank of the Tyne and near the road from Newcastle to Hexham, seven miles to the west of Newcastle. The Church of the Holy Cross is an ancient building in the early English style." Pevsner's *Durham* says it is the prettiest village on the south bank of the Tyne.

Without photographs of their wedding all that is certain about it is contained in the scant details on the marriage certificate. From them it is clear that Thomas Wilson's future brother-in-law Thomas Woof[105] acted as his best man and Dora's sister Jessie was her chief supporter. Thomas Woof was a farmer's son from Capplethwaite Hall just half a mile to the south-east of his mother's farm at Moss Foot and this choice of best man again indicates that Thomas Wilson was by now a fairly frequent weekend visitor to Firbank.

For his mother and siblings travelling from Sedbergh station, Ryton's location on the main Newcastle-Carlisle railway made it a relatively easy as well as attractive destination. The marriage was announced in the following week's *Consett Guardian*. In the same newspaper are found many stories relating to the miners' strike, the destitution it caused to the miners' families and the meetings of 'Colliery Relief Committees' working for their aid. Another news report indicates that on 14 May the Consett Iron Works stopped its plate mills from operating because of the scarcity of fuel. The strike was to last several more weeks until 3 June when the miners agreed to accept a ten per cent reduction in wages and the owners agreed to re-open the pits. The settlement was reached after a joint conference of the parties hosted by the Bishop of Durham at Auckland Castle. Evidently miners' strikes were not an exclusively twentieth century phenomenon but the successful intervention of the senior clergy in industrial strife today seems most unlikely.

At their October 1892 meeting the directors noted satisfactory progress on the new Garesfield to Chopwell railway. In November they discussed the expansion and improvement of Lord Bute's old line between Garesfield and the Tyne wharf at Derwenthaugh. Originally this was a wagon way where the coal trucks were released to run by gravity to Derwenthaugh and as they did, pulling up the empty wagons on the opposite line by the endless rope principle.[106] In his application to the ICE Thomas Wilson referred to it as the Garesfield and Derwenthaugh Incline and Railway and from the £42,000 spent it was almost as significant a project as the building of the line to Chopwell which cost £51,000. His use of the word Incline to describe it indicates the significant downward gradient between the mine and the river.

From the directors' minute book it is plain that the expansion included significant land acquisition and surveying and they agreed to retain George Laws's services. They agreed that Laws as consulting engineer was to be paid on the basis of a two and a half per cent commission on expenditure and then referred to "Mr T. W. Bracken acting under him as Resident Engineer & Surveyor in the pay of the Company. This arrangement is approved. For the increased responsibilities thus thrown upon Mr Bracken, Mr Logan is instructed to offer him a salary of £200 per annum."

A £200 annual salary was an attractive one for a 27-year-old civil engineer in 1892. In the following year Thomas Wilson was to be further rewarded by the directors when they agreed to give him the new Manager's House at Garesfield at an annual rent of £20. The tender of £850 for construction of this house had been approved by the board in March 1892 and in June 1892 they approved the construction of an additional room for it. Given the capital cost of the house the rent of £20 was hardly commercial and as it represented only a tenth of Thomas Wilson's salary it must have seemed a generous bargain to him.

It is unclear exactly when Thomas Wilson and his wife started to occupy this new house but it seems likely that they were in occupation by early July when Dora fell ill with a severe kidney disorder which developed into paralysis. After just five days under medical care she died on 11 July 1893 in their house at High Spen with her husband at her side. She was 25 and their marriage had lasted just over a year. Her doctor recorded the cause of death as 'chronic nephritis and apoplexy' and although he does not say so her condition was almost certainly a complication of pregnancy. Her bereaved husband announced her death three days later in the *Consett Guardian* but without giving details of her funeral and there is no obvious record of Dora's burial in Durham. She does not appear in any burial record for the parishes of Ryton, Winlaton, and Stella. A chapel-of-ease at High Spen dedicated to St. Patrick was opened in 1893 but the first burials in High Spen were not performed until 1897. After such a brief marriage and without a known grave or any photographs, Dora's presence today is very elusive.

Thomas Wilson suddenly made a childless widower at 28 seems to have reacted to her death in the usual nineteenth century way by concentrating on his demanding job and by increasing his involvement in his developing local community. For instance in 1893 he became involved with the new St. Patrick's chapel at High Spen and in the same year became the local agent of the High Spen District Conservative Association.[107] So far as his work duties were concerned, by the spring of 1894 the new railway to Chopwell was minuted as practically complete although it was not until the September board meeting that they were happy to regard the line as finished.

As this work came to a conclusion Thomas Wilson's work and attention shifted to the lower part of the old line to Derwenthaugh. At the July directors meeting held at the Garesfield Colliery office the board inspected both Garesfield and Chopwell collieries and the new railway in between and it is minuted "Mr Laws and Mr Bracken explained on the spot the proposed deviation and alterations to the Garesfield and Derwenthaugh Railway," and later, after luncheon with the directors it is recorded that Laws and Thomas Wilson joined the meeting to be told that their scheme should be revised on the basis that traffic would not exceed 1,500 tons per day. The revised scheme was presented in October 1894 when the scheme was authorised to proceed to working drawings.

At the same meeting the company architect's scheme for the new pit village at Chopwell was discussed. As well as houses this planned new community included a church, hotel and public house. The residents of the new village would not all be miners as in addition to the substantial new pit the CIC Chopwell scheme also included coke ovens. The building of this coke plant plainly impacted upon Thomas Wilson's workload. The August 1895 board meeting discussed and approved his scheme for a reservoir to supply boiler water and coke oven water.

The scale of the Chopwell operation is best illustrated by the number of men who worked there: following its opening in 1897 it employed 222 men, out of CIC's total mining workforce of 3,837; in 1910, CIC's peak pre-war year, Chopwell accounted for 2,240 of a total workforce of 8,188 and as such was CIC's largest single site. In the period up to the Great War, the mine yielded in the region of 300 tons of coal per man year labour, amounting to a peak annual production of circa 672,000 tons of coal.[108] Such a peak was rather in excess of the directors' calculation of rail traffic made sixteen years earlier when they had revised Laws and Thomas Wilson's original design.

The strength of this almost six year working partnership between George Laws and Thomas Wilson is probably best illustrated by his proposing Thomas Wilson for membership of the ICE in March 1897. Laws had been an ICE member since 1870.[109]

The Institution was and remains highly venerable. It had been founded in 1818, with Thomas Telford as its first president and with a galaxy of the nineteenth century's engineering stars as its members. Its current magnificent building sits on the site of Thomas Telford's house, opposite the Treasury in Great George Street, Westminster.

In support of his application for membership he wrote a now lost thesis and the proposal was seconded by nine other engineer members: among them was Sir Benjamin Chapman Browne who was Mayor of Newcastle from 1885-1887 and had started his engineering career as an apprentice to Lord Armstrong[110] at his famous Elswick Works in 1856. By the 1890s the Elswick Works in Newcastle competed with Krupps for being the largest armaments factory in the world.[111] Another seconder William John Cudworth[112] was the chief engineer of the southern division of the North Eastern Railway and in the 1880s was living at 3 Vane Terrace, Darlington, next door to Thomas

Wilson's old Darlington principal E. W. Lyall. His father William Cudworth had as a boy witnessed the opening in September 1825 of the Stockton and Darlington Railway and eventually he became chief engineer to the Stockton and Darlington Railway Company. The majority of his other seconders were 1897 residents of either Newcastle or Darlington but in a sign of how well travelled nineteenth century civil engineers were, two were living in Devonport, one in Fife and the ninth seconder member in West London. He was admitted to the ICE in February 1898 and would remain a member for the rest of his life.

His connection with George Laws also extended to his nephew Hubert Laws junior who had worked as his father's assistant prior to his death in 1891 before taking on the same role for his uncle George. Amusingly Hubert junior,[113] who had left Morpeth Grammar School with rather indifferent results aged seventeen before working in the offices of his father and uncle, did not impress the ICE when he applied for student membership in 1896. The membership committee rejected him notwithstanding his illustrious uncle being his proposer and the application to join was never renewed.

In the spring of 1897 Thomas Wilson's period of railway building for the great iron corporation came to a close when he left the north-east to work for the British Government building a railway thousands of miles away in colonial Africa. He executed his contract with the Colonial Office on 24 April 1897 at the home of his young friend Hubert Laws in Newcastle.[114]

Of course his engagement by the Government and imminent departure for Africa necessitated his resignation from the CIC. His boss William Logan reported his resignation to the board on 18 May 1897. In perhaps another sign of the closeness of all of their connections Logan proposed that George Laws should take on Thomas Wilson's duties at the same salary and appoint "a suitable man to be in constant attendance" all of which was agreed to: the 'suitable man' was to be his nephew Hubert.

7 – NEW ENGAGEMENTS

Why did Thomas Wilson give up his safe and secure job in county Durham for the pioneer and inhospitable tropical territory of West Africa? The answer is most probably his irresistible attraction to railway building, the domestic opportunities for which were now pretty much exhausted in England. The introduction to *A Gazetteer of the Railway Contractors of Northern England 1830-1914* neatly summarises the position reached by the 1890s:

> *There was in fact, on the face of it, little now left for them to do, in Britain, save perhaps the more prosaic enlargements, doublings and treblings of already established lines, works and stations. And so in sum… these contractors… were instead, henceforth, to take themselves off increasingly to major works abroad."*[115]

Thomas Wilson's career followed this pattern. His engineering career had been launched on the back of a youthful enthusiasm for and observation of the railway engineering marvels of the Pennines. That high ridge of hills forming the spine of England, was crossed and re-crossed by Victorian railway engineers before they actually pushed a railway along a significant part of it.[116] From its start in the 1880s his engineering career had moved with the opportunities for railway work. In 1882 they had taken him to Darlington, in 1890 to High Spen and the private lines of the Consett Iron Company; and as these were completed in 1897, so he moved again – although this time it was somewhat further – over 4,000 nautical miles.

Another attraction may well have been the £40 per month salary which was considerably more than his £200 a year salary in High Spen. He was also by the terms of his 'West African Railways – Engineers' contract to be provided with government quarters in the Colony of Lagos and a free first class passage home when the job was finished. A widower and in his early thirties, it is easy to see why such terms might have attracted him.

A third factor which, given his long-held enthusiasm for both the Empire and Christian evangelism, he probably did not consider minor, was the wider project to 'civilise' Africa and particularly to bring the message of the Gospel to the unknowing African races of the interior. A widely held view at the time was that railways in Africa would foster and assist the spread of British values and Christian civilization. In his YMCA work he had conducted domestic missionary work and had almost certainly come into contact with Anglican clergy who had ministered in Africa and India under the Church Missionary Society. In addition there were two Westmorland personalities who if they did not know him, or his family, were prominent local personalities by 1897 on account of their missionary links to Africa. The first was Anna Mary Livingstone, born in 1859 the youngest daughter of the great African missionary explorer David Livingstone. Educated at the Kendal Quaker School for Girls she went on to marry Frank Wilson a local woollen manufacturer and lived at Underfell, Kendal. Later as Mrs Livingstone-Wilson she went to Sierra Leone as a voluntary missionary.[117]

The second prominent African missionary was John Taylor Smith who was born in Kendal in 1860. After attending the Grammar School there, he went into partnership with his elder brother as 'Smith J & J T watchmakers, jewellers and engravers' with a shop at 26 Highgate, Kendal.[118] In many ways similar to Thomas Wilson, he was an enthusiastic member of the local YMCA, a keen cyclist and passionate about the natural beauty of the Lake District. Ordained in 1885, he was appointed Canon Missioner at Sierra Leone in 1891. While there he was appointed Chaplain to the Gold Coast Expedition and this brought him to national prominence as he ministered to the dying Prince Henry of Battenberg.[119] After taking the Prince's last words to a distraught Princess Beatrice and Queen Victoria his ascent was swift. Made an Honorary Chaplain to the Queen in 1896, within a year Taylor Smith was Bishop of Sierra Leone.[120] Thomas Wilson was both passionate about his native county and widely read and it is unsurprising if these two Westmerian personalities inspired his interest in Africa, if not actually causing him to follow their lead.

How he heard of the opportunity at Lagos is rather harder to guess although the railway's consulting engineer William Shelford[121] was a prominent member of the ICE with a seat on its council. It seems likely that he came across Thomas Wilson's application for ICE membership of March 30 1897 and approached him. Plainly by the time of his departure Thomas Wilson was aware of Shelford's ICE status as, seemingly in an attempt to boost his application, he wrote to the secretary of the ICE to advise the membership committee of his West African appointment under him.

This letter followed an interview with Shelford at his offices at 35a Great George Street, Westminster. Shelford, like George Laws, had a significant English railway building pedigree but in his case principally in 1860s London.[122] Thomas Wilson's recent railway work would have certainly appealed to him. At their meeting Shelford gave advice on the tropical climate and the risks it entailed to health. Practical advice was also given about suitable tropical clothing outfitters and other provisions and equipment which it was advisable to take.

How specific Shelford was about the danger of malaria is unclear but contemporary missionary accounts of Africa were full of tales of 'fever deaths' and Prince Henry's death of malaria had occurred just a year before. Other prominent victims of the disease, actually in Lagos, were those of Bishop and Mrs Hill within hours of each other in early January 1894. Bishop Hill fell to the rampant disease just six days after he had preached his first and last sermon as the first Bishop of Western Equatorial Africa[123] in Christ Church, Lagos.

In the light of his subsequent conduct, it is clear that concern for his own welfare did not come high in Thomas Wilson's list of priorities and he almost certainly also disregarded the risks of disease and death in 1897.

Following his resignation from the Consett Iron Company he took out a loan of £60 from the York City & County Banking Co Ltd, of 2 Collingwood Street, Newcastle. It was almost certainly borrowed as an advance on his Colonial Office salary and so he had a cash float with him for contingencies during the journey and on his arrival in Africa. Another reason for the loan may have been the financial responsibility he had recently assumed towards a nineteen-year-old woman. She was Polly Colman and was eventually to become his second wife and mother of his children.

Polly's antecedents and upbringing were quite different to his. Thirteen years his junior, she had been born on 2 April 1878 to Jane and Philip Thompson Colman in East Rainton, County Durham. East Rainton was in the heart of the Durham coalfield between Durham and Sunderland near Hetton-le-Hole. Both her surname and many of the local place names indicate that this had been a mining area for centuries. Polly's father, born in 1846 and married to her mother Jane Hutchinson[124] in 1866, is described as a colliery worker on her birth certificate. By the 1881 census he is listed as a coachman, although it is telling that all of their neighbours on the same East Rainton census page are listed as miners. She had four elder sisters and a younger brother Robert. All of her elder sisters were of school age in 1881 and are recorded as scholars. In 1880 school was made compulsory (although not free) up to the age of ten.[125] However the Colmans were not without the means to support their large family: their eldest daughter Frances Mary was still in school at fourteen, as was Elizabeth at eleven. The area was at that time a hard, dangerous and unhealthy one and a world away from Thomas Wilson's idyllic Westmorland. The year following the census claimed Polly's eldest sister at the age of fifteen and on 29 September 1883 her father died aged 37. On his death certificate the cause of death is given as 'phthisis eighteen months' which in modern medical speech is tuberculosis. He would have been increasingly incapacitated as his lungs slowly declined over the previous year and a half.

The death of the family's male income earner could have a devastating effect on Victorian families who could not call upon their community or wider family to support them. Without any social welfare provision the ultimate recourse was admission to the workhouse and the resulting division of families. Polly's mother Jane however was a local farmer's daughter with deep roots in the East Rainton area: there are three Hutchinson farmers listed in East Rainton in Kelly's 1890 *Directory of Durham* and as a result of this Hutchinson family network, she did manage to keep her young family intact until she remarried on 25 April 1888. The man she married was Thomas Trotter, a 54-year-old publican of neighbouring West Rainton, who had also been married before.

At the time of their father's death in 1883 Polly and Robert were five and three respectively and as such were probably cushioned the most from the effects of his young death. Their three elder siblings must have felt those effects far more. Elizabeth became a servant until she married in 1892 aged 21 and her sister Alice appears to have married at seventeen in 1890. Jenny seems to have been sent to live with a cousin Thomas Wilkinson and in the 1891 census she appears aged fifteen in his house along with his wife and son at 21 Howard Terrace, Chopwell. Of course Chopwell was the Consett Iron Company's new pit village and in 1891 Thomas Wilson was involved in linking it by rail with the existing pit at Garesfield. Wilkinson is described in the census as a 'pumping engineman' and as such he was almost certainly involved in the creation of the new mine and living in a house belonging to his employers. Wilkinson may well have actually worked under Thomas Wilson or just come to his attention through his general interest in steam driven machinery. Whatever the truth, this 1891 proximity between Polly's sister Jenny and Thomas Wilson is the best explanation of how Polly and her future husband met.

On the 1891 census, Polly and her younger brother are shown living in their step-father's public house, The Oak Tree Inn, West Rainton.[126] Their mother Jane is also shown, as is their half-brother William Trotter aged two years. Polly aged thirteen is described as a 'scholar' as is her younger brother Robert[127] aged ten.

After 1891 it is unclear where Polly was living but it seems likely that on a visit to her sister at her cousin's house in Chopwell, some years after Thomas Wilson became a widower in 1893, they became acquainted.[128] Family anecdote certainly suggests that Polly and her sister Jenny were close.

Also unclear is precisely when he reached an understanding or became engaged to Polly. Many years later his youngest daughter Betty (1911-1997)[129] stated that her parents did become engaged prior to his departure for Africa in 1897 and that her father arranged for her mother to stay with a vicar in Tiverton while he was away and until they were able to marry. Her use of the words 'able to marry' is significant because when he first left for West Africa in May 1897 Polly was only nineteen and would not be of age to marry in her own right until April 1899. Although her family would never have withheld their consent to such an obviously advantageous marriage being made prior to her 21st birthday, the fact that her father was dead complicated the situation. Thomas Wilson may have thought quite honourably that she should give mature and prolonged consideration before marring a widower thirteen years her senior. He also may have thought it unfair to marry her and then leave her in County Durham while he disappeared possibly forever to the part of Africa known as the white man's grave.

If such were his thoughts it was consistent to take steps to arrange a safe, comfortable and respectable environment for her to spend their necessarily long engagement. A further factor, given their quite different social and economic origins, may have been a desire to see her socially improved by her stay in Tiverton. They had been born into very different backgrounds. His was the world of the Westmorland yeoman farmer, going back centuries: hers the far more rough-edged and now lost world of the Durham mining community. Additionally, the world he mixed in as a successful and ambitious civil engineer and the one she would join on marriage were very different from her own youthful social network in the Raintons. It was almost certainly not akin to the cynicism and coldness of Shaw's *Pygmalion* but that he thought a period in the far more refined world of a Victorian vicarage would be advantageous to her is scarcely surprising for the time.

The explanation why Tiverton was chosen for Polly's sojourn is rather protracted. It came about through Thomas Wilson's connection with the Reverend Dr. Charles Storrs. Although Storrs was never a vicar in Tiverton he provided the link which enabled Polly to live there. Charles Storrs had been born in Doncaster in 1840. He was ordained a priest in 1864 in the diocese of Norwich and was a curate in Holbrook, Suffolk before leaving for the Punjab. His first daughter, Ethel, was born in Amritsar in 1869. After his return from India he held three Yorkshire parishes, including Snaith, near Selby, where he was Rural Dean from 1884-1885. From there he went to a parish in Somerset and then Torquay. He left Torquay for the Rectory of Selsey in the Diocese of Chichester in 1896 and in the same year became Dr. Storrs when the Western University of Canada[130] awarded him an honourary doctorate of divinity. In 1898 he became Vicar of St. John the Baptist's Church, in Palmeira Square, Hove, where he would remain until his death in 1904. St. John's was a fashionable church with seating for 931[131] drawn from his half acre parish and he had two curates under him.

Just how Thomas Wilson met Storrs is not entirely clear but the most likely explanation was their North of England connection. Thomas Wilson was aged twenty and a trainee civil engineer when Storrs left Yorkshire for Somerset. But more relevantly at this time he was an enthusiastic member of the Darlington YMCA and one of the YMCA activities was to undertake parish mission work often some distance away and in other counties. These visits usually targeted 'difficult' industrial areas and were especially welcomed by evangelical low-church clergy such as Storrs. It therefore seems most likely that during one such mission to the Selby coalfield area they met. Another possibility is that the link was made through one of Thomas Wilson's own parish vicars with whom he was invariably close. One of those vicars was the Reverend Arthur Hughes of Holy Trinity, Darlington, who like Storrs had a longstanding connection with the Church Missionary Society.

However, although his connection was with Storrs, Polly did not go to Hove but to St. George's Vicarage in Tiverton. The 1897 incumbent of St. George's was one of Storrs' former curates the Reverend John Hill who had married Storr's daughter Ethel in 1892. As to why Tiverton was preferred to Hove the answer was probably one of practicalities. The 1891 census discloses that the Rev. and Mrs Storrs had eight unmarried daughters ranging in age from 22 to ten in the house, plus four servants. Although by 1897 one of them had married, the vicarage in Hove was most probably a very crowded place. Conversely the vicarage in Tiverton had only Hill, his wife, adopted baby daughter and their servants.

Having made arrangements for Polly to stay in Tiverton, acquired his tropical clothes and organised his finances, on Thursday 20 May 1897 Thomas Wilson's friends and former colleagues made a presentation and formally said goodbye to him. The evening's events were very fully reported in the *Consett Chronicle*. As the newspaper was printed a week after he left the country Thomas Wilson may never have seen it:

> *On Thursday evening in last week an interesting gathering took place at the Assembly Rooms, High Spen, near Lintz Green, for the purpose of making a presentation to Mr Thomas Wilson Bracken C.E. who has been for a period of nearly seven years Resident Engineer for the Consett Iron Company's Chopwell and Garesfield Railway, on the occasion of his leaving the district to undertake a government appointment in West Africa.*

The report goes on to say that evening was presided over by Mr J. R. Gilchrist who was a director of the Consett Iron Company and mine manager at Garesfield. Also present was George Wishart the under-manager at Garesfield, the Reverend George D'Eath curate of St. Patrick's Chapel who had married Thomas Wilson in 1892 and two representatives of the Chester-le-Street Division Conservative Association. At the gathering, Thomas Wilson was presented with quite an array of gifts consisting of "a reducer, a barometer, a thermometer, a revolver, a calculator and a pair of field glasses. The articles were suitably inscribed." It was almost certainly George Laws who had advised on what gifts would be of most use and he may even have organised their purchase in Newcastle.

Of these articles the field glasses and revolver case have survived. The gun case is a large oak box with brass fittings and was made by W. R. Pape gun, pistol and rifle maker of 36 Westgate, Newcastle. On the top centre of the box is a medallion brass plaque bearing the inscription: "Presented to Mr T. W. Bracken C.E. on his leaving High Spen near Newcastle-on-Tyne for West Africa as a memento and mark of esteem from his numerous friends. May 20th 1897." The field glasses bear the same inscription and are still in the original purse-like leather case.

Sadly the pistol itself is no longer in the case, although it did survive until 1940 when Thomas Wilson's widow, in response to the emergency appeal for weapons, handed it in to the local police station.

Seemingly the other four gifts have not survived. Plainly the subscription raised to buy these things and to have each of them elaborately inscribed must have amounted to a substantial sum. It cannot be said exactly who subscribed but George Laws and the CIC directors Logan and Gilchrist were all wealthy men. Sir David Dale the CIC Chairman, who had been made a baronet in 1895,[132] was wealthier still, and it seems highly likely that substantial contributions were made by these men in addition to those of the ordinary residents of High Spen.

Returning to the report in the Consett newspaper it tells us that:

> The Chairman, Mr Wishart, the Rev. G D'Eath, Mr Paxton, Mr Robson and others alluded to the genial qualities of Mr Bracken and expressed regret at his departure and at the same time wishing him success in his new appointment – Mr Bracken feelingly responded and said he hoped to be back in England again before the twelve months were over. He had no idea when he came to Spen seven years ago that he was destined to make so many friends as he saw around him that evening and he hoped that the parting would not be of long duration. (Applause) – The formal proceedings terminated with a vote of thanks to the Chairman, the subscribers afterwards partaking of supper together. – Mr Bracken left for Africa last week.

On the evening of the following day he boarded the *S.S. Axim* in Liverpool, which sailed at dawn on 22 May 1897.

8 – AFRICAN ADVENTURES

The *Axim* had been built just four years earlier and weighed 2,808 tons.[133] It was part of the fleet of Elder, Dempster and Co. of Liverpool which owned both the British and African Steam Navigation Company (founded in 1869) and African Royal Mail Steamers, which had won the British Government's mail carrying contract to West Africa in 1852.

The journey from Liverpool to West Africa, via Madeira and the Canaries, took between three and four weeks. After the Canaries, Elder Dempster's ships called at Sierra Leone, Liberia, Ghana[134] and Nigeria. The list of passengers on board records twenty-one male passengers. Thomas Wilson's name appears first on the list made by the ship's master – whether because he was the first to embark or because the Colonial Office, which arranged and paid for his first class passage,[135] was the first to make a booking is unclear. The ship's crew was approximately 40 and so the 21 passengers would have been looked after extremely well.

Another advantage of first class was the amount of luggage it permitted. Aside from the array of gifts from his Newcastle and Durham friends and his surveying equipment he would, by modern standards, have taken a huge range of clothing so as to be dressed appropriately for all occasions. In order to decide exactly what was required he would have consulted one of the numerous guides for colonial officers which were published for each of the significant colonial postings. *The Lagos Offical Hand Book*[136] contains this section of 'Hints on Outfit for the West Coast of Africa':

> *Europeans wear on the West Coast of Africa the same clothing as in England in the height of summer, but the waistcoat is generally discarded in favour of the Cummer-bund. Flannel trousers, and suits of dark blue serge or of thin tweeds, which are specially made for the tropics, are much used.*
>
> *In the rainy season an ordinary English summer suit will not be too thick. A suit of evening dress clothes, and a thick black morning coat and*

waistcoat, should be taken out. White shirts with turn down collars are worn while indoors at headquarters. Flannel shirts are required while travelling.

Shoes are cooler than boots and are therefore considered by some to be more comfortable… others recommend boots as affording more protection against mosquitoes and sand-flies.

Officers whose work is out of doors should provide lace boots… and a pair of gamekeeper's leggings for crossing swamps, etc. A pair of high India rubber rain boots would be useful.

A complete set of winter clothes and winter underclothing and a thick overcoat or ulster should be taken out… leave of absence may take him to England in cold weather and warm clothing is required on board ship.

A helmet: light, pith, coming well over the temples and back of the neck should be worn at all times out of doors. A large silk handkerchief tied loosely about the neck is of immense protection from the sun… especially in stooping.[137]

Of the passengers who sailed with him only one other was bound for Lagos. The most common destination was Old Calabar further round the Gulf of Guinea and close to the current border with Cameroon. In 1897 Old Calabar was a part of the Niger Coast Protectorate. Other passengers were bound for the Niger Coast ports of Bonny and Burutu on the Forcados River, where the headquarters of the Royal Niger Company[138] was.

At the time no one thought of these ports as Nigerian. The concept of a state called Nigeria was to have a slow and haphazard creation and it was not until 1914 that the area essentially forming the modern state of Nigeria was established by Britain as a single administrative unit.

Britain's involvement in the area had first arisen from a desire to combat the area's active slave trade and as such was first confined to the coast, where British trading companies established themselves to buy the palm oil and other agricultural produce which the hinterland areas produced. The scale of import of West African palm oil was substantial by mid-century. As well as a lubricant for British machinery, it was used in the manufacture of both soap and candles and its by-product glycerine increasingly in medicines.[139] By the end of the century other significant exports from Lagos to Britain, apart from palm oil and palm kernels, were mahogany, rubber and cocoa.[140]

As the nineteenth century progressed, Christian missionaries such as

David Livingstone entered the interior of the 'dark Continent' for the first time. Their accounts of domestic slavery, outrages against missionaries and human sacrifice were avidly published by the British press, stirring public interest in the undiscovered continent.

Just how much interest there was is proved by Livingstone being given what was virtually a state funeral in Westminster Abbey in April 1874. His dictum of the '3 Cs': Commerce, Christianity and Civilization, to liberate Africa from superstition and slavery, proved irresistible to an evangelical Britain. The words on his tombstone sum up his mission and achievements:

> *For 30 years his life was spent in an unwearied effort to evangelise the native races, to explore the undiscovered secrets and to abolish the desolating slave trade of Central Africa.*

The history of the British in Lagos mirrors the history of British involvement in the rest of West Africa. Lagos was just one of the places along the coast where traders had established themselves. It sits on an island in the lagoon at the base of the river Ogun, separated from the mainland to the north of it. The only seaward access was over a shallow sand bar at the mouth of the lagoon beyond which lies the Gulf of Guinea and the Atlantic Ocean. Payne's 1893 *Principal Events in Yoruba History* describes the condition of the Lagos lagoon at this time:

> *This system of inland waters is called by the Europeans the 'Lagoon' and by the natives 'Ossa'. It varies very much in breadth, now spreading out into lakes and now contracted to half a mile across but always so gentle smooth and clear and so adorned on either side with trees of luxuriant foliage, that the beautiful 'Ossa' has become its frequent epithet even among European residents.*

Lagos had been an ancient Portuguese slave port and its name is derived from the Portuguese word for lagoon.[141] Its history as a Crown colony began in 1851 when the Royal Navy occupied it to extract a promise from its ruler to outlaw the slave trade. In 1853 a British Consul was appointed and in 1861 Lagos Island was annexed to the British Crown and governed as a dependency of the Gold Coast Colony[142] and administered from Accra. With a growing British appetite for intervention in the African interior a convenient pretext came in 1886 when, following a spate of tribal wars which badly affected

British traders in Lagos, the British government resolved to exert far greater control over the Yoruba tribe and the trading area of the Ogun, whose source is several hundred miles inland. As a result Lagos was given its own governor and administration. The policy of incrementally gaining control worked. In 1893 Governor Carter led an expedition to the interior of Yoruba and signed treaties with the native rulers leading to the interior towns of Ibadan and Abeokuta accepting British Residents under Lagos. In the Treaty of Friendship and Commerce signed by Carter on the Queen's behalf, at Abeokuta in January 1893, the Alake or King of the Egba tribe promised the British peace and friendship, free trade with Lagos and to protect and encourage ministers of the Christian religion.

To the east of the Colony of Lagos and further along the coast of the Gulf was the Niger Coast Protectorate and this territory along with that of Lagos would eventually form the coast of Nigeria. The interior area behind the Niger Coast was under the control of the Royal Niger Company which had been given a royal charter to control the trading area of the river Niger. From these three disparate units, a Crown Colony in Lagos, a British Government coastal Protectorate and a private English company, Nigeria was eventually created.

When it arrived at Lagos in mid-June 1897, the *Axim* was too large to enter the port owing to the sand bar and Thomas Wilson would have been lowered from the steamer to a smaller boat in the open ocean off Lagos in a 'mammy-chair'. A mammy-chair was a wooden box into which two chairs facing each other were placed: across the top of the box was an iron bar to allow the box to be lowered by rope from a derrick on the ship. Sir A. C. Burns in his *History of Nigeria* of 1936 vividly describes the journey from the steamer to the shore:

> *Passengers were transferred from the mail steamers to a tender in the open roadstead off Lagos in conditions of considerable discomfort and some danger. They were lowered over the side of the mail steamer, three or four at a time, in a mammy-chair, into a surf-boat, which rose and fell on a sea which was never still: crouched on the thwarts of the surf-boat as it… was paddled across by half-naked Krumen[143] to the tender and hoisted aboard in another mammy-chair… when they were finally landed on the wharf at Lagos they were hot, tired and not infrequently soaked to the skin.*

Arriving in 1892, Mrs Hill, described her and Bishop Hill's journey from the ocean steamer off the Lagos sand bar and their transfer to the branch steamer in a letter home:[144]

The bar on Saturday was unusually smooth; I was so thankful for it, for it was not smooth at sea and going from the 'Boma' to the branch steamer in a little rowing boat, it was very rough. We were let down by the crane in arm chairs; it is a very uncomfortable experience, but lasts only half a minute.

In the same letter she describes the view of their passage to the wharf:

Lagos has improved so very much since we were here in 1876 that I should hardly have recognised it. The township is far handsomer and the houses much better built than at Sierra Leone but, of course, it lacks the lovely mountain scenery of the latter.

Mrs Hill was certainly correct about Lagos's development. London had been linked with Lagos by telegraph in 1886, the Bank of British West Africa opened on the Marina in 1891 and the telephone arrived in Lagos in 1892. The 1891 census had recorded a population of 32,508 of which 12,071 were employed in commerce and of these just a few hundred were Europeans.[145] Payne's *History* also stated:

Lagos has had its ups and downs, but on the whole, she has made rapid strides in prosperity, and under proper management bids fair to become the Liverpool of West Africa.

Another description of contemporary Lagos is given in an 1898 edition of *The Engineer*:

The town of Lagos is on an island 3.5 miles long and 1 mile to 1.5 miles wide. The western part of this island is very thickly populated containing about 50,000 inhabitants of whom not more than 150 are Europeans.

At the western end of the island, closest to the sand bar was Government House. Behind it lay the official quarters, next were the mercantile quarters and finally the native quarters which were located in the north-west corner of the island.

The Engineer describes the view on arrival:

On entering the lagoon... the Government House is seen on the right and from it a broad road called the Marina runs along the front to the north-western corner of the island. It will be observed that wharves run out from the Marina into the lagoon, and at these the branch steamers discharge. The chief merchants and most of the Government officials have houses or offices on the Marina…

Although *The Engineer* omitted to mention it, another of the principal landmarks of the Marina was the tower of Christ Church Cathedral which was the first Church of England church in Lagos and had been dedicated in 1869. Christian worship in Lagos had been commenced seventeen years earlier by agents of the Church Missionary Society (C.M.S.) and by 1893 Payne lists fourteen other places of Anglican worship and over 30 Christian schools, including the C.M.S. Grammar School founded in 1859.

From the Wharf, Thomas Wilson took another boat to Ebute-Metta across the Lagoon on the African mainland where in June 1897 he reported to the Chief Resident Engineer, William Gee (1852-1905) at the Railway Headquarters Office. Like so many others, Gee's health was affected by the West African climate: at the age of 46 he was forced into retirement owing to ill health. Although he recovered sufficiently to resume duties, surveying the eventual route of the railway up to the Niger in 1900, he was dead five years later.

While taking this boat journey and the one from the ocean steamer to the wharf Thomas Wilson was in the hands of the Government Vessels Department which had been established to provide water transport between Lagos and such of the colony as was accessible by the extensive network of lagoons, rivers and creeks. The *Official Hand Book* describes the Department in 1898 as having:

A flotilla composed of one Governor's steam yacht, five steam launches, and a quantity of boats, canoes, etc. of various sizes and descriptions, stationed in various parts of the lagoon and rivers. A large amount of transport is carried on by contract with natives, also arranged by this department.

When he arrived construction work on the railway had already begun on the mainland opposite Lagos at Ebute-Metta[146] where, as well as the railway headquarters, staff quarters, workshops, engine sheds and a small railway hospital had been constructed.[147] In addition a photographic room had been built adjacent to the offices so as to enable both the Chief Resident Engineer in Ebute-Metta and the consulting engineer, Shelford, in London to see the construction in progress.[148] On this part of his journey he would have had his first view of the two bridges across the Lagoon then under construction: the first between Lagos and the intervening island of Iddo where the railway terminus was to be, and the second between Iddo and the mainland at Ebute-Metta.

The initial idea for a railway connecting Lagos with the interior of Yoruba land was contained in the Governor Carter's[149] despatch to the Colonial Secretary of 11 October 1893 in which he reported on his three month Interior Expedition to Abeokuta and Ibadan. Thereafter surveying and estimates for the Lagos railway commenced in 1894 following pressure on the Colonial Secretary from the Liverpool and Manchester Chambers of Commerce and William Shelford's survey was completed by May 1895.

Lord Salisbury became Prime Minister for the third time on 2 July 1895 and Joseph Chamberlain[150] was appointed Secretary of State for the Colonies, a post he was to hold for the next eight years. Chamberlain was, unlike his predecessors, determined to transform the Colonial Office, increase imperial trade and develop the under-developed parts of the Empire.

In a speech in July 1895 he set out his thinking:

Great Britain, the little centre of a vaster Empire than the world has ever seen, owns great possessions in every part of the globe, and many of these possessions are still almost unexplored, entirely underdeveloped. What would a great landlord do in a similar case with a great estate? If he had the money he would expend some of it at any rate in improving the property, in making communications, in making outlets for the products of his land.

The newspapers christened him 'Joseph Africanus'[151] and Shelford's West African survey could not have landed on his desk at a more opportune moment.

Unsurprisingly in this political environment, construction work began forthwith in Lagos in 1896 under the financial control of the Crown Agents for the Colonies. Shelford acted as consulting engineer to the Colonial Office in London, with a Chief Resident Engineer in charge on the ground.

Almost all of the materials required to build Nigeria's first railway were imported to the colony from England. The rails, sleepers and steel for the railway bridges were shipped from Liverpool and without a deep water harbour none of these materials could be unloaded in Lagos. Instead they were carried by the ocean steamers to Forcados and then transhipped in a much smaller boat across the Lagos sand bar. Given the quantities of material required the transhipment boats, drawing only nine feet of water, needed to make numerous trips to carry a single ocean steamer's Lagos Railway cargo.[152]

From a European staff list on the Colonial Office file dated 30 September 1897, the railway engineering hierarchy becomes clear. Under the chief resident engineer, were two district engineers; under them three assistant engineers including Thomas Wilson. The non-engineer European staff numbered around 30; consisting of medical officers, auditors, clerks and storekeepers. This small European group was dwarfed by the unlisted skilled and unskilled native labour force. Its size varied by many thousands during the construction period. *The Lagos Official Hand Book* gives a figure of 3,500 employed daily on 31 March 1898.

The Engineer described the railway labour force in the following terms:

> *In Lagos the workmen may be divided into three classes. Those coming from the Gold Coast, the Kroo Coast, and the interior of Yoruba. The earthwork is chiefly done by men from the interior, who seem to manage spades and wheelbarrows better than the natives of Southern Europe, but they try to do the minimum of work in the maximum of time, and are dear even at the usual rate of a shilling a day. Each gang must have an overseer of its own nationality, and these in turn must be supervised by a European foreman.*
>
> *The number of men at present employed on Lagos bridges and railways is over 2,000 natives and 47 Europeans, including two doctors.*

The initial stage of construction was the 22 mile section from Ebute-Metta to Otta and this section was still under construction when Thomas Wilson arrived in Lagos. Ebute-Metta was where his permanent quarters were but, although separated from Lagos by the as yet un-bridged lagoon, it was not particularly isolated, owing to the numerous boats of the Vessels Department. A Botanical Garden had been established there in 1888 and prior to that St. Jude's church was built by the C.M.S. to serve the Christians of Ebute-Metta. Thomas Wilson's quarters were provided free and furnished under the terms of his Colonial Office contract, and consisted of a sitting room, bed room and separate kitchen accommodation.[153]

The Engineer describes Shelford's plans for the railway terminus and the accompanying bridges across the lagoon:

The choice of a site for the Lagos terminus gave Mr Shelford a good deal of trouble. A railway station to which the inhabitants of Lagos could only gain access by boat would not be of very much use to them; and in view of the augmented commerce which the railway would probably produce, it seemed equally essential that the terminus should not be far from a deep-water wharf, to which not only the present branch boat could have access, but also ocean steamers, if the bar should be removed... there is an island called Iddo, between Lagos and the mainland; and it was decided to build a terminus and workshops on this island, and to connect it by bridges with Ebute Metta and with Lagos Island... the bridges... were named after the late governor, Sir Gilbert Carter, and the deputy-governor, Captain Denton, the Carter and Denton Bridges.

The Denton Bridge, 917 feet in length, linking Iddo with the mainland would serve as both a road and rail bridge,[154] whereas the Carter Bridge, of 2,200 feet with two swing openings to allow steamers to pass up the lagoon, would be for road traffic and a steam tramway to Lagos.

Within a fortnight of Thomas Wilson's arrival in Lagos, Queen Victoria's Diamond Jubilee was marked by a week of ceremonies in the colony. The colonial Government invited a huge number of tribal leaders and elders from the interior of Yoruba as the *Official Hand Book* records:

To celebrate Her Majesty's Jubilee invitations by the Government were issued to the Kings, Chiefs and Headmen, and representatives of every district to a Durbar held in Lagos. The ardour and enthusiasm manifested by all classes and sections showed that the people as a whole appreciated the importance of so memorable an occasion.

In June 1897, during the Jubilee week, over 3,000 people including several Kings and Chiefs and their retinues and horses, were conveyed to Lagos... to attend ceremonies held in honour of Her Majesty.

For Thomas Wilson, new to Africa, this great and colourful gathering or Durbar of the native leaders, paying tribute to their far distant Queen, was an unprecedented spectacle and one almost to rival the pageantry taking place in London, 4,000 miles away.

In charge of the Lagos show was the Queen's representative, the Governor, Royal Engineer Major Henry McCallum C.M.G. who had been in post since the previous January when he had replaced Governor Carter. One aspect of the celebrations was a state service at Christ Church Cathedral, on 30 June 1897, timed to coincide with the ceremony on the steps of St. Paul's which the increasingly infirm Queen witnessed from her carriage. All of the employees of the Colonial Government, including those working on the Lagos railway, were awarded a Jubilee holiday and this would probably have been the first occasion for Thomas Wilson to wear his formal morning and evening clothes.

The timing of the Jubilee in late June did not ensure appropriately fine weather in Lagos. For June is in the midst of the rainy season which usually commences in April and lasts until November; with the exception of six weeks during August to September which was known as the 'middle dry'. Meteorological records were kept by the Colonial Government for inclusion in the *Colonial Office Blue Book*. Those for 1899 record a not atypical annual rainfall of 73.92 inches, a mean shade daily maximum of 86.8 Fahrenheit and a mean minimum of 75.6. The dry season lasts from November to April with temperatures peaking in January-February. The 1900 *Blue Book* records the February 1899 average maximum as 91.5 Fahrenheit.

The first destination of the railway, Otta, was a town of circa 4,000 inhabitants and the railway passed up the river valley of the Ogun to reach it. In doing so the route went through dense tropical forest and after the route had been surveyed and selected, forest clearing was the first task for the huge labour force. Construction of necessary earthworks, culverts and minor bridges came next, followed by the laying of ballast and the permanent way. At the same time stations for this section were built at Iddo, Ebute-Metta, Agege and Otta. By September 1897 the track was laid to Otta and construction trains were running daily on it. Otta was the site of a missionary out-station of Lagos[155] and, although records are sketchy, it seems likely that Thomas Wilson visited this Mission while at Otta in late 1897. C.M.S. stations provided both a place of worship and a fairly safe and secure environment for the British in the Yoruba interior at this time and his knowledge of and involvement with such missions is referred to in his Carlisle Diocesan Magazine obituary.

Thomas Wilson may even have lodged at the Otta Mission in 1897 but as the railway building progressed into the interior camps were built for the workforce, including accommodation and office quarters for the engineers. From the surviving 1898 photographs of these camps it is clear that Thomas Wilson's quarters were of typical indigenous construction; timber framed, with walls and roofs made from palm and other vegetation, and open at one end so as to allow what breeze there was to provide some relief from the savage heat and humidity.

Whether this accommodation was entirely watertight must be doubtful and the Colonial Office files contain a letter from the Chief Resident Engineer for the railway describing the difficulties caused by the rainy season in the autumn of 1897:

> *There has been so much rain lately and the new banks near Otta are settling so much in consequence that it would be impossible for me to deplete the maintenance gangs and to keep the line open for traffic and even with the large number of men at present employed should there be much more rain it might be necessary for me to close the line beyond the 16th mile.*

As well as these foreseeable climatic difficulties of construction a political emergency erupted in October 1897 involving a French threat to the uncertain north-west frontier of the colony north of Saki[156]and the equally ill-defined border with neighbouring French Dahomey.[157]

The Engineer, in an article of 25 February 1898, accurately reflected these uncertainties:

> *Its northern boundary is not clearly defined: it is not easy to say where the Colony of Lagos leaves off and the Protectorate begins, nor even how far north the later extends...*

By Protectorate the Engineer was referring to the territory of the Niger Coast Protectorate under the control of the Royal Niger Company: the main cause of the crisis was the virtually unlimited interior territorial ambitions of that Company.[158] It had been founded by George Goldie in 1886 and given a Royal Charter to administer the trading area of the Niger River but just what were the limits of that trading area?

As part of its expansionist policy to turn the uncoloured parts of the map pink, the Niger Company, through its agent the great African explorer Captain Frederick Lugard DSO,[159] signed a treaty with the King of Nikki in 1894 – or rather, with the King's agent, as the King believed he would die as soon as he saw the face of a white man.[160] By its terms the company gained control of the territory to the west of the Niger at Bussa, 40,000 square miles known as Borgu. As soon as Lugard left Nikki with his completed treaty the French arrived and the King granted them an exclusive protectorate of Borgu. Armed with their own rival treaty the French now advanced to Bussa,[161] a key strategic point on the Niger just below the rapids, and the limit of the river's navigation. When news that the French tricoleur was flying there reached London in April 1897 Bussa found itself thrust to the centre of international politics. Chamberlain was prepared to risk war with France rather than succumb over Borgu and he despatched Lugard back to the Niger to deal with the French. He gave Lugard the creative title of Her Majesty's Commissioner for the hinterland of Nigeria and, with the temporary rank of Colonel, Lugard created what became known as the West African Frontier Force (WAFF). The WAFF troops were dispatched up the Niger in a dangerous game of brinkmanship to fly their flag alongside that of France.[162]

As a result of this potentially explosive Anglo-French struggle over Borgu, the Colonial Office also needed to secure Lagos Colony's own frontiers against the French and the troops of the 2nd West Indian regiment, who happened to be in Lagos at the time, were despatched to Saki in October 1897.

The railway with its workforce of several thousand was the best source of labour for the Colonial Government to commandeer to accompany them. On 13 October the Colonial Secretary wrote to the Chief Resident Engineer at Ebute-Metta informing him in the clearest terms that the emergency, and the consequent need for carriers to accompany the troops, were to take priority over railway construction.

I am desired by the Governor to inform you that it is of the utmost importance that the Detachment 2nd W.I. Regiment[163] now in Lagos should proceed to the N. W. frontier as speedily as possible. At the present time it is a very difficult matter to procure the necessary carriers to transport the baggage of the Detachment, and His Excellency will be much obliged if you can arrange to let the Government have 500 men at least from the Railway Works.

The men… will not be called upon to fight and the greater part will return to Lagos immediately after their arrival at Saki for fresh loads. They will have continuous employment for at least three months.

113

I am to impress upon you the vital importance of despatching the W.I. Regiment to the Interior at once, and I am to say that the Governor wishes all other work except that on the Bridges, to give way to this matter for some little time to come.

The *Lagos Weekly Record*, which was clearly aware of the Government's labour difficulties, was a willing agent in spreading the Government line in its edition of 9 October 1897:

Some misapprehension appears to exist in regard to the destination of the West Indian troops and which makes the natives reluctant to engage as carriers. The troops, who are required entirely for garrison duty, will not be employed beyond the boundaries of the protectorate of the Colony, so that there is no cause for any apprehension, and it will be a reflection upon the Colony if labour has to be employed... for a service which is at once remunerative and intended to serve the highest interests of the Colony.

On the ground, and in the forest clearing works surrounding Otta, news of the Government's appeal for carriers was communicated by Franklin Hurst, District Engineer to his two subordinates, the Assistant Engineers Thomas Wilson and F. H. Steinhaeuser. Hurst's notes of his actions relating to the military expedition have survived:

October 13th – *Instructed Steinhaeuser & Bracken as to Governor requiring 500 carriers for W.I. Expedition and asking how far they could gather these men from the surrounding villages.*

So far from being able to get outside labourers many of our own men ran away at the idea of their having to go.

October 21st – Went to Otta with Captain Thring (per special train) re carriers. Steinhaeuser had volunteered to go with our men, who refused to go without him and on the 22nd all our men going as carriers started to work erecting Sheds, Latrines, etc. at Otta for the reception of the troops.

October 23rd – There having been rumours of refusal to go to Saki I went to Otta per Special train and had a conference with Steinhaeuser & Bracken.

In essence the outcome of this discussion was that Thomas Wilson would

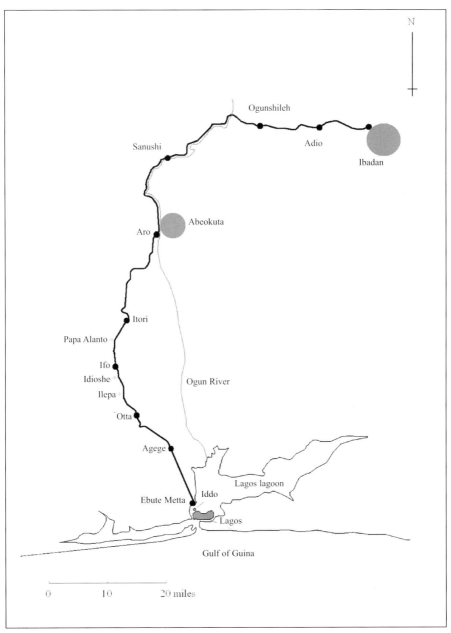

Lagos Government Railway.

remain in Otta on a holding operation in charge of the railway as so far constructed, while Steinhaeuser bravely accompanied the carriers in a journey that was to cost him his life.

On 21 October Gee, the chief Resident Engineer, responded to the Colonial Secretary's letter once Hurst had reported back to him on the situation in Otta:

> *agreeably to the instructions contained in your letter I have detached 500 men from the railway works to go as carriers to the W.I. Regiment. These men will be placed under the charge of Mr F. H. Steinhaeuser, Assistant Engineer, who will accompany the expedition as assistant to the Political Officer. Mr Steinhaeuser and his men are at Otta station ground awaiting instructions.*

In a later report to London the Chief Resident Engineer gave a description of the last weeks of Steinhaeuser's life:

> *The men refused to go unless accompanied by Mr Steinhaeuser under whom they had worked and who by his firmness and kindness had gained their confidence. As Mr Steinhaeuser was due for leave in six weeks, and at the time in robust health, and could not have continued the construction without his labourers, I readily accepted his proposal to accompany the Expedition as assistant Political Officer.*
>
> *Owing to the long delay in obtaining supplementary carriers from other sources, which prevented an early start from Otta and to the fact that the Colonel Commanding retained his services for some days at Saki to build camps etc. and he couldn't reach the coast in time to leave for England on the day he was due, and having contracted malarial fever on the march he died at Mr Shelley's camp on December 9th to the extreme regret of the whole Railway Staff and everybody who knew him.*

As well as providing carriers for the West Indian Regiment troops, the labour force of the railway was further depleted by the construction of a field telegraph between Lagos and Saki. The daily rates of pay for the telegraph workers were higher than those for the railway and given the military situation during 1897-1898 the Colonial Government considered it a higher priority. Shelford in London estimated that the telegraph work caused four months of serious disruption to the railway. A further problem was that when the carriers had finished their work in Saki they did not immediately return to work on the railway. The Chief Resident Engineer wrote a letter of explanation to Shelford:

Of the carriers who accompanied Steinhaeuser but a small percentage returned to work on the Railway immediately, as having en route drawn their 3d. a day subsistence allowance they had (for them) a considerable sum due to them in wages and preferred to go to their homes.

In late October *The Lagos Weekly Record* reflected what were most uncertain times for the Colony:

It is evident that we are on stirring and perhaps perilous times. The military preparations and movements going on around us have a sinister omen for the future. No one knows what "the scramble for Africa" will bring forth. For the present however, the whole country is precipitated into a condition of unrest and alarm and the dubiousness which overhangs the future is not calculated to give much assurance.

And then in the same newspaper on 6 November 1897:

The French Colonial Council are demanding that the French Government should insist upon the retention of Nikki and Bussa. The French appear to have a queer notion of their own in regard to treaties... They unscrupulously encroach on the rights of others and then insist on the fact of such encroachment as a title of right.

However the French Government in practice made no such sustained insistence. On 14 June 1898 France and Britain signed the Niger Convention and secure boundaries for what was eventually to become Nigeria were established. Britain retained Bussa and most of Borgu. All France acquired from the struggle was the extension of the eastern frontier of Dahomey 100 miles into Borgu[164] as far as Nikki.[165] For Chamberlain the outcome was a triumph and its further effects were to be the demise of the Royal Niger Company and the transfer of its territories, plus that of the old Niger Coast Protectorate, into the British Protectorates of Northern and Southern Nigeria. Each of these would be put under Colonial Office control.

At the end of 1899, the British Government paid the Royal Niger Company £850,000 compensation for its shares and the two new protectorates of Northern and Southern Nigeria to the east and north of Lagos were born. Chamberlain chose Sir Frederick Lugard[166] as the new High Commissioner of Northern Nigeria and gave him a virtual free hand to develop a new state out of what was virgin territory for the white man. Chamberlain's empire, like Queen Victoria's, was relentlessly expanding.

From the railway's European staff list for 1897 it is clear that Steinhaeuser was not the only staff fatality. The railway's chief accountant Mr Evans died in October and an engineer Mr Hamilton was invalided home in July. Also invalided was the chief storekeeper in December. Whether all of these were the victims of malaria is not clear but from the remarks of the Chief Resident Engineer made at the railway's opening in March 1901[167] it seems likely:

> *The greatest difficulty in Railway work upon the West Coast is however the deadly fever which decimates our European staff. Upon the work we hand over today to the Colonial Government, there have been 217 Europeans employed, out of these 29 have died and 31 have been invalided.*

Shockingly to us, from what must have been among a workforce of many thousands the far greater number of Africans killed and injured were not even recorded by the Colonial Office or noted by the Chief Resident Engineer. The *Official Hand Book* did at least note the unaccounted effect on native mortality which the editor seems to have attributed to climatic causes:

> *The season of 1897 was a bad one, from a health-point, the mortality amongst both Europeans and Natives being especially noticeable. Twenty five Europeans succumbed during the year to the evil effects of the climate – the death rate between the months of April and July being the most noticeable.*

The first developments in medical science relating to the linkage of the mosquito and malaria were only being made during the late 1890s.[168] In a later ICE paper which reflected the difficulties of constructing a railway out of Lagos, Frederic Shelford[169] refers to the:

> *railway officials being kept fully informed by books and pamphlets on the development of the Malaria Mosquito theory since it was discovered and detailed instructions were given on the site of camps, clothes, food and drink.*

Another problem for the railway staff was the unrelenting heat and humidity of the Lagos area. The 1900 *Blue Book* records an annual average humidity of 88% with an April peak of 97%. *The Engineer* in 1898 saw the possibility of escaping these climatic conditions as one of the benefits of the railway being built to Abeokuta:

It is probable that the construction of a railway will altogether change the conditions of Lagos as a residence for Europeans. Abeokuta cannot be reached in less than three days by horseback, even when horses can be obtained for the journey, which is not always possible. This being the case, Abeokuta and other inland towns are practically out of the question for anyone desiring change of air. The only alternative is to take ship for Sierra Leone, which is not a very inviting voyage and entails an absence of fifteen to twenty days. Missionaries and others who have resided at Abeokuta or Ibadan speak well of the climate, as compared to Lagos and the difference can be noted even a few miles from the coast. As soon as the first section of the line is opened, and it is possible to take periodical changes of air at no great cost either of time or money, Lagos is likely to become less trying to Europeans than it is at present.

The effects of the tropical climate on the health and morale of the railway staff led during late 1897 to the instigation of a limit of eight months of service in Lagos followed by four months home leave. Exactly when it was introduced is not clear although it is not formally reflected in the terms of Thomas Wilson's contract, which show a last revision in February 1897.[170] Its implementation was to have a significant effect on the numbers of engineer staff. From 1897 the number of District Engineers rose from two to six and the number of Assistant Engineers rose from three to six. A consequence of this expansion was the need to build more staff quarters at Ebute-Metta and these were constructed during 1898.

Having arrived in Africa in June 1897, under the new policy Thomas Wilson was entitled to take home leave by March 1898. The journey home again entailed crossing the Lagos sand bar in a small craft before being winched aboard the ocean steamer in a chair. The German Woermann shipping line[171] ran an accelerated service to Plymouth which was quicker than Elder Dempster's Liverpool service and took just nineteen days. However speed of passage was not the only consideration for Thomas Wilson as his

119

young fiancée was waiting for him conveniently in Tiverton. Before leaving he would have telegraphed his arrival date to her from the Marina office of the African Direct Telegraph Company.

As he left, *The Engineer* carried an article on the Lagos Railway which reflected minimal progress on the railway between October 1897 and March 1898, caused by the French emergency:

> *The track is at present laid and construction trains are running to a little above Otta; the clearing has been done for thirty miles and the survey has been finished up to 49 miles. It is not proposed to open the line to public traffic until the rails reach Abeokuta, which will probably be towards the end of next year.*

After six months of frustrating inactivity, accompanied by feverish political and military tension and the death of his friend and colleague Steinhaeuser, leave back to England must have been a very welcome departure for Thomas Wilson.

9 – THE EXERCISE OF PATIENCE

When he reached Plymouth on March 25th he went on by rail to Tiverton. St. George's vicarage was just round the corner from the church in St. Andrew Street, just to the north of the centre of the town and close to the Town Hall and the bridge over the River Exe. For reasons of decorum it is highly unlikely that Thomas Wilson ever stayed at the vicarage. The principal Tiverton hotels at the time were the Palmerston and the Angel, each a short distance from the vicarage, and he would have secured a room in one of them for the duration of his stay.

The incumbent of St. George's was the Reverend John Seymour Granville Hill MA. Perhaps unusually for the time, Reverend Hill and his wife had a one-year-old adopted daughter Aileen Millicent, born in London in 1897 and almost certainly 'rescued' at birth from a life of sin and vice in the capital. The 1901 census indicates the rest of their household. It consisted of three female live-in servants: a cook, a house maid and a nurse. On the same census return Polly Colman is listed after the family but before a four-year-old visitor friend of Aileen Millicent's and the three servants. Polly is described on the return as a 'boarder' aged 22. The word 'boarder' rather than 'lodger' suggests that she was being sponsored to be there rather than paying her own way.

John Hill had been born in Cranborne, Dorset in 1859 and was the son of a surgeon; where he was schooled is unclear but by 1881 he was in Cambridge, at Cavendish College[172] in Hills Road. He obtained his Cambridge BA in theology in 1880 and was ordained a deacon in 1882 and a priest in 1883. Hill had first come to Tiverton in 1882 where he served as curate in the old parish of St. Peter. His next curacy was at Christ Church Ellacombe, in Torquay where he served under the vicar and his future father-in-law Charles Storrs from 1891-1892. On marrying Ethel Storrs he became Vicar of Newport, Devon. After three years at St. John the Baptist's Church in Newport, Hill was inducted as Vicar of St. George's Tiverton.

St. George's was in Fore Street. With an approximate parish population of 2,000, he had a curate to help him cater for their needs. Tiverton had been a textile town throughout the seventeenth and eighteenth centuries and in the nineteenth century retained a significant lace making industry.[173] As a result, and in order to relieve pressure on the town's medieval church of St. Peter, a new Georgian church dedicated to St. George was built in the town and eventually a separate parish was created. The building was initially begun in 1714 and after a long interruption was completed in 1733. Its architect was John James[174] of London, an associate of Hawksmoor. With such a distinguished provenance it is hardly surprising that Pevsner regards it as, "Devon's best eighteenth century town church… dignified exterior of yellow sandstone with rusticated quoins and round headed upper windows." Between James' work and the end of the nineteenth century little changed apart from the seating, font and pulpit, and some alterations to the galleries. Pevsner again, "harmonious interior, little disturbed by minor later alterations."

While Polly was in Tiverton three services were held at St. George's each Sunday with a fourth on the second Sunday of the month and there was weekly Friday evensong. Crockford's indicates Hill's ecclesiastical income as 503 guineas per annum. His was in the middle of the contemporary league table of Anglican clerical incomes. As such, the arrangement he reached with Thomas Wilson was more of a favour than a financial transaction although, owing to his Colonial Office pay, Thomas Wilson was the richer of the two.[175]

Polly's new life in Tiverton was certainly different from that she had experienced in County Durham. The vicarage was substantial, with a very large garden on the sloping ground towards the river Exe, and the Hills had plenty of servants to cater for their needs. In this environment Polly's role was that of Mrs Hill's unpaid companion, accompanying her on parish visits. Certainly her wedding group photograph suggests that she made friends in the town and became part of the local community surrounding the vicarage and Hill's church. Otherwise, her days would have been taken up with sewing and needlework, and Aileen Millicent, despite having her own nurse, probably occupied her a good deal. It seems safe to assume she wrote to Thomas Wilson at least weekly as that was the frequency of the Elder, Dempster's Liverpool mail service[176] to Lagos.

In June 1898 he departed Liverpool for Lagos. He appears on the passenger list of Elder, Dempster & Co's ship SS Bakana sailing from Liverpool on 18 June 1898. This list was completed by the ship's captain on printed card which would have been handed out to the passengers on embarkation. The principal crew – captain, chief engineer, purser, surgeon and chief steward – are listed and the destination of each of the passengers is given. The captain then signed the card to certify that each passenger was on board on departure. However in the case of Captain Jones, in charge of *SS Bakana*, his certificate was plainly inaccurate: Thomas Wilson actually left on the Company's *SS Cabenda* a week later.[177]

Quite how this occurred cannot be precisely stated. Perhaps he was delayed en route to Liverpool and simply missed the boat; or maybe he was unexpectedly detained in England for health or other personal reasons. The *SS Cabenda's* Captain Dupen obviously took more care in certifying which of his booked passengers were on board: he has struck through the names of two no-shows before signing. This left twelve first class passengers and three second class passengers on board.

The *Cabenda* was a ship of 2,777 tons built in 1890. The sail for those on board – particularly those in first class looked after by Chief Steward Benson and his staff – would have been (subject to any unusual late-June weather) a very comfortable one. After Grand Canary, the ship called at Sierra Leone, the three Gold Coast ports of Axim, Cape Coast and Addah, and then Lagos before going on to Burutu and finally Brass.

As Thomas Wilson left Liverpool he would have known from the newspapers that the territorial dispute with France was now over, with the signing of the Niger Convention on 14 June. Less welcomely and unknown to him, his colleague District Engineer Thursby had died in Lagos the day before his ship departed from Liverpool and another railway District Engineer, R. E. S. Cooper had been invalided home on 15 March.

On arrival in late July 1898 Thomas Wilson saw the progress on the Carter and Denton Bridges which were slowly taking shape across the lagoon. Other infrastructure improvements were also occurring in the Colony and electricity first lit the streets of Lagos in 1898.[178] The Governor, a Royal Engineer officer, would have taken a close interest in all of these infrastructure projects and may well have been appointed by Chamberlain with them in mind.

To the north of Otta the railway continued to be pushed forward through dense tropical rain forest towards Abeokuta. Access to the railhead was provided by special construction trains running at low speed over the unfinished rails. Beyond, where surveying and staking out of the route was occurring, access was only possible by horse or on foot where the forest was impossible for horses. An insight into what his life 'up country' was like is provided by a photograph of him at Papa Alanto Camp on 21 September 1898. Shaded by his pith helmet he is enjoying a cigarette and is seated in the midst of his African staff. His personal servant is seated at his feet and his groom holds his horse to his left. The others appear both loyal and protective, with one holding a rifle and others surveying equipment. It is unclear why there is a separate group of workers to his right – possibly they are from a different tribe or of a lower status in the workforce hierarchy. His position, off centre and in the midst of his African staff negates any possible charge of hostility or colour prejudice. These men were his close companions during 1897-1898 for as an Assistant Engineer he was frequently isolated from the others of his grade and would only have seen his superiors when they came on inspections or when he was summoned to headquarters or permitted some leave to Lagos.

That position ended in November 1898 when Thomas Wilson was promoted to District Engineer in charge of the Otta to Abeokuta section of the railway. This promotion meant he now had his own Assistant Engineers and was accompanied by a doubling of his salary to £80 per month. Although it is notoriously difficult to translate the value of nineteenth century pay into modern terms, without virtually any overheads in Lagos this is probably equivalent to something between £8,000 and £16,000 in the bank per month today. Certainly it was fifteen to twenty times the typical monthly income of a coal miner and 113 times what Joseph Rowntree calculated as monthly food subsistence in 1899.

With his promotion Thomas Wilson's surveying role was increased and making measurements and detailed drawings of the route would have occupied him. Surveying the route brought him into contact with many unfamiliar birds, wild mammals and reptiles. So far as large wild mammals such as elephants were concerned, by the 1890s these had been either driven or shot from the forests of Yoruba land but leopards were still a feature of the forest and he and his servants would have carried guns for his own protection if not for sport.

As the railway remained on the same side of the river Ogun as far as Aro[179] no significant bridges were built on this section. The main constructional difficulty, aside from the climate, was the difficulty of surveying through the forest and then tree clearing. In his paper to the ICE in 1912 Frederic Shelford described some of the difficulties:

The surveying of the railways in West Africa was rendered difficult by the very dense forest which exists from the coast for a distance of about 150 miles towards the interior... the height and density of the bush varies but it is rare to obtain a view of a hundred yards...

On the matter of tree clearing Shelford states:

In order to render a line of railway through a dense tropical forest safe from interruption by fallen trees it is essential to cut down all trees which in falling would reach the railway or the telegraph wires. When, therefore the trees reach a height of 150 feet, as is not uncommon, it is necessary to cut a roadway 300 feet wide in addition to the width of the railway. This involves clearing about 40 acres per mile of line, and becomes a very serious matter when there are as many as 20 really large trees to the acre, as well as undergrowth. In such a case there would be about 80,000 trees to be cut in 100 miles of railway. Some of the trees in the West African forests are very large, measuring 20 to 30 feet in circumference at the base... such a tree will take two to three days to cut down by hand. Tree-felling machinery has not been employed extensively as the native labourers are more efficient and reliable.

A photograph of the railway running through thick jungle to the north of Lagos appeared in the 1902 Journal of the African Society.[180] A further difficulty was, due to the alluvial soil, there was no suitable stone for ballast en route. This meant that the tracks were initially laid unballasted; once stone-bearing land was reached, 2,000 tons of ballast per mile had to be railed back to secure the line's foundations.[181]

Between Otta and Abeokuta, stations were built at Ifo, Itori, Owowo and Aro and as at Otta these small towns supported Church Missionary Society out-stations providing a place of worship as well as a relatively convivial place for Thomas Wilson to spend breaks from his surveying duties. By 1898 a significant number of the missionaries he encountered were Africans as the figures in *Payne's 1894 Almanack* confirm: of the twenty missionaries recorded in Yoruba territory thirteen were native clergy. He almost certainly spent Christmas Day 1898 with some of these missionaries before returning to work at Idioshe Camp on Boxing Day. He was photographed there that day along with his boss Richard Knights, newly appointed Chief Resident Engineer and the Governor of Lagos who came with his uniformed bodyguards, on a tour of inspection of the railway works south of Abeokuta. In the photograph Thomas Wilson looks emaciated by the heat and humidity but is smoking a large cigar – possibly a Christmas present from Polly.

Abeokuta (which means 'the city under the rock'[182]) was at the time a city of 100,000 people and the capital of the Egba people. Because it lay on the other side of the Ogun river, a short branch line of 1.75 miles with a 500 feet bridge in three spans was built to the mainline station at Aro. The view across the river towards Abeokuta, showing a surveying tripod on a rock in mid-stream was also photographed as part of the Governor's tour on Boxing Day 1898. The line from Lagos to Aro was to be completed by April 1899 but the branch over the river and up to the walls of Abeokuta was not finished and handed over to the Government until December 1901.[183] In the interim ferries took passengers from the wharf at Aro to the Abeokuta side of the Ogun.

The Engineer in 1898 described the difficulty of transportation between Lagos and Abeokuta prior to the building of the railway:

> *a good deal of the Abeokuta produce comes down by the Ogun River and this is only navigable for large canoes for about a month at the beginning and the same time at the end of the rainy seasons. At all seasons except during the heaviest rains, the greater part of the goods… are carried on men's heads. The journey takes five days…*

In early April 1899 just as the rainy season broke Thomas Wilson took his second period of annual home leave. It coincided with the completion of the railway as far as Aro, effectively linking Abeokuta with Lagos.

Once again he took the faster German steamer to Plymouth before proceeding to the vicarage where Polly had just come of age and was now free to marry him.

In 1897 they had expected that the railway in Lagos would be complete at about this point in time, and for Thomas Wilson to have returned and married her. However he could not have foreseen the numerous delays and problems encountered in building the railway which had taken place during the intervening two years. In consequence their wedding was postponed for his conscience would not allow him to marry her and then swiftly return to Lagos where, due to the conditions and dangers, she could not accompany him.

His life plan was always to return to the north-east and set up on his own as a civil engineer – this was why he joined the ICE and gained life membership of the Institute of Mining and Mechanical Engineers in Newcastle. Acquiring a second wife and achieving a family probably went alongside his professional ambition but Polly was to spend over four years in Tiverton before his plan was realised. A small token of consolation was a portrait photograph of a very pretty and youthful Polly taken by Walter Mudford, photographer of 10 Fore Street, Tiverton, which he took with him on his return to Lagos. Polly faced the doubling of the time he was away and the consequent delay to their marriage with equanimity. She was already in her young life well used to life's disappointments and well aware of fate's hard knocks.

He did not spend the entirety of his leave in Tiverton: he was in Newcastle on 27 June 1899 when he signed his application for membership of the North of England Institute of Mining and Mechanical Engineers. The Mining Institute's building, along with its records, survives in Newcastle and is situated between the Royal Station Hotel and the Literary and Philosophical Society. The gothic revival building had been built by the Coal Owners' Association and completed in 1872. The Institute was formed in 1852 and gained its royal charter in 1876. Thomas Wilson was proposed for membership by his former boss and director of the Consett Iron Company, William Logan, and his application refers to his promotion to District Engineer of the Lagos Government Railway in the previous November. He was elected to membership on 14 October 1899 at a meeting held in the Nicholas Wood[184] Memorial Hall. In December 1899 he paid the Mining Institute £27 for life membership as opposed to the annual subscription of £2/2s. In 1899 £27 was a substantial sum and his choosing to pay it as a lump sum was a reflection of the level of his African salary.

On 2 August 1899 Thomas Wilson left Liverpool for the third time with Elder, Dempster: this time on the *SS Volta*. As in previous years he would have had both quiet and spacious first class accommodation as there were just five other first class passengers on board the 2,700 ton ship.

Just two days before his ship departed, on 31 July 1899 the first fare-paying passengers were allowed to use the railway in both directions between Ebute-Metta and the station at Aro 64 miles away. The first class fare for the one way trip was £1 and second class was 5/- with a journey time of four hours and stops at all five intermediate stations. As the Denton and Carter bridges were not yet complete passengers from Lagos had to take a boat from the Lagos Marina to Ebute-Metta to catch the train.

The notice[185] announcing the service was displayed in Lagos from July 18th and its terms made very clear the limitations:

> LAGOS GOVERNMENT RAILWAY
>
> *It is proposed to run mixed Passenger and Construction Trains on alternate Weekdays, leaving Ebute Metta at 8am on Mondays, Wednesdays and Fridays, and returning to Aro Wharf at 8am on Tuesdays, Thursdays and Saturdays.*
>
> *Owing to the line not being permanently ballasted, and the frequent sickness amongst the Staff, the Acting[186] Resident Engineer does not guarantee the regular running of these Trains. Passengers must travel at their own risk.*

Notwithstanding what was by contemporary British railway standards a slow, inconvenient, unreliable and expensive journey along what was probably uncomfortable unballasted track, the great excitement of travelling on the first Nigerian passenger train was probably enough to make up for the privations.

When Thomas Wilson returned to Lagos in September 1899 the Carter Bridge to Iddo was almost complete and, to the north, the next section of the railway covering the 61 miles between Abeokuta and Ibadan was under construction. As well as being the longest of the three sections authorised to be built by the Colonial Office it was in engineering terms the most difficult in that it passed over the highest ground and included three significant river crossings. The first river to be crossed in three 60 foot spans was the Oyan at the 67 mile point, three miles north of Abeokuta. The second was five miles further on where the line met the Opeki river and crossed it in a single 60 foot span. Finally at the 93 mile point at Onibuku the railway crossed the Ogun itself in three 100-foot spans.[187] To either side of this bridge over the Ogun an eight mile long cutting was dug to reduce the gradients between the stations of Eruwa and Ogunshileh as the railway passed over the highest ground of its route. This significant cutting is well marked on the large map of the Lagos Government Railway which is now in the British Library. From the stamps on it, it was first lodged with the Intelligence Division of the War Office on 8 July 1901 and held in the Map Room until 13 January 1923 when, with Nigeria secure, it was deposited with the British Museum.

As well as three railway bridges and the stations at Eruwa and Ogunshileh two more intermediate stations were built between Abeokuta and Ibadan at Sanushi and Adio. In addition the railway workforce, although now having locally available ballast, still needed to do significant rainforest clearing right up to Ibadan.

In order to counter these engineering difficulties, as well as to compensate for the unforeseen previous delays the Chief Resident Engineer increased the African workforce[188] significantly. In his 1904 ICE lecture, Frederic Shelford put the number of native labourers in August 1899 at 10,426.

During this era, the great powers of Europe were scrambling to acquire the unclaimed parts of Africa and just as Thomas Wilson arrived back in the Colony in early September, tensions were growing between London and the independent Boer republics in South Africa. On 8 September the Cabinet approved the despatch of 10,000 troops to reinforce the Cape and Natal. Once again the international crisis had been caused by Chamberlain's African territorial acquisitiveness. This time his agent was Sir Alfred Milner,[189] Governor of the Cape, who shared his master's determination to unite all of South Africa under the British flag. The diamonds and gold fields of the Transvaal made it the 'richest spot on earth' and meant that it was too important to be left out of the Empire.[190]

Provoked by this troop deployment the Boer republics of Orange Free State and Transvaal issued a joint ultimatum to London on October 10: two days later the Boers rode across the frontiers into the Cape and Natal. The South African War had begun. The Boer enemy, although well armed, wore no uniform, was not subject to the usual military discipline and form filling, did not do drill and did not even conduct roll calls.

In response Britain despatched the largest military force overseas since the Crimea. To the utter bewilderment of most people in Britain things did not go well for the British Army's 60,000 regulars in South Africa. After a week of military disasters the third week of December 1899 became 'Black Week' in London. Years of achieving easy colonial victories at little cost had led the British into complacency: this was severely shaken, and the popular reaction was one of great anxiety and nervousness. The feeling of vulnerable isolation was added to when it was learnt that the Boers had the assistance of a 1,600 strong volunteer foreign brigade consisting of Germans, French, Dutch, Russians and even Americans.[191]

Thomas Pakenham in *The Scramble for Africa* summed up the position that the British Empire in Africa had now reached:

> *For the twenty years of the Scramble the English had made war on the cheap, measured in British lives and money. Ever since Isandlwana and Majuba, the price for Britain's taking the lion's share of Africa had been largely paid by Africans… Now the elite of the British army had been sent to conquer 50,000 farmers at a cost of £10 million and they could make no headway at all.*

The British government's reaction was to sack the commander-in-chief Sir Redvers Buller[192] and to flood South Africa with reinforcements.

The initial troop deployments to Cape Town coupled with their reinforcement was to severely dislocate British shipping and was to have a significant effect on the arrival of materials for the continuation of the railway to Ibadan, over 3,000 miles away in Lagos Colony. Steamers to carry troops, weapons and other military supplies to the Cape and Durban took precedence over the shipping needs of all other African colonies from the autumn 1899 to spring 1900 and the already much delayed completion of the railway was put back still further.

On 6 May 1900, almost eight months to the day since his return to work, Thomas Wilson departed from Lagos for his third period of annual leave in England. He left as before on a German ship, this time the *SS Adolph Woermann*. The ship had started its voyage in Loango in the French Congo and after German Cameroon, called at Lagos on the 6 May, and reached Plymouth on 25 May. There six passengers left the ship, including Thomas Wilson and the Lagos Government Railway's Chief Storekeeper.

On disembarking they would have swiftly learnt that success in South Africa had been achieved while they had been on board. Mafeking had been relieved on 17 May 1900 after enduring an eight month siege by the Boers: they had missed the resulting remarkable scenes of jubilation which occurred right across Britain as months of stored up national tension was released.

By the end of May Thomas Wilson would have read in the newspapers that Johannesburg had been taken and then on 5 June the British flag was hoisted in Pretoria. Precisely how these events were celebrated by him in Tiverton is unclear but given the adverse effect the war had had on the railway, it seems likely that they were marked in some way. A small celebratory party may have been held at the vicarage[193] which he would have attended before retiring to his hotel for the night. There were more raucous celebrations in the town when on 27 August the Boers were routed at Bergendal and the South African War seemed to be finally over[194] just as the new twentieth century loomed.

Two days later on 29 August Thomas Wilson departed Liverpool for the fourth time for West Africa. As on his previous outward voyages his ship (this time the *SS Roquelle*) was carrying a mere fifteen passengers with nine accommodated in first class. As in 1898 he had not spent the entirety of his leave in Tiverton but had visited his family in Westmorland and been photographed, principally for Polly's benefit, by Brunskill of Windermere, the business of which had been carried on by his cousin's widow following J. W. Brunskill's death in 1890.

He was back in Lagos by 30 September when he appears on the railway's European staff list and is not shown on leave. As in prior years several staff on the list are marked 'deceased' or 'invalided'. He is still the second highest paid as a District Engineer on £80 per month coming after the Chief Resident Engineer on £120.

By the end of October the railway's utility in fostering closer links between the colonial government in Lagos and the tribal chiefs of the interior was graphically illustrated by the first visit of the Alake of Abeokuta and his Council to Lagos on 28 October 1900. The Alake was the ruling chief of Abeokuta and his title meant Lord of Ake (the principal quarter of Abeokuta). The council was the Council of Egba Chiefs and together they administered the city and surrounding area under the supervision of the British Governor of Lagos.

The senior railway staff who had enabled the Alake's visit were fully involved in the surrounding ceremony and Thomas Wilson enthusiastically attended the special service in Christ Church Cathedral, Lagos. The sermon was preached by Bishop Isaac Oluwole, Assistant Bishop of Western Equatorial Africa. Oluwole along with his fellow black African, Bishop Charles Phillips, had been consecrated at St. Paul's Cathedral by the Archbishop of Canterbury in 1893. Born to Christian parents at Abeokuta and ordained in Sierra Leone he had then spent his entire ministry in Lagos and the interior of Yoruba. As such it seems unlikely that this special service was the first encounter Thomas Wilson had had with the Bishop. The Bishop had visited both Keswick and Durham in 1893 where an honorary D.D. was conferred on him.[195] Oluwole had also been instrumental in the setting up of missions in the colony and knew the Westmerian Bishop John Taylor Smith, attending his consecration as Bishop of Sierra Leone in London in 1897.

By December 1900[196] construction trains were running up to Ibadan, which was planned to be the railway's northern terminus. At the time, Ibadan was located on the edge of the coastal rain forest belt and was a city built over seven hills and home to 180,000 Yoruba inhabitants. Governor Carter in his 1893 despatch to the Colonial Secretary had measured its circumference at twenty four miles and described it as "a very large town and well situated on high ground." Ibadan now has over four million inhabitants and competes with Lagos to be Nigeria's largest city.

The first missionaries from the CMS had reached Ibadan in 1853 and by the end of the century there were six mission stations within its walls. As he had done further down the line, Thomas Wilson would, when away from railway headquarters, have visited these missions, as work continued on completing the 61 miles of line between Abeokuta and Ibadan.

While the construction of the railway was nearing completion, news of the death of Queen Victoria on 22 January was cabled from London. In consequence on 2 February as her great funeral procession was occurring in London and then Windsor, right across her vast empire services and ceremonies took place to mark her death. In Lagos a Memorial Service for the Queen was held in Christ Church Cathedral. Even if not already based at Ebute-Metta that day, with his access to the now fully running line Thomas Wilson would in any event have been at the Cathedral to mark such a significant event.

A month later and after so many unexpected delays, trials and testings were complete and the railway was ready for handover to the Colonial Government. The Lagos Government Railway as it was to be known, could finally take public traffic over the entire 123.5 miles from Lagos.

Monday 4 March 1901 was declared a public holiday in honour of the railway's opening, and a special train between Aro and Iddo Island carried its first passengers consisting of the Alake and Council of Abeokuta. The railway opening day together with the following events took up almost the entire edition of *The Lagos Weekly Record* for 9 March 1901:

> *The event of the week has been the opening of the Railway, which has wholly absorbed the public interest and caused every thing else to pale into insignificance.*

The opening for use of the Carter and Denton bridges while affording great facility to the public served also as an object of additional interest and attraction, and by 10am an immense concourse of people was collected on the Island. The terminus and station were gaily adorned with flags, the long terminal shed being tastefully decorated with flags and palms and converted into a huge salle a manger for the entertainment of the people. At 10.30 o'clock a train gaily decorated steamed in from Abeokuta with the Alake and Council of that country as passengers. A guard of honour of Hausa[197] soldiers was drawn up at the entrance to the shed and the distinguished guests having alighted were conducted by the Honourable Acting Colonial Secretary[198] through the opening made by the cordon of soldiers into the spacious refreshment hall where they were received by the company which numbered thousands and represented every section of the community. A few minutes later his Excellency the Governor... entered the hall... shortly after Prince Eleko[199] and the White Cap Chiefs[200] of Lagos entered the hall. The whole company then sat down to luncheon...

Lunch was followed by a succession of toasts and speeches. The Governor of Lagos Sir William MacGregor[201] toasted the King, The Lagos Railway and then made the first speech:

Ladies and Gentlemen – I have asked you to come here today to assist at the inauguration of a great work, to take part in the opening of the Lagos Railway, by far the most important undertaking of the kind ever carried to completion on the West Coast of Africa. This day is therefore not only of deep significance to Lagos but it is also an event of much historical interest for the whole Coast. This inauguration will always be conspicuous as being the first one of the kind on this part of the continent. It will be followed soon by similar ceremonies in the neighbouring colonies in Dahomey, in the Gold Coast, and probably in Southern Nigeria.

He was followed by the Chief Resident Engineer, Richard Knights. He paid tribute to the 29 European staff who had died during the railway's construction and the 31 who had been invalided before continuing:

This great cost in valuable lives makes one's wishes all the more sincere when today we hope and trust that the Colony of Lagos has laid the foundation stone for the building up of a vast and mighty Colony.

In conclusion I would like to thank my Staff for their noble support. No one man can build a railway, the chief Resident Engineer must have the assistance of everyone, and all pull together to bring a work of this magnitude to a successful completion.

I am proud today and it will give me the greatest pleasure to report to the Consulting Engineers that the staff that has been employed has been most loyal and good fellows and I thank them for the way they have helped me and that hand in hand we have brought the work thus far as to a conclusion, we trust to the benefit of the Colony in every way.

A further six speeches followed. The fourth of these was by Chief Aromire on behalf of the White Cap Chiefs of Lagos:

We are thankful and appreciate very much what we see. We had heard a great deal about the Oko Ile (railway) but had no idea what it was. It has pleased God however by placing us under the rule of the late good Queen to enable us to realize what a railway means. We are very thankful to the Governor for giving realization to this great undertaking. By means of the railway Abeokuta which is distant three days journey can be reached now in four hours,[202] and Ibadan which occupies a journey of seven days can now be reached in one day.[203] The change means good and we are thankful for it. It is our hope that God will bless His Majesty King Edward VII, and make his reign long and prosperous. We trust that as his late mother loved the African His Majesty will follow her example and love the African too.

At the conclusion of the speeches the Governor declared the railway open; the first of two trains, carrying the Alake and the Egba Council back to Abeokuta, left. A second train carried the Governor and a train full of people for an inaugural excursion up to Aro and then back to the Iddo terminus, where tea was served and the day's events were brought to a close.

Thomas Wilson, as the second most senior member of staff, and who had been involved with the railway since 1897, travelled in the second special train after hearing the speeches and witnessing what must have been an amazing spectacle in the luncheon hall.

The opening ceremony did not end there though. On the next day the scene shifted to Abeokuta and once more the events were comprehensively described in *The Lagos Weekly Record*.

Early on Tuesday morning (5 March 1901) a special train carried 600 people with free passes to Abeokuta to witness the opening ceremony there. At noon a second train carried the Governor, his suite and guests there. The arrival scene is described in the newspaper:

> *The train steamed into Aro Station at 4.15pm. His Excellency was met at the station by the Alake and Council and an assembly of 5,000 Egbas, with their Chieftains and with drums and tomtoms resounding. The station was tastefully adorned with palms, with flags flying gaily, while an arch of palms gracefully set off the rail line and under which the train passed as it came to a standstill, while pennons fluttering everywhere denoted a gala day, éclat being added to the scene by the presence of a Hausa guard of honour.*

After dinner there were further toasts and speeches. The Governor spoke first:

> *Let the Alake and Council consider what they did yesterday. They had dinner at Lagos and returned the same day to Abeokuta. They were the first to accomplish the feat of making a return journey by the railway. I was concerned to accord them the honour of the first double journey because they deserved and merited it and I was very pleased to confer it.*

Two further speeches were made; one by the Colonial Secretary's representative another by Bishop Oluwole:

> *It is not only material benefit we look for from this railway. May we not expect moral and spiritual benefit from this free and easy intercourse with one another? May we not hope for those influences which produce habits that ennoble a people – truth, honesty, purity and temperance? I pray for God's blessing on this railway. As it joins tribe to tribe and race to race, may it join them for peace and not for war; for dealings of justice and mercy; for lawful and righteous commerce, and for whatever can elevate the whole man.*

He was followed by the Alake of Abeokuta:

> *At his Excellency's invitation we have met here again today, we, with all our people to enjoy His Excellency's bounteous hospitality, and notwith-*

standing our great number, we have all been feasted to surfeit... The only thing that has served to bring up a shadow of gloom upon the joyous festivities is the remembrance of the death of the great and good Queen. ...The late Queen our mother had done many wonderful things in her time. She sent Christian missions to Abeokuta, which have done great good. ...When we heard the railway was to be made, we had no idea that it would be to our advantage and benefit but now we find it so.

On the following day a similar third ceremony of dinner, toasts and speeches was held at Ibadan attended, according to the newspaper, by over 20,000 Yoruba. In its editorial the *Lagos Weekly Record* looked forward:

As to what the future will bring must be a matter of conjecture only, for with the river spanned with enormous bridges, and the railway carried to its present termination through almost insurmountable obstacles and difficulties one is forced to exclaim what has Mr Knights and his efficient staff wrought and what may not he or others achieve? What is most likely to be achieved and what the local community look forward to becoming another reality in the near future is the great undertaking carried to its naturally and rational point of termination the Niger.

Although the railway was now finished and was fully opened to regular public traffic on Monday 18 March 1901 this was not the end of Thomas Wilson's time in Lagos: he remained in the Colony until early July 1901. What was he doing during these final four months? There are two possible answers: either he was working on the bridge and branch line over the Ogun river between Aro and the mud walls of Abeokuta; or he was working on the steam tramway which was built between the eastern end of the Lagos Marina, over the Carter Bridge to the railway station on Iddo Island. These two projects were not quite complete when he left Lagos in July but, given he had by then exceeded the normal period of eight months' service from his last home leave by two months, it is understandable that he departed when he did. A further reason why his departure date was not wholly flexible was that, because he was not resident in Tiverton, he needed to be married by licence and on the application for that licence he had to nominate a specific date for his marriage quite some time before it was to occur.

He sailed home on the same ship he had used in 1900, the German ship *SS Adolph Woermann*, and disembarked at Plymouth on 23 July 1901. Nineteen other passengers disembarked at Plymouth: of them two others were civil engineers, and there were two American and one English mining engineer on board. Doubtless he told his fellow professionals over the voyage that he was returning to England to get married and the pending event was celebrated in the ship's saloon.

He was entitled to celebrate more than his impending second marriage. After spending a total of 34 months in the Colony he had seen the project through to completion and was, unlike many of his former colleagues, still alive and in good health. Also over the four years since he had taken the appointment he had earned a great deal of money and now had considerable capital savings to acquire a family home and to set himself up with his own professional practice in Newcastle-on-Tyne. However his satisfaction would not just have been material. The railway was there to spread peace and Christianity as well as commerce, and despite his modesty, he was surely entitled to feel considerable pride in the enterprise which he had played a very significant part in constructing.

If anything clouded his thoughts as he travelled home or soon after his arrival, it may have been the awareness that the new railways in West Africa[204] were attracting criticism in both parliament[205] and the press on account of their cost and the time taken to build them. He was probably more focussed on his impending marriage and may have hastily dismissed the criticism as ill-informed and unfounded.

However for William Shelford & Son, with hopes of further West African railway work and much greater responsibility for the problems identified, brushing aside the criticism was not an option. Shelford *père* was 67 years old, but Shelford *fils* took on the firm's critics in a series of lectures on these railways that he delivered in London to both the African Society and the Institution of Civil Engineers. Frederic Shelford's rebuttal of his critics worked: when construction of the railway beyond Ibadan was eventually authorised he was appointed consulting engineer to the Colonial Office; and when his father retired from practice in 1904 he was knighted.[206] The following year William Shelford died and when the next supplement to the Dictionary of National Biography was published, he was given an entry largely on the back of his pioneering West African railway work. His entry includes the tribute paid by the former Governor of Lagos, Sir William MacGregor on Shelford's retirement:

by his skill and perseverance he had overcome the formidable obstacles
of the unhealthy climate, the density of the tropical forests which the lines
traversed and the difficulty of landing railway material.

The lectures Frederic Shelford delivered provide a great deal of material
and facts which would otherwise be lost to history although he failed to provide a detailed justification of how and why the financial estimates provided
by his father proved quite so awry from the actual expenditure[207] constructing
the railways entailed.

Just over three weeks after Thomas Wilson disembarked at Plymouth, he
married Polly Colman in St. George's Church, Tiverton on Thursday 15
August 1901. John Hill officiated and completed their marriage certificate in
his precise clerical hand. Polly was 23 and Hill gives her address as his own
vicarage. Thomas Wilson was 36 and his address is merely given as
'Tiverton' suggesting that he was still staying in an hotel on the day of his
wedding. The couple probably spent their wedding night in Tiverton at the
Palmerston or the Angel.

One of the wedding presents he gave her, which now and possibly then
was an eccentric choice, was a bound limited *edition de luxe*[208] of the special
Church of England forms of service in commemoration of Queen Victoria to
be held in all churches on the day of her funeral or the most convenient day
within the octave. He inscribed it, "15th August 1901 to Polly Bracken with
her husband's love."

The witnesses on the marriage certificate are his best man Harold
Braithwaite Barkworth and her bridesmaid Dorothy Storrs. Dorothy Storrs
was twenty and the older sister of Ethel Hill and in the 1901 census she
appears in her father's vicarage at 22 Salisbury Road, Hove. Harold
Barkworth was a 22-year-old law student. He had been born at West Hatch,
Chigwell in Essex in 1878 the third son of Thomas Barkworth JP a City of
London colonial merchant with an office at 16 Austin Friars, London E.C.[209]
On census night 1901 Harold is listed along with his mother and three servants in Lancaster Road, Wimbledon, whereas his father now retired aged 59
and described on the census form as a 'paralytic' is recorded at 17, Second
Avenue, Hove, along with his two spinster daughters and six servants. Second
Avenue was and remains one of Hove's grandest streets running north from
the Kingsway seafront and Barkworth almost certainly moved there after
becoming an invalid. Just two streets from Second Avenue is Salisbury Road

where the Storrs family were living and Dr Storrs was the Barkworth's parish vicar. As such it seems highly likely that Thomas Wilson had visited Hove while on leave from Lagos, possibly accompanying Mrs Hill and Polly on a visit to the Storrs' vicarage, and while there he met Harold Barkworth his future best man.

The nature of Dr Storrs' services at Hove is made clear in his obituary in the Brighton Herald:[210]

> *At Hove Dr Storrs attracted crowded congregations of the kind that could be called fashionable. The character of the services was evangelical, though, by distinction from some churches that avoid all ritual, the musical standard has always been high.*

Five days after the wedding, an announcement appeared in the *Tiverton Gazette* but more significantly unlike Thomas Wilson's first marriage a wedding photograph has survived: not just a small one of the married couple but a large, clear group photograph of the entire wedding party of twenty people.

They are in the garden in front of the vicarage's wisteria-clad iron front canopy. Rugs have been laid on the gravel and two female children are sitting on them, one at each side of the photograph. Four ladies are seated with Dorothy Storrs identifiable by her large bouquet on Polly's left. Behind them stand the remainder of the wedding party. Thomas Wilson wears a black frock coat and Polly and all the other ladies wear long framed skirts and large straw hats elaborately decorated with flowers, feathers or silk. Anglican clergy at this time were yet to take up the Roman or Dog collar and so Hill on the far right is dressed in tails with a bow tie. He certainly looks like the person in charge and would have changed for the wedding breakfast after the service. Beneath him sits the younger of the two girls. She is boosted by a cushion and could easily be no more than four or five. She is Aileen Millicent Hill. Her head appears to be resting on the lower thigh of the lady seated behind her – her adoptive mother Ethel Hill.

Between Thomas Wilson and Harold Barkworth is an unknown older man, oddly dressed in pale clothing with a loosely tied silk cravat. Compared to the others he appears out of place and may well have just arrived from Africa without appropriate formal morning clothes.

Because the wedding also meant their departure from Tiverton for Tyneside there may have been some mixed feelings as they gathered before the photographer. The Hills had been kind, friendly and generous and after four years clearly regarded Polly as virtually a family member. Polly had acquired a new social circle in both Tiverton and on visits to Hove, and Aileen Millicent Hill had been used to Polly being there for as long as she could remember. If any of these thoughts were present they do not show. Together they form a most elegant happy and confident group: although the rest are unidentifiable it is a fair guess that they were Tiverton friends made from Polly's living at the vicarage and from Thomas Wilson's lengthy periods of annual leave from Lagos.

They probably saw it as a double celebration, the commencement of a loving marriage and the successful conclusion of his long African adventure.

10 – A THRIVING PRACTICE

Thomas Wilson and Polly's first matrimonial home in Newcastle was at 5 North Terrace, a pleasant rendered brick terraced house of three storeys between the city's two great green spaces, the Town Moor to the north and the Leazes to the south. To the west was Newcastle's substantial barracks and to the east what had become the fashionable late nineteenth century suburb of Jesmond. Leazes Park had been laid out as public park in 1872[211] and North Terrace probably dates from around that period. From the contemporary residential directories it was a solidly middle class street far removed from the industrial smog of the Tyne quayside. Its healthy respectable character is probably best attested by the adjacent Royal Victoria Infirmary which had been under construction since 1900. By 1901 the population of Newcastle had reached 215,000 and the city, clinging to the steep north bank of the Tyne was, in places, seriously over-crowded. As in other British provincial cities as transport links developed, the wealthier classes moved out to leafy suburbs, to avoid the noise, pollution and poverty concentrated in city centres.

The previous occupant of 5 North Terrace was a Mrs Rome and the neighbouring houses were occupied by a shipbroker, a stained glass artist, and a mining engineer.[212] In social terms it was not enormously smart and in Ward's directory of 1904 only one occupant is described as a gentleman, with the rest being either professionals, or from the more genteel trades of tea, books and wine. At number 8 was Miss Paige's Academy, a private elementary school that the elder Bracken children were to attend. Further along the street where North Terrace became Claremont Road, their parish church of St. Luke was conveniently located.

It was also pretty convenient, especially by tram, for the shops of Northumberland Street and the business and commercial district around Grey, Mosley and Collingwood Streets which lay beyond. The nearest tram route ran along Claremont Road, in front of North Terrace to Barras Bridge, down Northumberland and Blackett Streets to the Grey Monument and the Central Station. The entire tram system had just been electrified during 1900-1901 under the direction of the City Engineer, George Laws. By the summer of 1901 Laws, who remained Thomas Wilson's most significant friend and professional associate on his return from Africa, had been in post for twenty years and was 65 years old. He remained City Engineer until the end of 1901, when, having seen Newcastle's trams electrified, he retired although he was retained by the Corporation as Consulting Engineer.

Initially, Thomas Wilson combined both his home and office in the house, although that was to change as he found his professional feet in the city and his children started to take over the house. The first of those children, Dorothy, was born within a year of the marriage, on 4 August 1902. Familiarly known as Dodo, she was obviously named after Thomas Wilson's first wife, whose death in pregnancy eight years earlier had delayed his first fatherhood.

Soon after Dorothy's birth, she was taken by her parents to Westmorland to meet her grandmother. Elizabeth Bracken was now in her mid-60s. She had left Moss Foot in the late 1890s and in the summer of 1902 was living at Grassrigg, Killington, along with her younger son Robert. The reasons she did so were probably related to both her advancing age and her finances. Almost certainly the eroded profitability of the farm caused Robert to avoid taking it on as his means of livelihood. Instead he had taken a job on the Ingmire Estate as chief, or what the estate then called foreman, forester with responsibility for the management of its significant woodland.

With the job came Grassrigg, the same house where Robert had been born almost 30 years earlier. In August 1902 Elizabeth was photographed on the steps of Grassrigg holding her infant grand-daughter, Dorothy, who is dressed in an elaborate white gown and three cornered bonnet. Her grandmother looks older than her 65 years and she is, white apron apart, still dressed in black almost 30 years after her husband's death. This time the photographer was almost certainly Thomas Wilson. A fashionably dressed Polly looks on, standing next to a bicycle. The front of the house is covered in a climbing rose in full flower and burgeoning fruit trees occupy the orchard opposite the house.

It was evidently a warm and sunny day and the photograph presents a timeless image of rural life. The only 'modern' intrusion is the bicycle: perhaps its being there indicates that the day was a perfect one for bicycling along the local lanes. It would have been brought with them on the train for their holiday visit. Thomas Wilson almost certainly used it to visit his sister and brother-in-law, who were a short distance away, at Beckside. With its chain driven rear wheel, pneumatic tyres and proper brakes, it could achieve great speeds in comparison with the last century's penny farthings and bone-shakers. Bicycling side-saddle was impossible, and Polly's full-length skirt suggests that contrary to the initial impression, she had not just returned from a ride. Part of Robert's woodland estate forms the backdrop, and an axe and shovel are left handily adjacent to the door. Obviously posed at the photographer's direction, the photograph might almost be an assembled metaphor of the contrasts between the two brothers' lives.

Back in Newcastle, where Dorothy was baptised at St. Luke's on 31 August, the principal feat of civil engineering during 1902-1906 was the building of a second high level rail bridge over the Tyne connecting Gateshead and Newcastle. The first, also a road bridge, was one of the greatest products of early Victorian engineering and had been designed by Robert Stephenson (1803-1859) and Thomas Elliot Harrison (1808-1888) and was opened by Queen Victoria on 15 August 1849. The first bridge carried just three rail lines and by 1899 it carried as many as 800 trains per day.[213]

As well as being overcrowded, the old bridge necessitated both north and southbound trains arriving and departing from the same end of the station. This caused both delay and expense, in that steam trains unlike modern ones did not run with an engine at each end. In order to do away with this reversal inconvenience and to increase capacity, the directors of the railway company were happy to spend £0.5 million on a new bridge. It was designed up-river of the old one, by Charles Harrison (1848-1916) chief engineer of the northern division of the North East Railway Company, and was built over four years by the Cleveland Bridge and Engineering Company of Darlington.[214]

Charles Harrison was the nephew of Thomas Harrison, and had succeeded him in 1888 as chief engineer of the great railway company. Thomas or 'Honest Tom Harrison' as he was known to his contemporaries resides in the pantheon of early railway engineering. Together with Stephenson he was responsible for completion of the east coast rail route. In partnership they designed two significant bridges at high level; that in Newcastle and the Royal Border Bridge at Berwick. In 1854 when the North East Railway Company (N.E.R.) was formed, Harrison was appointed chief engineer to the company and retained that post until his death in 1888.[215] Between 1874 and 1881 Thomas Harrison's chief assistant was none other than George Laws[216] and in that capacity he was the first to support Charles Harrison's 1877 application for ICE membership.

Over twenty years later, Thomas Wilson would benefit from this chain of family and professional links and become well known to Charles Harrison. He was already acquainted with William Cudworth, chief engineer of the southern division of the N.E.R. as well as two of its more prominent directors, Sir Joseph Pease and Sir David Dale who until his death in 1906, chaired the Company's Way & Works Committee which was responsible for new engineering projects.

It is scarcely surprising that the rail enthusiast Thomas Wilson had chosen to return to the north east and establish himself in private practice in Newcastle in 1901. Of course in addition to his contacts with the great railway company, he was also in a position to benefit from municipal work sent his way by George Laws. The indications are that, after his return from Africa, their relationship was just as close as it had been during the 1890s.

On his retirement as City Engineer at the end of 1901 Laws vacated his office in the Town Hall, which occupied the triangle of land between the Cloth Market and the Groat Market. He then practised as a consulting engineer from his home at 65 Osborne Road, Jesmond but, either because he missed the city centre environment or because he was endlessly travelling there from Jesmond for meetings, he opened an office at 40 Grey Street in 1902. The fellow occupant of the three upper floors of the building was his protégé Thomas Wilson, who was to remain in practice at this very prestigious address for the rest of his life. From North Terrace to Grey Street was quite a leap for a 38-year-old civil engineer who was relatively new to the city and it seems safe to assume that, without Laws' involvement, this leap would not have occurred when it did.

The east side of Grey Street comprising numbers 18-78 had been designed in circa 1836 by the distinguished architect John Dobson (1787-1865) who Pevsner describes as the north east's "most prominent and most talented" nineteenth century architect. One of Dobson's principal patrons was the speculative builder Richard Grainger (1797-1861) who redeveloped a large portion of the centre of Newcastle in the neo-classical style during the 1820s and 30s. Grainger Town as it is now known was a planned commercial re-development on a scale without precedent in England. Pevsner sums up the effect:

Grainger and his architects brought a new sophistication to the town,

Papa Alanto Camp, 21 September 1898. Thomas Wilson (seated right) in midst of his personal staff and horse. His office and quarters are behind.

View across the Ogun towards Abeokuta and the Olumo Rock, 28 December 1898.

145

Idioshe Camp, 26 December 1898, showing Thomas Wilson's quarters and below a group photograph of the African workforce.

Idioshe Camp, 26 December 1898. Thomas Wilson enjoying a cigar (centre standing); Chief Resident Engineer, Richard Knights (left seated); Governor of Lagos (right seated) with the Governor's bodyguards and other engineers engaged on the Otta-Abeokuta section.

Ilepa Camp, 27 December 1898. Governor of Lagos (centre) with Chief Resident Engineer (left) and an assistant engineer (right).

Polly photographed in Tiverton for her 21st birthday, April 1899, by Walter Mudford of 10 Fore Street, Tiverton.

Thomas Wilson on leave from Lagos, summer 1900, by Brunskill of Windermere.

1900 view of Tiverton with St. George's Church in centre and Vicarage large white building in the right foreground.

In front of St. George's Vicarage, Tiverton, 15 August 1901, the wedding of Thomas Wilson and Polly (centre). Extreme right the Rev. J S G Hill, seated next left Ethel Hill, at her feet Aileen Millicent; to the right of Polly, chief bridesmaid Dorothy Storrs. Best man Harold Barkworth on Thomas Wilson's right.

North Terrace, Newcastle-upon-Tyne, 2007. Number 5 is in the centre.

Polly at Beckside, Killington, following her wedding, photographed by her husband with her sister- and brother-in-law, Hannah and Thomas Woof, and their children, left to right, Thomas, Dora, Agnes and Wilson, August 1901.

Thomas Wilson, engineer in practice, circa 1902.

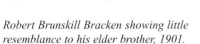

Robert Brunskill Bracken showing little resemblance to his elder brother, 1901.

150

Above, the sweep of Grey Street, Newcastle, 2007.

Left, numbers 36-40 Grey Street, Newcastle in 2007. Number 40 is the left-hand pavilion: Thomas Wilson's office comprised the upper three floors.

*Above, North of England Institute
of Mining Engineers, Newcastle,
2007.*

*Left, Conservative Union Club
building, Newcastle, 2007*

Grassrigg, Killington, August 1902. Thomas Wilson's photograph shows Dorothy in the arms of her paternal grandmother with Polly looking on.

Bowersyke, Killington, 2007.

Left, Thomas Wilson's photograph of Polly with 'Dodo' and 'Boyse' in Eldon Street, Newcastle, 1906.

Above, Jack with Polly on his first visit to the photographic studio of James Bacon & Sons, Northumberland Street, Newcastle, 1907.

Left, left to right: Dorothy, Jack, Mary and Robert, photographed by James Bacon, Newcastle, 1908.

Above, Mary and Jack on holiday in Westmorland, summer 1910, a photograph their father took and used for a 1910 Christmas card.

Right, Robert bound for Appleby Grammar School, autumn 1914. Photograph by Charles Nicol, Jesmond, Newcastle.

155

Rampson Cottage, Stainmore, a place of safety, on the family's removal there in 1915 to avoid the Zeppelin threat.

Mary enjoying her first summer on Stainmore, 1915.

156

Lieutenant T W Bracken RE, September 1915, looking impressively youthful when first awarded a commission aged 50.

Below, the Bracken children lined up at Rampson, summer 1916, in a photograph almost certainly taken to be sent to their father in France. Robert (centre, with buttonhole, watch chain and plus fours) at the age of twelve seems to have taken charge.

157

Embroidered silk greetings card 'Right is Might' 1915, purchased by Thomas Wilson in France.

Embroidered silk 1915 Christmas card showing allied flags, purchased by Thomas Wilson in France, December 1915.

A corduroy walkway running through Ploegsteert Wood, circa 1916.

A peaceful Ploegsteert Wood cemetery, 2008.

Neuve Eglise church exterior, November 1916, and below, the church and cemetery, 2008.

Arras in ruins, May 1917. Hôtel de Ville and bell tower (centre) with Petite Place beyond (to right). Below, Arras, May 1917, Petite Place and bell tower (left).

Arras Cathedral, May 1917.

Left, carved wood panel Thomas Wilson retrieved from the ruins of Arras Cathedral and brought back to England, and right, a matchbox holder brought back from Arras also in 1917.

Grand' Place, Arras, as reconstructed, 2008.

163

Left, Lieutenant Bracken, 9 June 1917, in Lillers en route to Ypres - having survived Arras and exhibiting a steely determination that the war should be won. Right, Captain Bracken home on leave, Rampson, September 1918.

Andes Farm, Belgium, 2008. The spire of Ypres Cloth Hall can be seen in the distance.

and a grandeur combined with Picturesque planning influenced by Nash's London developments. Where brick had reigned supreme, there were now smooth stone fronts; where details had been modest floor and sill bands and classical doorcases, there were now giant classical orders, with rusticated basements supporting giant pilasters and full entablatures.

Howitt[217] writing in 1842 described the transformation in graphic terms: "You walk into what has long been termed the Coal Hole of the North and find yourself in a city of Palaces; a fairyland of newness, brightness and modern elegance."

The central thoroughfare of Grainger Town is the gently rising and curving Grey Street with its Theatre Royal of 1837 and the Column to Earl Grey of 1838. No less a figure than Gladstone described it as "England's finest street" in his diary entry for 7 October 1862. At the centre of Dobson's east side range was numbers 42-50 and on each side of it Dobson designed a pavilion building, like a "house with projecting wings" as it was described in 1842. The lower five bay pavilion comprising numbers 34-40 Grey Street had on completion been occupied by The Queen's Head Hotel.[218] It had four street doors giving rise to the numbering and a central arch leading through to a courtyard.

In 1903 the ground floor and basement of number 40 were occupied by a jewellers shop, giving Laws and Thomas Wilson the run of the three floors above. Each floor would have consisted of two to three rooms and the scale of it is confirmed by Ward's 1896 Directory which lists a separate business occupier of each of the four principal floors. The relationship between Laws and Bracken, even if not a formal partnership, was close enough to justify joint business cards to advertise their service from 40 Grey Street. Unsurprisingly Laws's name comes first and he describes himself as 'M.I.C.E., Consulting Engineer' with an age-dictated lighter workload of 'Arbitrations, Valuations, Property Cases and Sanitary Reports.' Thomas Wilson is described as 'A.M.I.C.E., M.I.M.E., Civil Engineer and Surveyor' and there follows a long list of his specialisms. Unsurprisingly the focus is on railways, mining and quarrying, hydrology and sewerage. However the list does contain a few surprises such as 'Land Surveys,' 'Floating Hospitals' and 'Roads and Bridges.' Other categories derive from both his experience in Darlington and with the Consett Iron Company ('Preparation of Parliamentary Plans,' 'Tramways,' 'Inclines and Light Railways'). Prior to the cards being printed they had joined the subscription telephone service and acquired 'National Telephone No. 171.' Laws's nephew Hubert, already rejected by the I.C.E. was now rebuffed by his distinguished uncle who did not invite him to join them in Grey Street but left him to practice on his own from his house at 22A Normanton Terrace.

Given his status it seems likely that Laws occupied the first floor front office and Thomas Wilson the office above. The arrangement gave both a magnificent view, into the curve of the west side of Grey Street. Their clerks, (and they would have employed at least one each), together with assistants and pupils would have occupied the rooms at the rear and top. Opposite was the Newcastle Branch of the Bank of England, at numbers 33-37, forming the centrepiece of the west side design. The corresponding grand centrepiece of the east side[219] was occupied by Thomas Wilson's bank on its move from Collingwood Street. The bank, originally the York City and County, following its 1909 merger became the London Joint Stock Bank, and the Midland Bank in 1918. Other prestigious occupiers were his old employer the Consett Iron Company at number 19, the French Consulate at 58 and the U.S. Consul at number six. The Argentine and Spanish consulates were located on the same street and those of Russia, Germany and Austria-Hungary were nearby. Of course the population of early twentieth century Newcastle was not particularly international: these diplomats were there to represent the interests of their governments in commercial negotiations with the local armaments and shipbuilding giants of Armstrong, Whitworth & Co., Swan, Hunter & Wigham Richardson Ltd. and R & W Hawthorn, Leslie & Co.[220]

As well as being prestigious, Thomas Wilson's Grey Street office was also practical, in that it was highly convenient for his clients. A large number of the Durham and Northumberland colliery owners and companies retained an office on Grey Street, which was also convenient for Neville Hall where both the Durham and Northumberland Coal Owners Associations were based. The same building housed the Institute of Mining and Mechanical Engineers and in its library, lecture theatre and luncheon rooms, Thomas Wilson would have started to recoup his 1899 investment in life membership.

On 2 June 1910 Thomas Wilson submitted a written paper as a contribution to the discussion at the London meeting of the Mining Engineers held at the Geological Society, Burlington House,[221] on the means of delivering coal from the railway truck to the ship's hold. This suggests that his practice continued to be concerned with the north east's coal trade, which was now reaching dizzying heights. Between 1881 and 1911 the export value of British coal and coke increased two and a half times and in 1913 the peak was reached with the shipment from Newcastle of 20.3 million tons.[222]

Also a short walk away from Grey Street was Newcastle's magnificent Central Station, which then housed the N.E.R's civil engineering department, as well as allowing easy access to more distant clients and their civil engineering projects.

Having successfully established himself in the city over the two and a half years since returning from Africa, 1904 brought less welcome developments in the form of three significant deaths for him. The first occurred on 20 January when his sister Hannah, aged 36, died at Beckside, Killington, of a thrombosis following the birth of her sixth child. Next, on 24 March, the Rev. Dr. Charles Storrs died suddenly at Hove of a heart attack. His funeral took place in his church in Palmeira Square two days later. The suddenness prevented Thomas Wilson's attendance but his wreath was among the 100 sent, which according to the *Brighton Herald* of Saturday 2 April 1904, filled two carriages. The two wreath carriages along with fifteen others formed the procession to the church behind the open funeral car. The funeral service was taken by his clergyman brother, the vicar of Sandown,[223] and his cousin John Storrs, a Canon of St Paul's and Rural Dean of Westminster, who in 1913 would become Dean of Rochester. In the *Herald's* obituary much was made of the "tragic significance" of the text of his last sermon being "ye know not what a day may bring forth."

The third death of 1904 was that of George Laws, suddenly of heart disease on 22 December at his house in Jesmond. After just two years in practice together, Thomas Wilson was suddenly deprived of his mentor. Also for the fatherless Thomas Wilson, it is not hard to see that Laws had occupied the role of father figure. His long experience spanned many of the engineering triumphs of the previous century and therefore he was a ready source of advice and guidance. His death must have been a heavy blow to Thomas Wilson.

His funeral service was taken by Canon Boot, the vicar of St. George's, Jesmond. After the family, Thomas Wilson was unsurprisingly the first listed among the Christmas Eve mourners in the Boxing Day edition of the *Newcastle Daily Chronicle*. Others present were Laws' successor as City Surveyor, several aldermen and councillors. Three days earlier the same newspaper published an obituary which referred to his birth 68 years earlier at the Manor House at Tynemouth and his upbringing at Prudhoe Castle, both on account of his father's employment as the Duke of Northumberland's land agent. His "fine bridge at Wylam" was also mentioned along with his significant work for the North British and North Eastern Railway Companies prior to his appointment as City Engineer in 1882. "His chief work latterly has been the system of tramways which superseded horse drawn vehicles. He retired in November 1901 and was appointed Consulting Engineer to the Corporation which post he retained at his death."

As both of Laws's sons were doctors, Thomas Wilson effectively inherited his civil and consulting engineering practice and doubtless moved downstairs to occupy his first floor office. However in a sign of Thomas Wilson's self-confidence and just how thriving his practice was, Laws's place was not to be filled by either a replacement or a partner, and he along with his assistants, pupils and clerks, now became the sole occupier of the upper floors of the building.

Thomas Wilson's connection with the Laws family did not end there though, for the splendidly named Dr Cuthbert Umfraville Laws, of 58 St. George's Terrace, Newcastle, was the Bracken family doctor from 1901 to 1915. He was George Laws' elder son and the choice of the name Umfraville provides an erudite reference to the earlier thirteenth century owners of Prudhoe Castle – it was only in the next century that Prudhoe came into Percy Northumberland hands.[224]

There were two far happier developments in 1904. The first was the birth of a second child, a boy, born on 8th May at 5 North Terrace. Seven weeks later he was baptised Robert Colman Bracken and this time the names he was given did not reflect an earlier marriage. Robert was a family name of both the Colmans and the Brunskills, and commemorated both Thomas Wilson's Brunskill grandfather, and Polly's deceased brother Robert Colman. To the family he was initially known as 'Boyse' and later 'Bob'.

The second celebrated event was the founding of the Cumberland and Westmorland Societies. These societies were set up to promote the interests of those connected with the two counties. The first society was established in London in the spring of 1904. Its prestigious early members included both Speaker Gully[225] and the Deputy Speaker[226] of the House of Commons, the Bishop of Hereford[227] who was a native of Brough, Lord Hothfield,[228] Lord

Lieutenant of Westmorland since 1881, Claude Lowther MP[229] and both Westmorland's MPs. All were tied to one of the two counties by birth or residence and their early enthusiasm illustrates the strong county loyalty that existed at the beginning of the twentieth century.

On Tyneside there was a rapid move to follow London's lead, although Thomas Wilson was to claim the idea had existed already in Newcastle for some years. There were five initial promoters and Thomas Wilson's primary role was to seek newspaper publicity for the proposed association, in order to attract members. Evidently he remained an avid reader of the Westmorland press, which had subscription postal services for those living outside the circulation area. He initially made contact with Daniel Scott, the editor of the *Penrith Observer* in April 1904. The *Observer* had been founded in 1860 and covered both Stainmore and Kirkby Stephen. His grandfather Robert Brunskill had used it in 1864 to announce his daughter's wedding and it would have been known to Thomas Wilson since boyhood.

One of the editor's then columns was headed 'Facts and Gossip of the Week – Leaves from a Northerner's Note Book' and it was under this column that Thomas Wilson's charmingly polite approach was reported:

A correspondent – a professional gentleman on Tyneside – who desires to hide his identity for the present sends me the following interesting letter which is dated April 20th:

May I ask a little of your space to say that a movement is on foot to provide a common meeting ground for Cumberland and Westmorland men resident on Tyneside either on the lines of the Cumberland and Westmorland Association recently formed in London and that proposed at Manchester, or otherwise as may be found best.

It is felt that there is some difficulty in bringing this to the knowledge of all natives of the two counties in the locality, who although they may be equally interested in such a project, are in a good many cases unknown to one another and no better means of making it known exists than through the columns of the Weekly Press of the two counties, on which many of us, now at a distance, depend largely for news of our old homes and home days.

Those Tyneside readers who were interested in joining the project were invited to contact Thomas Jackson, a Penrithian living in Newcastle, who

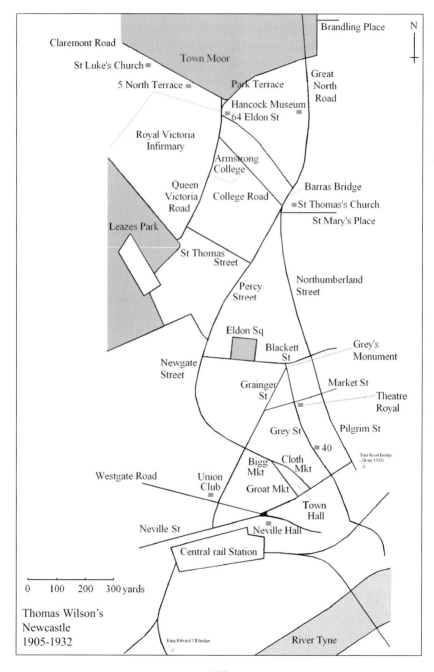

Thomas Wilson's
Newcastle
1905-1932

would become the first secretary of the Tyneside Association later that year. Evidently the response made to Jackson was satisfactory because by late June the venture was back in 'Leaves from a Northerner's Note Book' and this time Thomas Wilson was happy to loose his anonymity:

The project of establishing a Cumberland and Westmorland Society for Tyneside is I am glad to hear making good progress... Mr T W Bracken A.M. Inst. C.E. Newcastle tells me the idea has been in several minds for some years. He has now sent me a draft proposed constitution. The aims and objectives of the proposed Society are to be as follows:

To preserve and promote social intercourse.

To take a kindly interest in, afford introductions and guidance to young persons coming from Cumberland and Westmorland to the district.

To encourage the recollection of and preservation of the dialect, folk lore, customs and sports, to study their history and keep in mind their interests.

To give assistance in the way of procuring work for any applicant the Committee may consider worthy.

To give an opportunity for members to be helpful to their countrymen in the two counties and to be a means of them keeping in touch.

The conditions of membership are to be birth in either county, descent from parents born in either county, or a husband or wife of a person so qualified.

The inaugural meeting was held in the Grainger Street Rooms on the evening of Monday 10 October 1904 and 70 applicant members attended. The Resolution to form an Association was moved by Councillor William Harker who had a carpet business in Grainger Street and was seconded by Councillor Richard Millican of Reed, Millican & Co glaziers and glass makers of Croft Street. The presence of two Newcastle councillors in the founding group of five demonstrates the strength of Thomas Wilson's Newcastle Town Hall links.

When it came to choosing a President, perhaps surprisingly Canon Rawnsley, since 1893 a canon of Carlisle, was approached (probably by Thomas Wilson) and was unanimously elected President of the Tyneside Association. He would remain in the post until 1911. As a former disciple of Ruskin, Thomas Wilson and his fellow proposers may have had an initially ambivalent attitude towards him.

Following his election Rawnsley gave what the *Penrith Observer* report referred to as "an interesting address in which he gave his audience some excellent advice and especially appealed for higher things than those of mere financial consideration." The *Newcastle Daily Chronicle* of the following day reported the Canon's "praise of the Western Counties and his advice to his audience to foster the literature of the two counties at their meetings above all else." These high-minded words seem rather removed from the world of his audience.

However Rawnsley did not share Ruskin's more extreme dislike of all railways and industrialisation generally, and had confined himself to saving the natural beauty of the Lake District and to co-founding the National Trust in 1894. Since the 1880s Rawnsley had published both prose and poetry on the subject of 'The English Lakes' – most recently in 1903 when his *Lake Country Sketches* had appeared.

There were two other aspects of Rawnsley's past which would have had Thomas Wilson's approval. First in the 1870s he had conducted 'unconventional' mission work among the poor of Bristol while Chaplain of Clifton College and as a result had been dismissed. Second he had masterminded the national chain of bonfires to mark Queen Victoria's Golden and Diamond Jubilees.

From his subsequent letters and articles written for the *Observer* it is clear that Thomas Wilson took pride in his role in the establishment of the Association and later considered it, perhaps modestly, as the major achievement of his life. Also his openly expressed pride in the unspoilt natural beauty of his native county, during the twenties and early thirties, suggests that he was either converted to Rawnsley's way of thinking, or always shared his views.

In the month following the foundation of the Tyneside Association, a sensational political development brought the northern half of Westmorland to national prominence when its MP Richard Rigg abandoned his party's whip and prompted a by-election. Rigg was a discontented Liberal who, disagreeing with the policies of his party, submitted his resignation to his constituency association in Appleby and joined the Tory party. He had first been elected in the 'khaki' election of October 1900 when Liberal opposition to the conduct of the Boer War produced a Tory landslide. North Westmorland had bucked the national trend and ejected the Tory member since 1892, Sir Joseph Savory. In 1892 Savory, who had just served as Lord Mayor of London, had no connection with Westmorland. He swiftly contrived to create one by purchasing Wharton Hall but in 1900 when he faced a far younger, moderate Liberal, from Applegarth, Windermere, Rigg deprived him of the seat with a majority of 579. The Unionists had held the seat without interruption since 1885, the year when Gladstone's conversion to Home Rule was announced and with Rigg not opposing the conduct of the Boer War, nor favouring Home Rule for Ireland, the 'local connection' factor was evidently responsible for what would otherwise have been a freak result. The reaction of the local conservative association to this electoral defeat was to select a new candidate for the next election, Major Noble, again from outside the constituency. While they could have replaced him with Rigg, when Rigg became a Tory, they chose not to.

Reflecting on these events and Rigg's resignation, Thomas Wilson again entered the *Observer's* columns in a letter to the editor of 10 December 1904. In so doing he claimed to speak for the silent majority of the constituency's electorate:

> *Sir – May I ask a little of your space to set forth a view held by the less strictly partizan electors of North Westmorland – a not negligible body as the last election proved, and which as yet does not seem to have been expressed through the Press.*
>
> *They have not forgotten the attitude of Mr Rigg at the last election on Home Rule and on Imperial questions generally…*
>
> *These not strictly partizan electors, sinful as it might seem in the eyes of party managers and more or less eloquent frequenters of caucus and other meetings, and regrettable as even you regarded it at the time, gave their votes where they thought them most deserved, some even with a lingering doubt, and coupled with a hope that the vote would be more fully deserved in the future. So one told me himself some months after, saying with an enigmatical smile "where there's youth there's hope."*

The 'one' he here refers to is almost certainly his uncle Richard Brunskill and this conversation would have occurred on a visit after his return from Africa in the summer of 1901. He continues, praising his uncle's opinion:

> *How true the presentiment and how well that hope has been fulfilled is now seen. With Mr Rigg a new and enthusiastic member of the*

Conservative Party, and just admitted a member of the Constitutional Club, what at the present time, when Imperial questions are so much in the forefront, is there to prevent his adoption to contest the seat at the bye-election against any Radical comer. In such a course the Conservative Candidate brought into the field in readiness for the general election, having regard to his well-known patriotic principles and chivalrous disposition, would doubtless be the first to concur and wait till the general election came around.

He signed himself 'An East Westmorland Tory' and the anonymity, given that elsewhere in the letter he referred to Sir Joseph Savory as a "somewhat alien member," is perhaps unsurprising. In the paper's editorial the editor drew attention to the letter before roundly rejecting the idea of Rigg's candidature being limited to the by-election, and condemning the proposition that Noble who had already dedicated time and effort to the constituency should stand aside. Openly confident of a Tory victory the editor concluded, "Omitting the lapse of 1900 which really had little to do with the great question at issue (namely the Boer War) – it is scarcely open to doubt that the constituency will return to its old faith."

Thomas Wilson was obviously not prepared to let the matter rest there and in the following week's newspaper a second letter from an East Westmorland Tory appeared. Perhaps stung by the editor's implied criticism of his party loyalty, in this letter he displayed his firmly partisan alignment while not conceding the issue of candidate selection:

Sir, I thank you for being allowed to call attention to opinions held by many who are little in the habit of giving loud expression of their views and are therefore apt to be (and at times have been) mistakenly left out of the count; and am largely in sympathy with the point of your remarks, although not able to concede that an understanding come to with reference to a general election is binding at all costs for a bye election on candidate or constituency in such altered circumstances; or to abandon a strong belief in the old saying "where there's a will there's a way."

That either Mr Rigg or Major Noble can and will give Mr Leif Jones or any other Radical candidate from gallant little Wales a most complete beating at the present time I have no manner to doubt.

In the event Major Noble declined to step aside, leaving Rigg with the unpalatable option of standing as an independent and forcing a three-cornered fight. He did not do so as this would have virtually guaranteed a Tory defeat. Even so, the March 1905 result of the dual contest was not to the Tories' liking and the 'gallant Welshman' Leif Jones won with a majority of 220.

Far too polite to actually say 'I told you so' Thomas Wilson could not resist responding to the outcome by a further letter in the first *Observer* edition following the result and this time he let his mask slip slightly by adding his location to his sobriquet:

Sir, Having expressed in your columns certain views held by a good many electors prior to the selection of candidates, will you now permit me to add a word of appreciation of the fine fight made by Major Noble, who did all that any outside candidate could, and by the help of Mrs Noble who did more than it was possible for any man to do in the effort to win back the northern half of the county to its traditional colour.

The result on a square political fight between outside candidates, with the division polled out as never before, practically to its last man, has been disappointing and, it may as well be admitted, not that expected when the contest began.

What conclusion under these circumstances are we to draw? Is it that North Westmorland no longer affords a fairly safe Conservative seat? Perhaps so, but the writer feels none the less confident that he will again see Mr Richard Rigg member for North Westmorland, and that before long. To begin toward the recovery of the seat some little infusion of modern ideas into the party management might do no harm.

Yours, etc.,

An East Westmorland Tory, Newcastle-on-Tyne, March 11 1905"

11 – A WESTMORLAND TORY

Thomas Wilson's professional income evidently allowed him both the time and leisure to become an inveterate newspaper correspondent and heavily involved with the Tyneside Cumberland and Westmorland Association. Another indication of just how successful Thomas Wilson's private practice was proving to be was that the family moved in 1905 from North Terrace after less than four years there. The move was a very short one beyond Queen Victoria Road to Eldon Street. This was a classic street of 1820s terraced houses set back from the road behind railings and lined with trees. The houses were of four storeys. Number 64, the new Bracken home, was at the end of the terrace and as such was on a larger plot and of a larger size than the neighbouring houses. Unsurprisingly given the houses' size, in social terms the occupants of Eldon Street were of a higher order than North Terrace. The previous occupier of 64 is described as a gentleman in the 1904 Directory, as are many of the other occupants of the south-west end of the street. Their immediate neighbour at number 62 was Captain Tizard. Number 21 was the Portuguese Consulate. Others were ship owners, surgeons and solicitors.

It is not clear exactly when Eldon Street had been first laid out but it was roughly contemporaneous with its more famous namesake Eldon Square which had been designed and built by Dobson at Grainger's behest between 1825 and 1831. In Thomas Oliver's *A New Picture of Newcastle upon Tyne* of 1831 he writes, "Eldon Street and Eldon Place, together with Brandling Place have all been recently built and become a very important improvement to that part of the Town." From Oliver's accompanying map of 1830 it is clear that Eldon Place and Street together with Claremont Place were the only streets in existence to the west of Barras Bridge and the area must then have had an almost rural feel.

Interestingly George and Robert Stephenson are recorded as having lived at 33 Eldon Place from 1824-1825 and a tablet to that effect is noted in *Baedeker's Great Britain* of 1890. If those dates are correct, then the street pre-dated Eldon Square. One oddity of it was that its eastern end was named

Eldon Place and its western end Eldon Street. From *Oliver's* map of 1830, this is explainable by the Place houses being built on one side only with gardens opposite, whereas the Street houses occupy both sides, on larger plots and with gardens front and back.

Both Square and Street were named after one of Newcastle's most famous sons, John Scott, first Earl of Eldon (1751-1838) who rose from coal merchant's son via the law to be Lord Chancellor from 1801-1806 and 1807-1827. In politics he was to become a famously unyielding High Tory and eventually an implacable opponent of his fellow Northumbrian, the Whig Prime Minister Earl Grey (1764-1845) and the 1832 Great Reform Act. Amusingly in the city of Newcastle where reform was popular and Grey a hero, Eldon benefited from collective amnesia, being honoured after 1832 for his 1772 elopement from Newcastle to Scotland with a wealthy banker's daughter.[230]

This coincidence of name and date raises the issue of whether Eldon Street was also the product of another co-operation between John Dobson and Richard Grainger. If it was the product of at least one of them, as seems likely, this seems to have gone unrecorded. Of the two, Dobson was engaged in 1827 on the design of St. Thomas' Church and St. Mary's Place on the other side of Barras Bridge.[231] In the 1820s Barras Bridge was indeed a bridge carrying the Great North Road from Newcastle to Edinburgh, over the now hidden river of Pandon Burn.[232] As such, the area around Barras Bridge was the contemporary gateway into Newcastle and these leafy and fashionable terraces adjacent to it were designed to be seen and admired by those travelling by coach into and out of the city. In this regard as early as 1811, building plots at Barras Bridge were being advertised for sale with John Dobson named as the agent/architect.[233]

The houses in Eldon Street were not, when built, as large and fashionable as those of Eldon Square but by 1904 most of the houses of Eldon Square had already been converted to professional and commercial usage. Over the following 60 years the Square's houses declined further until most of them were demolished to make way for a shopping centre of the same name. Sadly, Eldon Street fared no better and was demolished in 1961-1962 to make way for the University of Newcastle. In 1964 the authors of *Tyneside Classical* regretted this loss of "the last complete street of domestic Georgian architecture in Newcastle." It now seems inconceivable that an entire 1820s terrace where the Stephensons, father and son, had once lived, should be bulldozed –

however worthy the replacement – but plainly Newcastle's 1960s planners felt differently. The former site of Eldon Street is now covered by the University's Merz Court building.

In the summer of 1905 when the move from North Terrace to Eldon Street occurred, Polly was heavily pregnant with her third child. As a result she, together with Dodo and Boyse, spent the late summer and early autumn at Killington where their grandmother and uncle had, in 1902, moved the short distance from Grassrigg to Bowersyke. It was one of the most attractive houses of the Ingmire estate and suggests either that Robert Bracken was highly regarded as the estate's head forester, or that Thomas Wilson was subsidising his rent payments in order to provide a house large enough to accommodate his family on holiday visits. Bowersyke had been occupied by a Bracken relative[234] and his descendants for most of the nineteenth century and continuing the tradition may well have appealed to Thomas Wilson's keen sense of history.

The house, although far older, had been given a Georgian-era makeover by its Upton owners and was rendered and whitewashed in the classic Westmorland style. Set back from the lane behind a high walled garden it would have been an ideal alternative to Newcastle for Polly and her young family – added to when Mary was born there on 12 September. In testament to the length of this stay in Killington she was baptised at All Saints, Killington, on 29 October 1905. In this she was unlike all of her siblings both earlier and later, who were baptised at St. Luke's in Newcastle. Mary was named after Thomas Wilson's maternal grandmother and his repeated choice of Brunskill family names indicates a preference over those selected by his father and his forbears.

This stay at Bowersyke may have been so long because the house in Eldon Street needed improvements or redecorating. If this was so Thomas Wilson would have stayed in an hotel through the week and taken the train to Sedbergh for weekends. When his family did move into the new house in Eldon Street they had the advantages of more space and garden as well as easy access to Leazes Park and, compared with many Newcastle children growing up in the industrial areas by the Tyne, theirs was a relative idyll of quiet and clean air. On wet days the Hancock Museum built for the Newcastle Natural History Society[235] and home to its huge collection of stuffed birds and mammals since 1884 was just across the street from their house.

For Polly the shops of Northumberland Street, including J. J. Fenwick's department store which had opened in 1882 and pre-dated his London store by ten years,[236] were a short walk away, as was Miss Paige's elementary Academy when Dorothy reached school age. Family anecdote suggests that Polly had a children's nurse to help her look after the infant children and Thomas Wilson's return of the 1911 Census form lists a household servant, Florence Maddison, a local woman who lived in and ensured that the family awoke to lit fires and hot water. Other servants almost certainly attended daily and the absence of a nurse on the form is probably explainable by their youngest child being close to four, on the census night of 1911.

On Sundays they were now in the ancient Newcastle parish of St. Andrew but by the baptisms, they seem to have continued to worship in the much nearer Victorian church of St. Luke. Another convenient alternative was Dobson's fine church of St. Thomas the Martyr, just across Barras Bridge.

At about this time the Bracken children became early fans of Beatrix Potter's stories which had started with the publication of *Peter Rabbit* in 1902 and swiftly followed by the publication of nineteen more before the end of 1913. Thomas Wilson with his great love for his native county, its fells and lakes, birds and mammals, doubtless inspired and nurtured this early source of reading. It was far lighter and more secular than his S.P.C.K. tracts of 40 years earlier. After acquiring 64 Eldon Street, Thomas Wilson both lived and worked in some of the finest architecture Newcastle possessed. He himself had designed numerous terraced and detached houses in 1880s suburban Darlington and perhaps the surveyor in him made him a great appreciator of Dobson and Grainger's work. However, as is perhaps to be expected in a civil engineer, he was not unappreciative of the benefits of modernity as his passion for bicycles, cameras and the telephone testifies.

An unwelcome intrusion into this comfortable world for the profoundly Tory Thomas Wilson, were the national political developments of 1905-6. In July 1902 Arthur Balfour had succeeded his uncle Lord Salisbury as Prime Minister and, still in possession of the landslide Tory majority of 1900, saw no need to seek his own mandate. Increasingly though his party tore itself apart over the issue of free trade versus tariff reform based on imperial preference.[237] The great imperialist Joseph Chamberlain, concerned by the rise of rival manufacturing in both Germany and the United States, favoured a system whereby the empire's imports and exports between Britain and her colonies were favoured and those of foreign competitors penalised. Others in the Cabinet were far from ready to slaughter the sacred cow of free trade. Their resolve to oppose Chamberlain was strengthened further because his proposals included the re-introduction of duty on foreign grain and other foodstuffs, which might lead to unpopular rises in the price of food. Balfour, not the first or last indecisive Prime Minister, sat in the middle of the controversy and for doing so was lampooned in verse by his Liberal opponents:

> *I'm not for Free Trade, and I'm not for Protection;*
> *I approve of them both, and to both have objections.*
> *In going through life, I continually find*
> *It's a terrible business to make up one's mind.*
> *And it's always the best in political fray*
> *To take up the line of the Vicar of Bray.*
> *So, in spite of all comments, reproach and predictions,*
> *I firmly adhere to Unsettled Convictions.*[238]

In November 1905 the tariff controversy came to Newcastle when the city hosted that year's meeting of the National Union of Conservative and Constitutional Associations. The National Union had been founded under Disraeli, as the Party's chief organisation in 1867, and its annual meeting had previously been held in Newcastle in 1881 and 1894. A third great congress in the city was a considerable civic honour and ensured the presence of the Prime Minister, the Cabinet, almost the entire parliamentary party and a huge number of political agents and activists. The 1900 general election had left Newcastle with two Conservative MPs and with the next general election due in 1906 the gathering was seen locally as a necessary boost to the party's chances of holding on to the city. The two day annual meeting was at that time organised by the local Newcastle association and Thomas Wilson, an active member since his return from Africa, involved himself in the preparations. The meeting itself was held in the Grand Assembly Rooms at Barras Bridge, just minutes from his house in Eldon Street. In his opening remarks the Chairman, commenting on the recent defection of Winston Churchill to the Liberals, stated that the Conservative Party was "stronger for his loss" and that he would be "a source of future weakness" to the Liberals.

The remainder of the conference seems to have been conducted under a cloud of similar illusion and the motion in favour of Imperial Preference and for the erection of tariff barriers against the goods of foreign competitors, was, embarrassingly for the leadership who along with most Mps disdained to attend and vote, carried by 698 votes to two. The supposed high point of the gathering was Prime Minister Balfour's speech on the evening of the first day. The following day's *Newcastle Daily Chronicle* reported that his remarks on tariff reform "simply platitudes intended to be a plea for unity" were received with "ominous flatness." The editor perceptively continued:

> *Mr Balfour has the fatal gift of seeing both sides with the result that he is unable to choose either...*
>
> *Mr Balfour's complaints about the want of definiteness in the attitude of the Opposition leaders evidently led many of his hearers to expect something more definite from him.*
>
> *Mr Balfour may perhaps think that he gave a lead to his party last night but it was a lead which if followed will end in the ditch of defeat.*

Thomas Wilson doubtless found the entire gathering a depressing affair that had merely served to worsen the party's electoral chances in the city. His great enthusiasm for the empire, and his subsequent specific writings on the issue of food prices, indicate that he was not one of the two who voted against Chamberlain's tariff proposals.

Unsurprisingly, the next month Balfour resigned and the King sent for the Liberal leader Sir Henry Campbell-Bannerman. The formation of a Liberal government was rather a novelty for people of Thomas Wilson's generation – the Unionists had been in power for 22 of the previous 30 years. The new Prime Minister, unlike his predecessor, wasted no time in seeking a mandate and taking advantage of his opponents' division, fought the general election on the easily understood slogan that voting Tory was the same as voting for an increase in the price of bread.

The outcome in February 1906 was a Liberal landslide. The results repre-sented a seismic shift in the political make-up of Parliament. The Unionists won only 156 seats as opposed to 402 in 1900. Among the great swathe of Tory casualties, even Balfour lost his seat. The triumphant Liberals won 397 out of a total of 670 seats and the infant Labour party increased its seats from two in 1900 to 29 in 1906. In the city of Newcastle where two members were returned, traditionally one from each of the major parties (but in the 'khaki' 1900 election two Conservatives) both Conservative candidates lost and the Labour candidate was not only a winner for the first time in the city's history but gained 446 votes more than the Liberal who came second. The Labour majority over the highest placed Conservative was a massive 6,927 votes.

The result in Thomas Wilson's beloved North Westmorland seat, while extremely close, was no better in terms of outcome. Although Major Noble, whose health had been broken by the rigours of the 1905 by-election, had stood aside, the selection committee ignored Thomas Wilson's earlier plea to select a local candidate, preferably in the form of the old Liberal member Richard Rigg. Instead they went for someone with a nationally high profile. He was Lord Kerry, the elder son of the 5th Marquis of Lansdowne, who had been Foreign Secretary since 1900 and leader of the House of Lords from 1903. Kerry had other attractions: he was a Major in the Irish guards and he had won the DSO in South Africa. Scion of one great political dynasty, he had married a niece of the Duke of Devonshire; but for all of his very grand pedigree he had no connection with Westmorland and even the Tory editor of the *Penrith Observer* tentatively expressed the view, in December 1905, that only a local candidate could regain the seat for the Tories.

His doubts were well founded and Kerry lost to the Liberal, Leif Jones, by three votes.[239] However, as Colonel Bagot of Levens Hall, re-standing for South Westmorland, was also swept from Parliament in the 1906 Liberal onslaught, it seems doubtful that any Tory candidate could have won the northern or Appleby division of the county.

Thomas Wilson's response to what he regretfully regarded as the 'radicalisation' of politics after 1906, was not without professional danger for him in Newcastle. His views were now obviously out of step with those of most male citizens but more dangerously many of his contacts on the City Council were Liberals. Formerly this had not much mattered but as the implementation of the Liberal Government's programme turned up the heat on Tory-Liberal Party rivalry, an overly vocal response might have led to a waning of his connection to the corporation. That this did not happen was probably due both to his own prudence and the influence of the Cumberland and Westmorland Association which ensured that he continued to socialise with Liberal city councillors. He along with Councillors Harker and Millican remained officers of the association throughout the heated political period of 1906-1910, thereby avoiding any rupture in relations. The bi-partisan nature of the Tyneside Society was emphasised by Richard Rigg on a visit to the city in 1911 when he, a past President of the London Association, praised the organisation for providing a venue where "men of all views, irrespective of sect or of party, might come together with the place of birth as the common magnet."

The programme of meetings they arranged also catered for a variety of interests and intellect. Among the more demanding was probably the 1906 lecture by the Dean of Durham, Dr Kitchin, who shared with them his youthful reminiscences of Cumberland. Other lectures were illustrated by lantern slides such as the Chairman Councillor Harker's lecture themed 'A trip to Lakeland' in 1907. Other evenings provided music, songs, recitals, card games and even 'an evening of impersonations of characters from Dickens.' An early and fixed feature of their meetings was that they ended with the singing of *John Peel*.

By the summer of 1906 the new high level rail bridge with its lattice girder spans and carrying four new tracks was ready for opening by King Edward VII.[240] The King did so from a special platform built in the centre of the bridge at which the Royal Train halted. Prior to pushing an electric switch to lower a cord which had been laid across it he met Charles Harrison the bridge's chief design engineer. From photographs of the opening a large number of invited guests were present on the platform and Thomas Wilson may well have been among them.

The King accepted a silver miniature of the bridge which he had agreed should be known as the King Edward VII Bridge, before proceeding on to Alnwick Castle. The following day 11 July he returned to Newcastle with the Queen and the Duke and Duchess of Northumberland. He opened two new buildings in the city and honoured the mayor and corporation with his presence at luncheon. Both of these buildings, Armstrong College and the Royal Victoria Infirmary, neighboured Eldon Street and the royal carriage procession with its mounted escort would have been easily visible from the end house as it proceeded down Queen Victoria Road from Park Terrace to Armstrong College. In a sign of how significant an event this was, stands were built for spectators along the processional route from the central station but Polly and her young children would have had an equally good view of the spectacle from the upper floors of their house.

Armstrong College was immediately south of Eldon Street and College Road was the parallel street to it. Both the college office and the Durham University Union Society were, after 1910, located in Eldon Street and the undergraduates, lecturers and professors would have been a familiar aspect of the neighbourhood. Newcastle's College of Physical Science, as it was originally known, had been founded in 1871 jointly by the University of Durham and the North of England Institute of Mining and Mechanical Engineers. In 1888 it moved to the College Road site, which was further extended in 1894. In 1904 the college was re-named after Lord Armstrong. The King was opening the college's second extension with a tower and three hundred foot frontage on Queen Victoria Road and overlooking the Leazes.[241] Eventually the college was to de-merge from Durham when the University of Newcastle upon Tyne was formed in 1963.[242]

After declaring the new college building open the King did the same at the Queen Victoria Infirmary, further down the same road and occupying a ten acre site that had been carved out of the Leazes. In his speech at luncheon in the Assembly Rooms the King paid tribute to Newcastle's remarkable recent achievements in the fields of shipbuilding and engineering. As he did so the *Mauretania,* the largest ship ever built on the Tyne, was nearing completion at the Wallsend yard of Swan Hunter and Wigham Richardson Ltd.[243] The King's audience included Newcastle's substantial contingent of foreign Consuls and Vice-Consuls as well as Thomas Wilson's friend and fellow civil engineer Sir Benjamin Browne the former mayor and alderman and a director of the engineering and shipbuilding giant R&W Hawthorn Leslie & Co.

Later that day after the Royal party had returned to Alnwick, the newly knighted and first Lord Mayor of Newcastle held a civic reception in Leazes Park. Thomas Wilson and Polly's names appear on the guest list printed in full in the special Royal Visit editions of the city's newspapers.

As in earlier summers, following the Royal visit, the Bracken family went to Bowersyke. At this time the Ingmire Estate had reached its zenith – its owner Mrs Upton-Cottrell-Dormer was still buying up local farms and land in 1904. Her husband had died in 1880 leaving her *châtelaine* of Ingmire, as well as Rousham, Oxfordshire with its famous William Kent designed garden and a house in London's Berkeley Square. Endowed with this very significant landholding, on her death in January 1907, she left a huge fortune to be distributed among the survivors of her fourteen children. Her fourth son John inherited the Ingmire estate of 4,430 acres and upon doing so changed his name, by deed poll, to that of his maternal Upton ancestors.

12 – RECALL TO AFRICA

As 1907 prepared to slip into 1908, many thousands of miles away from Newcastle and unknown even to Thomas Wilson events in Northern Nigeria were occurring which were to threaten the Bracken family's harmonious and settled routine, based as it was on Thomas Wilson's professional success in the city and the consequent trappings of wealth it brought to his family. In the same way as Polly's financial security and future marriage had been threatened by the prolongation of construction of the Lagos Government Railway between Lagos and Ibadan in 1897-1901, so now delays and difficulties with the Lagos Railway's Northern Extension up to and beyond the river Niger[244] were to threaten her happy and relatively carefree life in Edwardian England.

In the summer of 1901 when Thomas Wilson had last been in Lagos the extension of the railway was already envisaged and a survey of the possible route between Ibadan and Jebba had already been conducted. However implementation of the survey route was delayed by a dispute between Lagos and London over the route and its cost and viability. As the Colonial Office and its advisers grappled with the issues, external agencies continued to apply pressure for more Nigerian railway-building.

In 1903 the Manchester Chamber of Commerce petitioned the Colonial Office for the extension of the line beyond Ibadan. Their fear was that French railway construction in Dahomey threatened to divert trade away from the Lagos hinterland. The Manchester merchants were followed by the British Cotton Growing Association who petitioned the Colonial Office to bring the cotton fields of Oshogbo within their reach by means of the railway. Oshogbo was not within the 1901 surveyed route and their petition succeeded: on 16 February 1905 construction of the 70 mile Ibadan to Oshogbo section commenced, following the approval of the Consulting Engineer's estimate for it of £429,012.

The Colonial Office's decision to sanction the extension to Oshogbo was vindicated by the statistics relating to the Lagos Government Railway in the 1907 *Blue Book*. Railway net receipts reached £65,312 in 1907, passenger numbers were up from 116,267 in 1904 to 188,419 and the weight of goods carried had grown from 46,203 tons to 82,900 tons over the same period. By the end of 1907, four million tons of Oshogbo cotton had been exported from Southern Nigeria to Britain.

After Oshogbo was reached, a further 60 mile extension to Ilorin in what was then the Protectorate of Northern Nigeria was sanctioned by Whitehall. On 16 June 1908 the railhead reached Ilorin and the Ilorin section was opened for public use on 27 August 1908.

The extension beyond Oshogbo could certainly not be justified on economic grounds. Northern Nigeria was only solvent due to imperial hand-outs. Government revenue in Northern Nigeria was just £178,444 and without £290,000 of Imperial Grant in Aid from London and £70,000 from Southern Nigeria, the state was not viable. Its recorded exports, mainly of ivory and tin, were worth just £24,573: they compared most unfavourably with the contemporary exports from Southern Nigeria worth £3.8 million.[245] In this economic context extending the railway into the infant Northern Nigeria could only be justified in terms of re-inforcing and securing its rather loose connection with the rest of the Empire.

After Ilorin the next strategic destination for the railway was Jebba, on the river Niger, 56 miles away and 306 miles from Lagos. On 30 October 1907 the Secretary of State approved not only this section of railway, but also, because Jebba was no more than a landing stage on the Niger, a ferry (and ultimately a bridge over the river[246]), and an onward section of circa 120 miles to Zungeru. At Zungeru the new line would link up with the other Northern Nigeria railway then being built between Baro and Kano.[247]

News of the severe construction difficulties encountered on the 176-mile section between Ilorin and Zungeru reached Thomas Wilson in the summer of 1908 via an appeal for help from the consulting engineers in London addressed to those civil engineers who had had experience of the pre-1905 pioneer days of railway building in Nigeria.

The headquarters for the northern section were established on Government Hill, Jebba, which had previously been used as the military headquarters of Frederick Lugard during the 1898 Anglo-French crisis over Borgu.[248] In 1900 when the British Government bought out the Royal Niger Company and appointed Lugard as High Commissioner with a remit to create a new imperial possession, Lugard initially chose Lokoja further down the Niger as the first capital but after two years, as his control over the territory grew, he rejected Jebba as a candidate for capital and moved Government House to Zungeru on the Kaduna River, in the centre of the country.

Therefore contrary to the indications of its name there was precious little government or other essential facilities on Government Hill, when the railway staff arrived there on 10 November 1907.[249] In fact the primitive conditions at Jebba were such that the clearing of bush and scrub on the hill and down its slopes took until October 1908. This delay in clearing delayed the erection of proper staff quarters and in these exposed conditions the European staff were ravaged by malaria and other forms of sickness during 1907-1908. According to the 1908 and 1909 *Blue Books* for Northern Nigeria this sickness among the European railway staff at Jebba led to seven deaths. Even in the usually restrained language of Whitehall, the scale of illness at Jebba, at its severest, in May 1908, was referred to as "an epidemic of sickness."

Another difficulty in Jebba related to the arrival of supplies which were, as river levels allowed, to be shipped the 537 miles up the Niger from Forcados[250] to Lokoja and then in a smaller craft to Jebba. From the reports submitted by the consulting engineers supplies were so scarce during 1907-1908 that the labourers attached to the survey parties beyond Jebba deserted for lack of food.

A major part of the problem at Jebba was that, unlike the Lagos hinterland and the coastal region of Southern Nigeria, the indigenous population were almost entirely unused to and untrusting of the white man. In Lagos they had experience of white traders for centuries and of British officials and missionaries for many decades but this far up the Niger and in the interior between Jebba and Zungeru the situation was very different. In much of Northern Nigeria it was only Lugard's recent show of arms that had reluctantly incorporated the remote and scattered population into the Empire. Both missionaries and traders were extremely rare. The 1908 *Blue Book* estimated the native population of Northern Nigeria at 7.1 million and the European population was counted as 499. Of this total 399 were civil and military officials, and 100 traders and missionaries. Elsewhere the *Blue Book* records just six Anglican missionaries attached to the Church Missionary Society working in the Protectorate and they were almost exclusively ministering to the tiny, white and largely official population. These demographic and cultural conditions meant that recruiting a local labour force to construct the railway was to prove far more difficult than it had been in Yoruba land ten years earlier.

Other more predictable difficulties arose from the adverse weather and the rapid growth of vegetation. Although the contemporary *Blue Books* do not contain weather records for Jebba, those for Ilorin and Zungeru were published. There is little difference between them and they record some of the highest temperatures in Nigeria. The average yearly 1908 temperature at 9am in Zungeru was 81 degrees Fahrenheit, with a highest recorded day's shade temperature of 104 and an average mean daily maximum of 92. Added to the stifling heat, in 1908 Zungeru received almost 59 inches of rain. In these conditions progress was minimal and financial estimates were being exceeded across the board. As the 120 mile Jebba to Zungeru section risked descending into chaos the Resident Engineer was recalled to London for consultations.

As a result of his recall the Joint Consulting Engineers, Cooper and Shelford contacted several civil engineers with relevant West African railway experience. One of those contacted, doubtless via the ICE annual address book, was Thomas Wilson who had known Frederic and his late father Sir William Shelford since gaining his 1897 colonial appointment. The post they offered him was that of District Engineer on the troubled Jebba-Zungeru extension. The grade and pay was similar to what he had been paid when last in Lagos. By domestic standards the pay remained generous but it seems likely that, unlike in 1897, pay was not a major reason why he accepted the

Lagos Railway Northern Extension, 1908.

post. All the indications are that his private practice in a generally booming Newcastle was exuberant. It therefore seems that duty and sentiment may have been the motivating factors in his decision to return. A self-confessed imperialist since his school days, he obviously believed in the completion of the Lagos Railway project and doubtless the wider one to develop, 'civilise' and integrate Northern Nigeria into the Empire. Possessing the relevant experience to aid the ailing project, he probably felt that it was his patriotic duty to go.

As to whether he was wise to do so, he probably never considered the question for if he had done so seriously he should have declined. His non-financial circumstances were also very different to 1897. He was married with four young children: the youngest Edmund John, or 'Jack' to the family, was just over a year old having been born in May 1907 at 64 Eldon Street. Unlike his siblings he was given names which did have a Bracken family pedigree. John was the name of his long-dead Bracken grandfather and Edmund was the name of the latter's younger brother born at Newfield, Firbank in 1841. Jack was baptised on 30 June at St. Luke's and later photographed in his christening gown standing on a cushion, supported by his mother. When she learned of her husband's decision to return to Africa, this time she knew of the danger he would face and how many of his former colleagues between 1897 and 1901 had never returned. On 17 October 1908 when he left Liverpool for Lagos on the *SS Sekondi* she surely wondered if they had just spent their last summer together.

On board in first class were two other District Engineer appointees bound ultimately for Jebba. Eighty other passengers of all classes were on board – suggesting the development of British West Africa since his previous Liverpool departures when the number of passengers had never exceeded 21. Before leaving he was issued with the *West African Pocket Book – A 1905 Guide for Newly Appointed Government Officers*, containing information on clothing, hygiene and malarial prevention: an innovation since his last appointment.

Eight days before the *Sekondi* sailed the consulting engineers wrote reassuringly to the Acting Resident Engineer holding things in Jebba:

Mr Brounger[251] *and a considerable additional staff of experienced District Engineers and Assistants are leaving on October 17th, although some may be a week later.*

Approximately sixteen days later Thomas Wilson arrived in Lagos and was doubtless fascinated to see the changes seven years had brought to it. The population of Lagos had grown considerably since 1901 – almost certainly aided by railway enabled migration. Christianity was also on the increase and the 1907 *Blue Book* for Southern Nigeria lists 82 Church of England churches with a regular attendance of over 12,000. After his long voyage he almost certainly visited Christ Church Cathedral and renewed his acquaintance with Bishop Oluwole and the clergy missionaries whom he knew of old. When he left Lagos the train trip from Iddo Island to Ibadan must have awakened many old memories for him and he almost certainly broke the journey with stops at some of the mission stations he knew. After Ibadan it was virgin territory to him all the way to Ilorin, the passenger terminus, in Northern Nigeria.

In Ilorin he was for the first time in his life in an Islamic city without a Christian church or even a mission station. Revealingly the 1908 *Blue Book for Northern Nigeria* lists just nine native Christians in the country and the rest of the 7.1 million native population are described as either 'Mohammedan or Pagan.'

After Ilorin he went onwards by construction train but as the railhead did not reach Jebba until April 1909, the final part of the journey was covered on horseback with carriers following. After so long a journey through the Nigerian interior his first crossing of the great river Niger must have been a welcome one. Although impossible to be precise about dates it was probably mid-November before he reached Jebba and Government Hill.

According to the Colonial Office files the situation he found there was much improved from earlier. The staff bungalows were now completed and additions advised by the medical officer underway. A tennis court had been provided and racquets sent out from London. A cricket pitch, railway institute and recreation room were also in the process of being provided.

However personal accounts and Government files often tell very different stories. He provided his account of his arrival in Jebba and the conditions he found there in a December 1929 letter to the *Penrith Observer* which was primarily concerned with his hunting hero John Peel and the song which bears his name:

Illustrating how the mind travels homeward, some twenty years ago arriving at a works camp which had endured a bad time of stress and trial the first thing that met the eye was a piece of board nailed to a stick as a finger post and on it pencilled figures which read four thousand odd miles 'to Cumberland.' Enquiry revealed that a West Cumbrian had left a few days before, and 'John Peel' was known there.

His words hardly fit with the existence of a tennis court but even if the court was serviceable it seems unlikely he and the other newly arrived District Engineers were given much time to enjoy a game before embarking on the job of surveying and staking out the 120 mile route to Zungeru. He would have welcomed a church or mission station just as much as recreational games but there were none. The nearest Church was St Ebenezer's in Zungeru but, given the distance, it seems highly unlikely he ever saw it or Lugard's newly built Government House.

The surveying task was divided into 25 mile sections with a District Engineer with assistants and a survey party of African labourers being allocated a section each. One of the many difficulties they faced was in finding a line which satisfied the maximum gradient of one in a hundred. Which 25 mile section Thomas Wilson was allocated and how far north-east of Jebba he reached cannot be determined. They were surveying virgin scrub and bush and there would have been plenty of wild mammals, including elephants to see. Ivory was Northern Nigeria's largest export in 1908 and he and his survey party would have carried guns for their own protection as well as possibly to secure fresh food.

He was back in Jebba, probably having been relieved, on 29 January 1909 when he fell ill. It was as well that he was, because had he been up country, without the medical officer to treat him and the possibility of evacuation from Jebba by river, he would most probably not have survived. He had contracted blackwater fever, a complication of malaria. The name blackwater, however, is not derived from the shadowed stagnant water where mosquito larvae thrive but the awful symptom whereby the sufferer's urine turns raven black. The red blood cells become parasitized and burst, causing the red haemoglobin to leak into the blood plasma. This in turn causes liver damage leading to blood in the urine causing a dark discolouration – hence the name. In fatal cases the urine's flow is stopped or severely restricted by the leaking blood obstructing the kidneys' tubules. Other symptoms are the more predictable ones of a high fever, nausea and exhaustion.

Northern Nigeria in 1908-9 only had two hospitals; one impractically far in Zungeru and the other down the Niger at Lokoja. From Jebba, Lokoja was

130 miles away and the river steamers, held up by the low depth of the river at this point, took five days to reach it. It is most unlikely that the Jebba steamer had a doctor on board but the crew were almost certainly used to caring for the disease's many victims.

At Lokoja the smaller river steamers met the larger craft which could travel far faster over the river's remaining 407 miles to Forcados at one of the many mouths of the delta.[252] At these higher speeds Lokoja to Forcados took just five days. Given he took three weeks to undergo a ten day journey it seems safe to assume that he was admitted to hospital on arrival in Lokoja. According to the *Blue Book* statistics there were four Europeans admitted to Lokoja Hospital with blackwater fever in 1909 and all were successfully treated. However the disease was certainly potentially fatal. In the previous year the hospital attributed one death to the disease and in 1909 one homeward bound passenger from Lagos to Liverpool died of the disease while on board one of Elder Dempster's steamers.[253]

The level of service and comfort on the Niger River Steamers was, like so much else in Northern Nigeria, both varied and unpredictable. This is confirmed by the Rules and Regulations reproduced in the 1908 *Blue Book*:

Cabin Accommodation – Intending passengers should always provide themselves with a camp bed and a mosquito curtain as cabins are not always available.

Electric Light and Ice – The five larger vessels are fitted with electric light and the Corona and Sarota are fitted with refrigerators.

As such his accommodation and level of comfort on board must remain in doubt. Also in doubt must be how many of the amazing sights and sounds of the long journey along the great curving river his fever allowed him to take in. On 19 February his river steamer reached Forcados where they were timed to meet and draw alongside the international steamers to Plymouth and Liverpool. Forcados was Southern Nigeria's second port after Lagos and there was a frequent homebound service. His steamer met the ocean steamer *Burutu* and he was winched aboard in a chair. After eighteen days under the care of the ship's doctor, he left the ship at Plymouth on 9 March 1909.

Having reached Plymouth in the morning he took the train to London – the detailed chronology of his return from Jebba to England is so clear because later that day he set out the details in a surviving letter to his government employers. It indicates that he was staying at the Albemarle Hotel on the corner of Albemarle Street and Piccadilly and as the letter is typed he either had a portable typewriter with him or the hotel offered a typing service. This is unclear but according to Baedeker's *London* of 1900, the hotel offered "excellent wine and cuisine."

In the letter he sought the Colonial Office's approval to see its medical adviser Sir Patrick Manson. In order to hasten the appointment Thomas Wilson evidently delivered his letter by hand as the recipient, who next day sought permission to make the appointment, has written "Mr Bracken looks ill" in his letter which has also survived on the Colonial Office file.[254] He was almost certainly still suffering from jaundice and after two days wait the government granted his request and sent him to see Manson at its expense in order to seek advice and treatment but on the clear understanding that he was resigning and post-recovery would not be returning to Jebba.

Sir Patrick Manson was the best in his field and Thomas Wilson was wise to press his employers for the appointment. Manson in 1894 had first reached the then novel conclusion that mosquitoes were the intermediary agents in malaria. Then in 1897 Chamberlain appointed him adviser to the Colonial Office and he was afterwards instrumental in the foundation of the London School of Tropical Medicine.[255]

Of course details of the medical consultation are not on the government file but Manson almost certainly sent him home to Newcastle with advice, a prescription and a letter explaining the disease to Dr Laws. He obviously eventually made a full recovery as his subsequent acceptance by the British Army demonstrates, but how long that recovery took is less clear. It may have been six months; for exactly six months after his arrival at Plymouth he applied for a gratuity on account of his injury from the Colonial Office. His letter of application of 9 September has not survived but it was made against the terms of his Class 1 West African Railways Agreement which provided for pay to the date of resignation or medical certificate of incapacity and a free first class passage to England but with the express proviso "that he shall have no further claim on the Government."

Doubtless Thomas Wilson quite reasonably argued in his application that the consulting engineers having sought him out and expressly asked him to go and abandon his practice in Newcastle, a further sum ought to be paid to him. This argument apparently succeeded in that on 15 October 1909 the Colonial

Secretary agreed to pay a gratuity of six months pay on account of his injury while on service.

In Northern Nigeria construction of the Jebba-Zungeru section continued at a slow and expensive rate. It was June 1911 before the link between the Lagos Railway and the Baro-Kanu Railway was completed at Zungeru.[256]

By late September 1909 Thomas Wilson was well enough to attend the 6th annual meeting of the Tyneside Cumberland and Westmorland Society. He was re-elected to the committee and to the role of treasurer. After the formal business which included his re-election as President, Canon Rawnsley gave a lecture illustrated with lantern slides on the life of Nelson.

13 – SWIMMING AGAINST THE TIDE

In December 1909 the prolonged parliamentary battle over Lloyd George's controversial budget measures reached a climax when the House of Lords, in breach of precedent, rejected passage of the budget by the massive majority of 350 to 75. Asquith, who had become Prime Minister in 1908 on the death of Campbell Bannerman, obtained a dissolution of parliament to put the issue before the electorate in January 1910. North Westmorland had lost Lord Kerry to West Derbyshire and the Tory party had selected the barrister Lancelot Sanderson KC to represent its cause in Appleby. Sanderson had an established Northern Circuit practice and had been born in Lancaster but like his predecessor candidates could not really be considered local.

The day before polling began[257] Thomas Wilson, prompted by the Liberals' continued use of the free trade issue they had used four years earlier, could not resist an appeal from Newcastle to the electors of his native county. As in previous years it was addressed to the editor of the *Observer* in Penrith:

Sir, One feels refreshed to see again, after four years, the big free trade loaf on the bill-posters' stations and in committee room windows. Induced by the sight of it, I have spent a little time to-night in going over the old bills relating to household accounts, which my wife puts away on her file and this is the result: The prices in the first column are taken from the local tradesmen's accounts for the early part of 1906. Those in the second column from the same for the later part of 1909, and except two items only, the items are from the same tradesmen, and precisely the same in 1909 as in 1906.

The long list that follows, provide some insights into their domestic life in Eldon Street, as well as demonstrating Polly's impressive household accounting and record keeping – doubtless taught to her in the Tiverton vicarage in the final years of the last century. They indicate that the house was lit by gas but heated with coal. Sugar was delivered to the house in a solid half stone loaf and Thomas Wilson had acquired a taste in Africa for savoury or Patna rice – a food item probably unknown to many of his Westmorland readers. He concedes both that the prices given are town not country prices and that bread is absent because it is baked at home. Instead he lists bread's ingredients and how they have risen between the two elections. He calculates flour has increased by 20%, wholemeal by 22%. Oatmeal has increased by 6.5%. The largest rise shown is in the price of bacon which he calculated had risen by 43%. It is followed by his Patna rice at 33% and then flour and wholemeal. Commenting on the figures he continues:

It may be noted that oatmeal, which is mainly grown at home, has gone up but little, whilst flour and oatmeal, and bacon, both largely imported and liable to be controlled by American capitalists and other rings, have gone up enormously. The rise in flour is equal to something like 8 shillings per quarter of wheat, or more than four times the duty the wildest tariff reformer proposes. Now this has taken place in spite of the statement made in 1906 that if a Conservative Government was returned to power "our food would cost us more" with its underlying inference that if only a Liberal Government was returned it would not do so, or would cost us less.

Such was the statement in 1906, when as we know a Liberal Government was given power. Whatever dreams may have been dealt with then, we are now in 1910, and this much is certain, the files with their tradesmen's accounts, and with their prices as above, are actual facts; and we are left sitting on the solid bedrock of indisputable fact that unemployment has become greater in England during the past four years, whilst the prices of the necessaries of life have gone up.

To come to the practical question, what are we to do? Retain Mr Lloyd George and his party, whose loaf must needs contain 20 per cent more gas if it is even to look as big as the loaf of 1906, or give the other side a chance? They can't do much worse, and they can be dealt with in their turn, some four or five years hence if they don't do better.

Yours etc., Westmerian, Newcastle-on-Tyne, Jan 14th 1910

His measured and perhaps deceptively bi-partisan appeal to do no more than 'give the other side a chance' was answered in that both Westmorland seats were regained by the Tories with respectable majorities. The *Penrith Observer* of January 25th 1910 in reporting the results was far from measured.

Its editorial headed "Well Done Westmorland" contained the following sharply biased statement:

The two divisions of Westmorland on Wednesday took a splendid share in the revolt against Modern Radicalism and Socialism as represented by Mr Asquith's Government.

Newcastle did not share in the 'revolt' and the Liberal and Labour candidates were returned with majorities of over 4,000 votes. Perhaps Thomas Wilson's letter might have been more usefully aimed at his fellow voters in the city but the problem with doing so was that his clients and associates were largely of Liberal or Labour persuasion.

Nationally the Liberals lost 100 seats and the Tories gained a similar number, leaving the two main parties evenly matched; but with the support of the 82 Irish Nationalist MPs the Liberal Government had a workable majority, even if it unexpectedly fell out with all of the 40 Labour MPs. Such an outcome was no Tory triumph and with the Irish now holding the balance of power, a third attempt at Home Rule was now a certainty. Hitherto, the House of Lords could be relied upon by the Tories to prevent Home Rule: but now the government proposed a Parliament Bill which would govern relations between the two houses and remove the Lords' veto.

Outside politics 1910 brought Thomas Wilson several distressing family developments. The first was in Westmorland on 8 March 1910 when his mother Elizabeth Bracken died at Bowersyke aged 72. He ensured that her death was announced at both ends of the county in the *Westmorland Gazette* and the *Penrith Observer*. Each newspaper referred to her long widowhood and the *Observer* additionally to her Stainmore birth, although incorrectly crediting her as being the fourth rather than third daughter "of the late Robert Brunskill, Barras House, Stainmore." She was to be followed in September 1910 by her brother Richard Brunskill at the age of 78. Thomas Wilson as his closest surviving relative organised his funeral and settled his affairs. They were much diminished from the days of his being master of Barras House and its accompanying acreage. Plagued by the absence of offspring, his advancing years and the worsening profitability of agriculture, he had left Barras in the early 1890s first for the Slip Inn, Stainmore, and then for a cottage in Brough Sowerby where he died.

Richard Brunskill was the last survivor of the six siblings and according to the contemporary Directories the last of the Brunskills living on Stainmore. After over four centuries a significant family presence had come to an end. His two spinster sisters Sarah and Mary Isabella who had lived with him throughout their lives died respectively in 1891 and 1895. His younger brother Robert had died in 1901 and the following year claimed his elder sister Ann Simpson. For such a large family to leave so small a footprint seems remarkable and Thomas Wilson seems to have keenly felt the loss of the Brunskill name and the complete demise of his maternal family. That he did is demonstrated by his giving the Brunskill name to each of his three youngest children. The first of the three was born at home in Newcastle at the end of August 1910. He was named Richard Brunskill Bracken and died the following day, owing to his lungs not opening properly. Dr Laws who had failed to save him certified his death. He was baptised just before he died by the vicar of St. Luke's and poignantly the age recorded on his death certificate is 29 hours.

Within six months Thomas Wilson had suffered three deaths. Whatever the effect on him, they did not diminish his work and private activities. In November his name as treasurer appeared alongside that of Canon Rawnsley in a joint letter by all five Cumberland and Westmorland Societies appealing for more members. By 1910 the original three, London, Newcastle and Manchester, had been joined by Liverpool and Glasgow. Birmingham was soon to follow. The *Observer* was an enthusiastic reporter of the activities of what it termed "Lakelanders in the Cities." The letter demonstrates that by now women were just as welcome members as men with equal subscriptions payable. Those subscriptions were, just like so much else in Britain of 1910, highly stratified: the 'Ordinary Annual Member' paid 2/6, the 'Honorary Annual Member' paid 10/6 while 'Life Members' paid five guineas.

The new Parliament was dissolved after just nine months and a second general election called for December 1910. Unsurprisingly the latest crisis was precipitated by the House of Lords rejection of the Parliament Bill. Just prior to the dissolution, Balfour who seems to have found a voice on this issue, had told an audience in Nottingham "smash the House of Lords in order that we may get Home Rule – that is their cry" and on Asquith specifically "it is in order to get what the people of this country have twice refused that he is asking you for all time to shatter your constitution." Unsurprisingly, the Government preferred to categorise the crisis as 'People versus Peers'.

The second election changed almost nothing. The Liberals lost three seats but because of the success of the Irish Nationalists, the Government's effective majority increased from 124 to 126. This outcome meant that the Liberal Party had won three successive elections. It was a triumph without precedent since 1832 and it severely shook the Conservatives' self-confidence.[258]

In Newcastle, the Conservative candidates were again defeated. In Westmorland they repeated their victory of January. In North Westmorland Lancelot Sanderson's electoral slogan was 'Vote for Sanderson and a United Empire' and above the results the *Observer's* headline was "Westmorland stands true in its opposition to Home Rule." But irrespective of Westmorland's view, the issue of Irish Home Rule was a matter of when not if, as soon as the House of Lords passed the Parliament Bill – as they did in the following August.

For Thomas Wilson the Unionist position in the city of Newcastle now seemed hopeless. More widely, what had been the natural party of government throughout most of his adult life seemed to have lost its winning touch and, at the time, there seemed no obvious way for the party to come back from this malaise.

At least Westmorland remained loyal to his way of thinking and following the contest he and his family went there for Christmas at Bowersyke and to attend his brother's wedding at Killington. His 42-year-old bachelor brother perhaps made an usual bridegroom. Since the death of his mother he had been alone there and to bring that situation to an end he married his 29-year-old second cousin Alice Jane Bracken. Possibly his mother had opposed the match: Alice had spent her entire life at Grassrigg and they were long acquainted by 1910. For her, an attraction may have been moving to Bowersyke where her grandfather William Bracken had died in 1885 and her father John William had been born 75 years earlier. By this consolidation another stitch was placed in the closely woven Firbank-Killington Bracken tapestry.

Between 1911 and the outbreak of war there was an unprecedented rise in trade union militancy. It was as if the struggle with the Lords had awakened a sharp sense of working class grievance. Innumerable disputes often of a seemingly quite petty nature blew up in manufacturing businesses across the country. They were often under-reported; but it was impossible for the press to ignore disputes concerning the two great contemporary giants of capital and labour, the railways and coal, with each of which Thomas Wilson had close professional links.

Trouble had been foreshadowed a year earlier in July 1910 in Newcastle and was precipitated by the suspension of a railway engine shunter called Goodchild. He worked in the goods yard at Gateshead and when asked to go from one part of the huge yard to another had refused and was suspended.

His suspension led to somewhere between 7,000 and 10,000 North East Railway staff going on strike. As they had withdrawn their labour without notice, the strike was illegal and the participants liable to the company in damages. However the shocked directors, who had never experienced anything similar before, swiftly offered that there would be no legal action if they returned to work. They also offered hearings into general grievances and specifically those of Goodchild who would be re-instated. Their terms were accepted and after three days the strike was over.

However as the Railway Union leaders doubtless observed, even over three days, it had a huge effect on the large business users of the railway, such as the coal industry, fishing, shipping and the docks on the Tyne; as well as, obviously passengers. The local newspaper correspondents, used to a small army of porters and other uniformed railway staff on duty, were obviously stunned:

> *The Central Station presented an extraordinary appearance on Wednesday. Scarcely a man in uniform was to be seen, the porters and ticket collectors to a man having ceased work. Clerks unaccustomed to the job were fumbling with fistfuls of tickets... passengers with luggage had to manage as best they could, and it was a common sight to see a fashionably dressed man gravely wheeling his own luggage along the platform on a station barrow.*

This was an age where no man of status would carry much more than a cane or umbrella and the railways were at the peak of their importance in national life. In August 1911 such scenes were repeated across the entire country when a national rail strike was declared. Although the railways were owned and operated by private companies the Government could not ignore a situation which was rapidly leading to national paralysis. Asquith met with and threatened the Railway Union leaders with "use of all the forces of the Crown" to keep the railways open. However in the event, the army was not required, as the offer of a Royal Commission into the dispute, ended the strike after the country had endured three days of chaos.

This environment of industrial strife caused Thomas Wilson to ponder the causes and in particular the issue of food price inflation which he had last publicly addressed in 1910. His conclusion in 1912 was effectively that Chamberlain and the tariff reformers had been substantially vindicated by subsequent events, and that it was the rising cost of imported food and the pressure it caused to workmen's wages which had precipitated the current industrial unrest. He found support for his conclusions in two surprisingly radical quarters and these he shared with the readers of the *Observer* of 30 January 1912:

> *Sir, For twenty years and more a former Penrith resident, an old friend, has sent me at odd times copies of the 'Bulletin' a well known Australian paper. The 'Bulletin' is one of the most Radical of the Australasian papers, and one more critical of and disrespectful to the aristocracy and landlord interests, and more antagonistic to these, as such it would be hard to find... an article appeared in that journal on October 26th. It is not a complimentary article nor very respectful... but some of your Radical readers at home and elsewhere might like to see it, and slightly abbreviated this is what that very democratic paper, speaking from the other side of the world, says:*
>
> *A few days ago the cable reported... that sundry new strikes and riots had broken out at Swansea (England). Various premises were mentioned as being wrecked... and the country is full of such shindies as it hasn't known for more than half a century. The working Bull...[259] still believes in free trade (theoretically and as a matter of form) just as he believes in Heaven... and a personal Devil with a caudal appendage. From ancient habit, he is content to hear his candidate state at election time:*
>
> *1) That he is the freest, best-fed, and best-paid workman on earth.*
>
> *2) That he enjoys cheap food, and the big loaf.*
>
> *3) That under Protection he would have dear food, and a small loaf, and be glad to eat horseflesh.*
>
> *He listens to these statements... just as... he listens approvingly on Sunday to the statement that he is a miserable sinner. But on week-days, and when he is not listening to the free trade candidate, he knows that his wages are going down and the price of his food is going up.*

When he opened his ports to foreign food supplies in the early days of free trade, all continental Europe had victuals to sell. Competition gave him cheap food and Bull's own agriculture was allowed to go to perdition... Now the food supply isn't anything like so great, in proportion to the demand, as it used to be, and the suppliers are able to put up prices heavily against the one great country which having practically no supplies of its own, is at their mercy.

It was all right when he bought foreign food cheap and sold manufactured goods to foreign nations dear. But gradually it is becoming the case of buying food dear and selling manufactured goods cheap, because other countries have learnt to manufacture, and the struggle to find a foreign market grows more and more intense.

Now the 'Bulletin' being such a very Radical paper... if they disagree it will be of little good that any of your said Radical readers should write through you at me, for I oft times disagree with the 'Bulletin'. But it might be kind to put the editor right... the 'Bulletin's' address is Sydney, New South Wales.

Confirmation of facts sometimes comes from quarters where least expected... that distinguished English Radical, the Right Hon. Thomas Burt,[260] is by a coincidence reported... as saying yesterday:

"At the present time there is a great deal of industrial perturbation. That unrest was widespread and effected nearly all trades. There must be some cause for it. He believed there was more than one cause. One was that the workmen did not believe... they participated... in the wealth which they did so much to produce. Another was that the cost of living had been increasing... more rapidly than wages."

So the 'Bulletin's' diagnosis of the disease is endorsed from an unexpected quarter... Doubtless on the subject of treatment the 'Bulletin' and Dr Burt hold different views, and I do not for a moment suggest they would prescribe the same remedies at present. But the first step in a consultation is to diagnose the disease.

Yours, &c, X. Grey Street, Newcastle-on-Tyne, January 20th 1912.

Archly sarcastic as it is, the letter illustrates how many Tories felt about the Liberal's deceitful election tactics over free trade; and the fact that one of the consequences of it was that the government was plagued with industrial strife, was no consolation to patriots like Thomas Wilson.

In late February 1912 the first national coal strike occurred when over a million miners stopped work. It was the worst coal stoppage in the North-East since the Durham miners' strike of 1892, which Thomas Wilson had experienced in the Tyne and Derwent Valleys while working for the Consett Iron Company. The miners sought a national minimum wage and within a fortnight it was estimated that a further 1.25 million workers in other industries had been put out of work due to the lack of coal. The Government's rapid response was the Coal Mines (Minimum Wages) Bill which was swiftly enacted by Parliament. The miners voted to accept the Government's scheme and returned to work in April but the *Observer* editor did not exaggerate when he wrote on April 9, that the strike had been "a gigantic struggle without parallel in the whole of British industry."

Proof that Thomas Wilson's practice was still tied to the coal industry and its engineering work is found in *The Times* of 10 May 1911. In the paper's Engineering Contract List, he invited tenders on behalf of the Stella Coal Company for the diversion of a railway line and the construction of a tunnel near Ryton, Durham. In this, to him, unpalatable political and industrial world he sought distraction in his young family and the undisturbed peace of Westmorland. Another place where harmony still reigned was at the meetings of the Cumberland and Westmorland Society where during the miners' strike the members attended a slide illustrated lecture titled 'A Scamper through the United States.' In 1911 Thomas Wilson stood down as Treasurer of the Society and in 1913 he received 'a warm tribute' from the Chairman as he left the committee of the organisation he had helped found in 1904. His reasons for doing so were not recorded: perhaps he felt he had done enough for the organisation which now had branches in Winnipeg and Vancouver, with others planned in Calgary and Alberta. Also, of course, his life membership ensured that he did not entirely lose touch with them.

Another possible and understandable reason for his departure was to enable him to spend more evenings at home with his wife and young family. He was not the remote and distant father figure of Edwardian stereotype. Also in these years his already large family continued to grow. In November 1911 Betty Brunskill Bracken joined her four elder siblings on the upper floor of 64 Eldon Street. Betty had been the name of Thomas Wilson's great aunt Brunskill who had lived at Barras after her widowhood and in his earliest years.

Then 28 months later in March 1914 his youngest child Erik Richard Brunskill Bracken was born. Erik[261] with its Swedish-inspired spelling was the only non-familial name he chose for his seven children and may have been a reflection of Newcastle's historic links with Scandinavia. Erik's other given names were very familial – Richard Brunskill commemorated his elder brother's day long life and his great uncle Richard Brunskill.

Just prior to Erik's birth in February 1914 Thomas Wilson made his final *Observer* contribution before the outbreak of war. The previous week's paper had listed sixteen Bishops and Archbishops who had been born in Westmorland and it was this list that stirred him to do so. The editor in his column 'Facts and Gossip of the Week' readily conceded that he had made omissions a week earlier, which had not gone un-noticed:

> *Witness the following postcard from Newcastle dated Wednesday – "the Rev. Henry Lowther Clarke, the present Archbishop of Melbourne and Metropolitan of Victoria. He is the son of the Rev. W. Clarke, a former Vicar of Firbank, spent his early boyhood in Firbank, and the writer thinks, was born there but of this is not certain." The same writer also reminds me of Bishop Taylor-Smith formerly of Sierra Leone and currently Chaplain General of His Majesty's Forces.*

It demonstrates his impressively retentive memory of a conversation he must have once had, long before, with his mother about her earliest memories of married life in Firbank and the teenage son of the vicar, who was living next door. It also perhaps demonstrates his pedantic appetite for accuracy. It plainly never occurred to him to make any distinction between the occupants of English sees and colonial bishops.

14 – INTO UNIFORM

In the months prior to August 1914 the great political controversies were not concerned with international relations and the threat they posed to world peace. Rather, within Parliament the main issue was Irish Home Rule and the almost interminable progress of the legislation as it was debated and re-debated, to satisfy the provisions of the new Parliament Act. Outside the Parliamentary arena, the main issue was the violence of the women suffragists. In June 1914 they had even set off a bomb in Westminster Abbey, which damaged the Coronation Chair.

Although Thomas Wilson did not state his views publicly at the time on either issue, it is not hard to surmise that his views on Ireland exactly matched those of his party. In the summer of 1914 the Government's Irish Home Rule Bill had just provoked extreme opposition from the Conservative party, virtual mutiny in the British Army, and surprisingly fierce dissent from Buckingham Palace.[262] For the whole of Thomas Wilson's adult life, Unionism – i.e. the defence of the union with Ireland – had been a central tenet of the Conservative party. In 1886 when Gladstone flew his kite by having his son announce his conversion to Home Rule for Ireland, it is not hard to guess what Thomas Wilson felt. He had been in the city of Cork just a few years previously while surveying the route for a light railway extension and if Ireland, Britain's first Imperial possession, was to be surrendered, what hope was there for the future of the rest of the Empire? To him and many of his contemporaries there was no distinction between Cork and Westmorland, Midlothian and Glamorgan.

Into this polarised world came the international crisis which appeared with unexpected suddenness. Seen through the prism of the *Penrith Observer* which he would have read, there was nothing relevant between the report of the assassination of the heir to the Austrian throne in the 30 June edition and that of 28 July when "The Worst Crisis of this Generation" was gravely reported. On the Tuesday following the Penrith editor was already writing of "The Great War" in his 4 August edition.

Of course in Penrith as the printing presses ran the newspaper staff were not sure that Britain would treat German troops entering neutral Belgium on 3 August as a *casus belli*. As soon as it was known that this was so, a common British reaction to this unexpected state of war, occurring over an August Bank Holiday, was a belief that the Royal Navy would soon favourably resolve the matter and there were many popular demonstrations of enthusiastic patriotism. Although this reaction was encouraged by a powerfully jingoistic press it seems, to us who know what was to follow, almost obscene. In the defence of the many 1914 enthusiasts, they probably thought you could have a war in which only foreigners got killed. Many of the minor colonial wars of the previous century had been like that and even the Boer War had caused small casualty lists compared to what followed. The Prime Minister, Asquith, found the hysteria of the London crowds that August highly distasteful and recalled Walpole's remark "now they are ringing their bells; in a few weeks they'll be wringing their hands."[263] Unlike Asquith though there were numerous complacent commentators, who predicted swift and inevitable victory and that it would all be over by Christmas.

What was Thomas Wilson's reaction to the momentous events of August 1914? His patriotism was never in doubt but in his fiftieth year he had long experience of the difficulties and unexpected complications of life. His time in West Africa had taught him that Government planning and predictions were liable to be badly awry. He could easily remember the Boer War which had similarly started on a wave of popular enthusiasm but also degenerated into a prolonged and far from glorious struggle. In Newcastle the South African War Memorial still dominates Haymarket, at the far end of Eldon Place, beyond Barras Bridge and it would have served as a daily reminder on his way to and from his office in Grey Street of the sacrifice of the Northumbrian regiments.

We know his party politics: his hostility to Asquith's Liberal government would have been in his mind like any party member witnessing the performance of the opposing side in power for a long period. However as the crisis broke, so very unexpectedly, such raw feelings were put aside at the prompting of a Conservative Party leader who offered the government "unhesitating support" and stated that "in everything connected with it [the War] there would be no parties."[264] Thomas Wilson an avid newspaper reader and loyal party member since the 1880s, would have quickly followed Andrew Bonar

Law's lead in putting party aside and embraced his country's and his government's cause.

In the days which followed he, like many other non-Liberals, would have been helped in their patriotism by Asquith's reluctant appointment of the military hero Kitchener of Khartoum as Secretary of State for War.[265] For Thomas Wilson, Kitchener had two attractions: he had a long pedigree of distinguished military service in Africa and he was a Royal Engineer who had constructed a railway to ensure the conquest of the Sudan in 1898. Thomas Wilson had first encountered the Royal Engineers in the guise of Major-General Hutchinson as an adolescent trainee civil engineer in Darlington in 1882. In the 1890s he had encountered another Engineer officer, Major McCallum who served as Governor of Lagos from 1897-1899. In 1915, 33 years after meeting Major-General Hutchinson, he was himself to become an officer of the regiment.

To us Kitchener is of course best known as the stern face staring from the recruiting poster sub-titled 'Your Country Needs You'. His campaign for recruits began immediately on 7 August. Its effect, when coupled with the appalling early losses, would be to sweep away much of the ethos of the old British Army for ever. Within eight weeks 761,000 had responded to Kitchener's call.[266] In recruiting his new citizen army Kitchener was wise enough to harness local loyalties by using mayors and corporations, and committees of local industrialists, to raise recruits. Recruits often joined new units which were bolted onto the local county regiment. One of these new units was the 16th Battalion of Northumberland Fusiliers (known as the Newcastle Commercials[267] and raised jointly by the Chambers of Commerce of Newcastle and Gateshead) and Thomas Wilson almost certainly knew many who joined this new part of a proud and famous county regiment in the early months of the war.

The age range for Kitchener's recruits in August 1914 was 19 to 35. In the following May the upper limit was raised to 40 but Thomas Wilson, aged 50 and without previous military experience, was very obviously ruled out. His reaction was like that of many older men in war-time both before and since: a feeling of wistfulness at fate ruling him out of a military contribution the signs of which were all around him. The rate of enlistment in the Durham and Northumberland mining villages was particularly impressive and Thomas Wilson with his strong connection to the mining industry witnessed first hand this depletion of labour. Amazingly his old colliery village High Spen pro-duced two soldiers who were awarded the Victoria Cross. The first to do so was Billy Dobson who was working at the Garesfield Colliery in August 1914 when he was hastily recalled by his former regiment. By late September 1914 he was serving in France as Lance Corporal F. W. Dobson of the Coldstream Guards when he won his V.C. The second was awarded to Private Thomas Young of the Durham Light Infantry in March 1918.

The great response to Kitchener's call to arms in the city of Newcastle is marked still by the War Memorial at Barras Bridge. The bronze figures of a recruiting band are followed by men in uniform as male civilians behind rush to down their tools and embrace their wives and children before joining the colours.[268] Beneath is inscribed "Non Sibi Sed Patriae[269] – The Response 1914."

However, prior to the assembly of Kitchener's new citizen army it was the old British army, highly proud and small in number, with its officer class, largely aristocratic in background and exclusively schooled on the basis of nineteenth century colonial wars (where the enemy had consisted of either lightly armed native Africans or more recently rebellious Dutch farmers), which first embarked for France on the night of 14 August 1914. The most influential – and smartest – regiments were the cavalry regiments of Hussars, Lancers and Dragoons: but across the army, no regiment had any experience of continental warfare since the Crimea. They were massively outnumbered by the advancing forces of the enemy. But notwithstanding the obvious numeri-cal difference, the men of the British Expeditionary Force seem to have shared the general thought that they would easily dispose of the enemy and rode and marched off to France with corresponding enthusiasm. Another disadvantage of the great rush to France which was rapidly exposed was that the Army was seriously under-equipped and its artillery very short of ammunition.

As is well known the initial stages of the war did not go well for the British Expeditionary Force (BEF). Its first engagements with the enemy and the planned advance quickly became the retreat from Mons on 24 August. Although this and other battles slowed the German advance it was September before the German advance on Paris was halted at the river Aisne, where the Germans securely and immovably dug in. Facing deadlock here the BEF switched its attention to the north and the so-called race for the sea aimed at securing the French Channel ports but here too the hoped for breakthrough

was not achieved. The initial complacency and confidence in an easy victory evaporated as the casualty figures were digested. Within a month the BEF
lost more than 20 per cent of its strength killed, missing, or wounded in
action.

At the time such awful statistics were not even particularly clear to the War
Office and to those such as Thomas Wilson reliant on press reports the early
wartime situation was very unclear and confused. The *Observer* reports
swung from pessimism to optimism and back from week to week. Although
the war now completely dominated the newspaper certain former features
were retained. One was '50 years Ago' and the 22 September paper, slightly
prematurely, focussed on its previous edition of 4 October 1864. At the bottom of the column, the second wedding report was that of Thomas Wilson's
parents, on 24 September 1864. As he undoubtedly read it he was almost
exactly five months away from his 50th birthday and if his premature conception was previously unknown to him, it was now totally clear.

As autumn turned to winter, the lines of trenches in which the armies sheltered from the deadly machine-gun and artillery fire grew inexorably from
Switzerland to the Channel. By early 1915 the pattern of the Western Front
as a horrendous immobile attritional war, in which tens of thousands died for
the sake of the same few miles of territory as the opposing armies attacked
and counter-attacked from their respective trenches, was established. So
much for the war of movement which all of the armies involved had planned
for. Instead they were enmeshed in a largely static struggle between ever
denser defences.

This unexpected turn of events was to have two principal consequences for
Britain and its Empire in 1915. The first was the search for other new theatres of war such as the Dardanelles in which it was hoped a decisive blow
could be struck whilst circumventing the deadlock in France. The second was
a serious shortage of material and suitable ammunition which eventually contributed to the fall of the Liberal government and the formation of a cross-
party Liberal-Tory coalition in May 1915.

Curiously Asquith made a visit to Newcastle in April 1915 and the widely
reported speech he made there was to aid the demise of his Government. He
made the visit in recognition of the city's great armaments industry, to con-
gratulate it on its work and to refute the recent newspaper criticism. However
far from defusing the 'Shells Scandal' he exacerbated it. Maintaining that

there was no cause for recrimination or blame, he then made the staggeringly complacent and obviously incorrect statement:

I don't believe any army or navy has ever either entered upon a campaign or been maintained during a campaign with better or more adequate equipment.

A secondary mistake was to acknowledge that Kitchener's unregulated recruitment campaign had damaged the productivity of the coal mines and other vital industries. His admission that day was to increase pressure for conscription and government control of industrial labour and cause the Prime Minister further political difficulty during 1915-16.

Even after 90 years the figures in Asquith's speech are eye-watering: 217,000 had enlisted from the mines, almost 50% of the miners of military age, but in consequence mining employment was down 14% and output down 12% while demand for coal due to the War had risen sharply. Seemingly all a wartime Prime Minister could do in response was to appeal to those in these vital industries to stay where they were, by using the words "they are serving their country just as well at the coal face in Northumberland or Durham as if they were mining the trenches in Flanders and France."

It is clear from the *Newcastle Daily Chronicle* report that many who applied for tickets to the Palace Theatre, where Asquith spoke, were unsuccessful but the *Chronicle* lists two of Thomas Wilson's friends being on stage behind the Prime Minister, Sir Benjamin Browne and Councillor Millican. Their presence, plus his Town Hall contacts, indicates that Thomas Wilson was in the audience that night. After his speech Asquith stayed in Newcastle and on the next day visited the huge armaments works of Armstrong, Whitworth & Co.

Contrary to what Asquith said, there was little material for building the trench shelters which had become necessary as a result of the stalemate, and even a shortage of spades to dig them with. Trench mortars and periscopes were also a rarity among the soldiers of the original BEF. This form of warfare demanded a far greater degree of engineering skills than had been planned for by the War Office. The grand plan for rapid advance,[270] involving huge numbers of cavalry troops who in the event spent years sitting idly in reserve before eventually fighting dismounted, precluded all planning for an engineers' war and left the Royal Engineers seriously under-represented at the highest level of the War Office.

A further problem in securing proper representation for both the Engineers and the Artillery in the pre-1914 upper echelons of the British Army was that their officers were frequently the victims of snobbery and suspicion. They were commonly seen as overly technically minded and intellectual: then a disadvantage given the abiding cult of army amateurism. An additional problem was that RE and RA officers were trained at Woolwich rather than at Sandhurst. Also the Army's smarter regiments had long memories and did not forget that it was only the Engineers and Artillery which had abandoned the purchase of commissions prior to Gladstone forcing the issue in 1871. With the general ethos and expense of officer life being unchanged by the abolition of commission purchase, some officers in the grander regiments up to 1914 thought RA and RE officers 'not necessarily gentlemen.'[271]

The first catalyst for the rapid post-1914 expansion of the Royal Engineers was the hasty abandonment of the plan that the French would carry out all services for transportation, bases and lines of communication.[272] More generally in the form of warfare which transpired, trenches and other defences needed to be constructed and maintained, and the communication routes to the front line needed to be increased and repaired as they were put under severe pressure by the continual passage of huge numbers of men and supplies over small heavily congested areas. The statistics relating to the strength of the Corps of Royal Engineers speak volumes about what most certainly became an engineers' war. In August 1914 the total strength was 25,000: by November 1918 it was over 314,000. So far as the officer strength was concerned it in turn increased tenfold from 1,569 to 15,000.[273] As Peter Barton has recently written in his 2007 book *Passchendaele,* "The Western Front was quite simply the greatest engineering exercise in world history."

Even when the Corps expanded to meet the task in hand, the work the Engineers did during 1914-1918 was often seriously under-reported. This was because although vital it was often unglamorous and unrecognised – even following victory where in the morass of untangling highly complex events, historians found it easier to focus on the bravado and panache of other more visible fighting units. The significant contribution of the Engineers, often working at night, unseen and even underground, can easily be overlooked.

At the start of the war Corps officers with full regular commissions were trained as formerly at the Royal Military Academy, Woolwich, and at the

School of Military Engineering in Chatham where they received technical instruction. Prior to the war this training lasted for four years but after war was declared this was shortened to a year.[274] Aside from Territorial officers, the other class of Royal Engineer officer consisted of those given temporary commissions for the duration of the war. Prior to the passing of the Compulsory Military Service Act of 1916, which first introduced conscription for men aged[275] between 18 and 41, these recruits were all volunteers. Many of these men were civilian engineers who were interviewed and recommended by the Institution of Civil Engineers (ICE). It is again perhaps indicative of the War Office's lack of preparedness that it employed an external civilian agency to recruit engineer army officers. These recruits were young temporary officer cadets, many of them being ICE student members and the maximum age prescribed was 30. Once they had been medically examined and their appointment was confirmed by the War Office they were trained in a course of just seven weeks (later extended to eleven) at Chatham, Newark or Deganwy and were then despatched to units in the theatre of war.[276]

Thomas Wilson had been a member of the ICE since 1897 and would easily have passed through the technical qualifications, which the interview was there to test, and on to recommendation: but his age remained a bar. Some of these young engineer officers came from the not insubstantial Newcastle engineering fraternity and Thomas Wilson would have known several who joined the officer class of the Royal Engineers in this way. Some may have even been his former pupils and assistants. The western screen in Newcastle Cathedral records the war service of eight Northumbrian Royal Engineer field units who would, so far as practicable, have been led by local men. The same screen also records the huge expansion of the Northumbrian Fusiliers from its initial seven battalions of regulars, reserves and territorials at the war's outset to some 36 by its close. Above it hang eighteen World War One regimental colours in testament to Newcastle's huge contribution towards the war effort.

Undoubtedly before conscription came in much of the contribution was garnered by great peer pressure to enlist as is evidenced by the growing practice of ladies to present white feathers to young able-bodied men who were not in uniform. The practice was particularly prevalent at railway stations and although Thomas Wilson was too old to be at risk of feathering in his frequent travels he may have witnessed the practice which became so widespread that the Government issued khaki armlets to those who had attested their willingness to serve but had not yet been called up.

Against this fevered background and growing casualty lists, at the end of July 1915 the War Office, realising that the siege conditions demanded huge amounts of engineering on the Western Front, sanctioned a further expansion to the Corps of Royal Engineers by the formation of Labour Battalions. Eleven of these battalions were eventually raised. The men were recruited from the construction industry and the officers were selected from civil engineers directly by the Fortifications and Works department of the War Office. The idea was to create a dedicated construction workforce in uniform to deal with broader and more technical construction needs of the army than were catered for by the Royal Engineer field units. Also as the War Office wanted to avoid the delay that would be caused by the imposition of the usual officer training period, it only wanted highly experienced civil engineers to form the officers of the battalions. In consequence no age limit was imposed on officers and they were given direct commissions as Lieutenants and Captains in the Corps.[277] This was Thomas Wilson's chance: all the available evidence is that he seized it with alacrity and immediately volunteered to the War Office. They were probably impressed by his previous service to the Colonial Office and by his longstanding membership of the ICE, to which the War Office remained close. Subject to a medical, they readily accepted his offer to provide his engineering skills to the British Army.

What were his motivations for volunteering? A high level of patriotism and a desire to play a useful and active part in what was proving to be a very difficult chapter in the British nation's long history would seem to be the principal ones: after the War he was to write of the psychology "of the Englishman generally, with whom experience has shown the graver the trouble the greater the keenness to enlist."[278] England was certainly in trouble on the Western Front with no progress and enduring colossal casualties by the summer of 1915. Elsewhere, in the Dardanelles, a disaster on an epic scale had been suffered and on the Eastern Front, Russia was in full retreat from Galicia and was soon to be deprived of Warsaw and most of Russian Poland. In such a dire military environment it is perhaps unsurprising that he felt providing his engineering skills on the home front, to the undeniably vital Northumbrian and Durham coal mines and railways, was not a sufficient contribution to pacify his conscience.

More minor motivations were perhaps a desire to be where the action was and a spirit of adventure which he had already exhibited on his previous forays to West Africa. As to his bravery he had already demonstrated it in the dangers he had faced in Nigeria and in particular his brush with death there in 1909. Clearly Thomas Wilson was a man who paid little attention to his personal safety. He had a strong Christian faith and seems to have been happy to place his trust in God as to whether he was to live or die. Of course he was going to be serving in a support role providing engineering services to the army and as such was not going to be put in the front line and told to lead his men over the top into a hail of machine-gun fire. Nonetheless he would still be facing the ever present dangers of artillery fire, aerial bombardment and gas attack: how much he knew as to exactly what role he would be expected to play and the dangers he would face must remain very doubtful.

What most certainly did not attract him was the amount of officer pay he would now receive. A lieutenant's pay in 1915 was considerably less than that of a successful civil engineer with a booming practice but in making that financial sacrifice he was no different to many officers and men who had enlisted in response to Kitchener's call. In April 1915 the Lord Mayor of Newcastle had specifically addressed the financial sacrifice made by skilled men when calling upon those who had stayed at home to work harder in the local munitions factories:

> *Thousands of men at the Front have sacrificed remunerative positions to respond to their country's call and whether in the Naval or Military Forces are doing their duty with only a fraction of the pay they formerly received.*

For someone without previous military experience being given a commission at 50 was highly unusual: none of his ineligible contemporaries would have criticised him for declining to answer the War Office's appeal. All the indications are that when he eventually returned to Newcastle and civilian life in 1920 his professional peers and clients did not forget what he had done almost five years earlier.

One of the consequences of his volunteering was to leave his wife and six children, the youngest Erik at just over a year old, but in this he was acting no differently to thousands of other volunteers and he probably dismissed it as an objection to his going. His return to the Lagos Railway in 1908 had proved that he was a man of his time and his career and interests came before those

214

of his wife and children. Whether Polly was of the 'Women of Britain say –
Go!' school or if she attempted to dissuade him from volunteering, will now
never be known but if she did, she was plainly unsuccessful.

An important consequence of his departure from Newcastle for his military training was that his wife and family left the city for Stainmore,

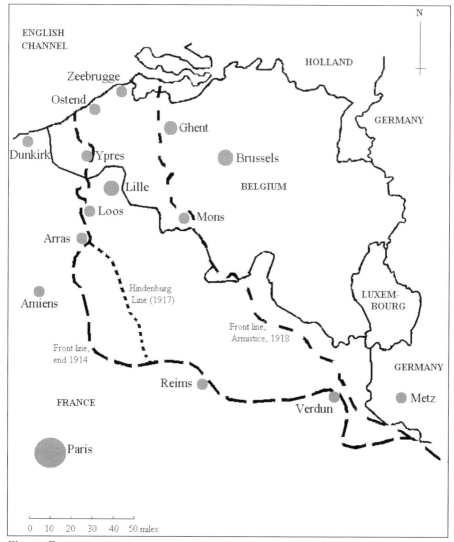

Western Front.

Westmorland, and the area of his birth and upbringing. The motive for this move from their house at 64 Eldon Street was their safety, for by the summer of 1915 it was becoming clear that the east coast of England was the most dangerous location for civilians. German battleships had famously shelled Hartlepool, Whitby and Scarborough in December 1914 and the first Zeppelin raid on London took place on 31 May 1915. One on Hull followed in June: later in 1916 there were further Zeppelin raids on both Sunderland and Edinburgh. Newcastle with its huge armaments and shipbuilding works was perhaps a more obvious strategic target and it was quite reasonable to fear for their safety that summer. Although by comparison with the 1940s the risk was slight[279] the danger perceived by a civilian population entirely unused to attack was not. This new danger of aerial bombardment caused significant civilian panic throughout the war and provided the catalyst for the Bracken family to move out of the city to the safety of rural Westmorland. A second reason may have in part been financial retrenchment necessitated by his army salary meaning a much reduced family income. However any retrenchment had limits in that he maintained his office in Grey Street throughout the war – sending his clerks and other staff to volunteer and locking it up when he left Newcastle for his own military training. The ground floor of number 40 was, by 1915, occupied by a photographer and doubtless he kept an eye on its dust-sheeted upper floors.

Stainmore as well as being a place of safety was where his eldest son Robert had been living since entering Appleby Grammar School in October 1914. His school record survives and records him as first lodging at an address called Rakestraw, Stainmore. When he entered the senior school in 1918 aged fourteen he is shown as boarding at school. Robert's admission to Appleby and his acceptance there prior to the outbreak of war, initially puzzles. Why did he not attend the nearby Newcastle Royal Grammar School? As a passionate Westmerian and founder member of the Cumberland and Westmorland Association on Tyneside, the decision to send Robert away to Appleby illustrates Thomas Wilson's natural determination that his eldest son should share some of his own Westmorland roots, even if it meant his having initially to live with an old friend or distant relative. Another factor may have been that 64 Eldon Street had become rather crowded with children by 1914.

He was unable to enter his father's old school because in 1908 Kirkby Stephen Grammar School became a girls school and Appleby Grammar

School was from then on exclusively for boys. So Appleby was the next best thing for Robert and – partly as a result of their evacuation from Newcastle – Thomas Wilson's daughters would attend his old school. Thus all of his children had a Westmorland education, fifty years after his own.

Thomas Wilson retained a great affection and nostalgia for Stainmore and Rampson to which the family moved in the late summer of 1915 had been known to him since his boyhood. In fact there were two farms at Rampson: the principal farm belonging to Christopher Kipling – a distant cousin of the famous author Rudyard's – and a subsidiary farm behind, now known as Rampson Cottage, occupied in 1915 by William Bell. Although no distinction was then made between the two properties in address terms, it is clear from surviving family photographs that the Bracken family moved to Rampson Cottage. It was an attractive stone built house of the Georgian style with an attached barn; behind it was a large walled garden leading down to the Argill Beck. Compared to Eldon Street it may have been quite cramped for Polly and her six children but this was wartime: as a place of refuge from the perceived dangers of Newcastle it would have been hard to better.

Exactly what arrangement Thomas Wilson reached with Bell is unclear but it seems likely that he rented the farmhouse from him leaving Bell to farm the land while living in a neighbouring house. Similarly, what Polly made of this uprooting from the urban north-east to an isolated rural location cannot now be known. It did have the advantage of re-uniting her with her eldest son and Westmorland was far from virgin territory for her following the frequent holiday visits to Bowersyke since their marriage; but for someone who, apart from her time in Tiverton, had spent her entire life in the industrial or urban landscape of the north-east the peace and quiet of Stainmore may have been quite a culture shock. Of course there is the question why Bowersyke was not chosen as the place to evacuate them to, as Thomas Wilson's brother and his family remained there. Probably re-uniting them with Robert was a preferable solution and, as his newspaper letter-writing had demonstrated, his first loyalty was always to the north of the county.

Polly may well have felt the loss of Newcastle's theatres, cinemas, shops, galleries and museums, along with her social network. Newcastle was at this time quite a theatrical centre. In addition to the Theatre Royal there was the Tyne Theatre, Palace, Empire, Pavilion and Hippodrome. Many of the plays came up on tour from London and in the summer of 1915 *Charley's Aunt* and

What The Butler Saw were on offer.

Cultural deprivation may have been low on the list of Polly's complaints as she may have genuinely feared for their safety in Newcastle and she now had the sole care of six children, two of whom were under five. It is unclear what paid help she retained in Westmorland, but her new wartime life without Thomas Wilson can have been far from easy. In the spirit of the times she doubtless uncomplainingly got on with it. The available indications are that the family, doubtless helped by their father's connections and ancient local pedigree, were a popular addition to the small rural community. There is a photograph in Dawn Robertson's history of Stainmore *'The Plains of Heaven'* which shows Dorothy and Robert Bracken sitting on the bridge over the Argill along with the vicar's wife and daughter. It presents an idyllic picture of his children's wartime life there. Certainly the effect on Jack, the second son, who was removed at the age of eight from a private day school in Newcastle and placed in the local South Stainmore primary school, was profound. He was to become a great countryman, a lover of nature, birds, fish and flora, which but for the Great War would probably never have happened.

As his family settled into their new life on Stainmore Thomas Wilson travelled south to commence his military training in Southampton and from now on, courtesy of his company or battalion war diary, there is a daily record of what he and his unit were doing. These diaries were required to be kept under the 1907 Field Service Regulations. They were often scribbled in pencil in haste and on the flimsiest of paper.

He joined the 11th Labour Battalion on its formation and when he first entered the army and its war diary opens in the very neat pencil hand of the adjutant Lieutenant Crocker. The strength of the Battalion was initially fixed at twelve officers and 1,040 other ranks. This was a very high officer to men ratio due to the fact that it was not a fighting unit but in effect a military construction workforce. The first officers of the Battalion arrived in Southampton on 20 September 1915 and the officer strength was complete by 10 October 1915. Within this time frame it is uncertain as to the precise date Thomas Wilson arrived in Southampton but the announcement of his commission as a Lieutenant was made in the *London Gazette* of 1 October 1915 and took effect on the following day. The war diary tells us that the officers were instructed in "military matters, interior economy of a company, infantry training, military laws, etc." The etcetera would have certainly covered horsemanship, weapons training and animal management. This training period amounted to just three weeks prior to the arrival of recruits on 11 October. Although some further training probably continued up to the point of embarkation for France on 28 October this was the shortest training period for officers with temporary commissions within the Corps of Royal Engineers. Unlike other RE officer recruits, these men were both experienced and mature and it therefore seems unlikely that these labour battalion officers stood out from the rest of the regular RE officer class. Certainly Sir John Cadman, a civil engineer who advised the War Office, said he could never tell during the war whether he was talking to a regular or temporary engineer officer.[280] Thomas Wilson, aged 50, with a rural upbringing certainly knew how to handle both guns and horses and his times in West Africa had taught him how to lead large numbers of men in the field and given him more recent riding and probably shooting experience. As such his length of officer training was probably more than was required to meet the usual regimental standard.

While the battalion was being created at Southampton during September and October 1915, across the Channel the British Army was fighting one of the most significant battles of 1915 at Loos. By now Kitchener's new armies had superseded the old BEF which had been decimated by the fighting in the final months of 1914. Two armies were initially created under Commander in Chief Sir John French. The First Army was commanded by General Sir Douglas Haig and the Second by General Sir Herbert Plumer; eventually three more would be created.

Haig's 1st Army saw action in the Battle of Loos. It was the biggest offensive conducted by the British army to date and also marked the first British use of chlorine gas following the German use of it five months earlier. The attack began on 25 September and the success of both British troops and gas was patchy. The British plan was simple enough: once the German first position was broken by I and IV Corps, IX Corps would pass through the gap. In reality, the arrival of IX Corps into position was delayed by congestion on the approach roads and this gave the Germans a chance to move up their own reserves. Consequently it was the afternoon of the second day before the Reserve IX Corps advanced. German observers saw them advance as if on parade and without covering fire. Amazed by the ease of their target the German machine-guns opened fire at 1,500 yards and within seconds men were falling in their hundreds. A German regimental history recorded the

219

work of its machine-gunners "with barrels burning hot and swimming in oil, they traversed to and fro along the enemy's ranks unceasingly: one machine-gun alone fired 12,500 rounds that afternoon." Some of the attackers actually reached the German wire but, confronted by it after all they had endured en route, the survivors turned back. The Guards division now attacked to stabilise the situation and in consequence Rudyard Kipling's only son John was killed. In total the British lost 43,000 men[281] when the battle ended on 11 October. In terms of territory captured apart from the town of Loos itself it was back to the old British line. The French 10th army's attack to the right had fared no better against the Germans. Although they reached Vimy Ridge they failed to take it and it was to remain in German hands for another eighteen months until it was famously captured by the Canadians. This debacle at Loos was eventually to cost Sir John French his job as Commander in Chief even though his successor Sir Douglas Haig as 1st Army Commander was probably just as culpable.

It was into this military environment that the 11th Labour Battalion was born. Returning to the battalion's new and pristine diary we learn that at the same time as training was underway the quartermaster obtained the Battalion's clothing and equipment so that when the men started arriving on 11 October (just as Loos was ending) they first visited the quartermaster's store. Thanks to the wonderful detail provided by the adjutant we know that they were issued with a mess tin, knife, fork, towel and soap before being medically examined. After this they proceeded to the orderly room where they were issued with regimental numbers and then those passed as fit were marched back to the quartermaster's stores to be clothed while those marked unfit were placed on fatigue duties. After bathing the men got into their uniform for their first inspection by the officer commanding and were inoculated before drawing their equipment. Thereafter the fit were instructed in drill while the unfit continued in fatigues until discharged or transferred.

It is apparent that during this early period a significant number of recruits supplied were unfit for service. The diary states that during the three week period of formation 128 were discharged on medical grounds. Commenting on this the adjutant writes scathingly "this might easily have been obviated had the men been properly examined by medical officers prior to enlistment. A letter on this subject was addressed to the Chief Recruiting Officer, Whitehall." The recruitment process of 1914-15 brought to the attention of the authorities and the higher classes that a very large number of young men, especially those from urban backgrounds, had appalling health. The adjutant's rather naïve and doubtless futile protest illustrates the general ignorance of the condition of the poor among the officer class. From 22 October the battalion went under canvas at Southampton Red Camp for just six nights prior to orders being received to embark at Southampton Docks.

While describing the details of this embarkation the diary first refers to Thomas Wilson by name. The entry dated and timed 28 October 9am reads "Lt Bracken, Lt Ray, 40 other ranks with horses mules and transport moved to Southampton docks and embarked on the SS City of Chester at 12 noon." The reason for this being such a small advance party of only two officers and 40 men was that the ship also carried the battalion's transport of 250 horses, 8 mules and its horse drawn wagons and carts. Surprising as it may seem, the battalion was only supplied with two items of modern transport in the form of a single bicycle and a motor car. At 11.30am the *City of Chester* docked at Le Havre where the detachment disembarked and proceeded to camp which was designated "no. 1 Red Camp." At 6.30pm on the same day the battalion commander Lieutenant Colonel MacDonald, the adjutant Lieutenant Crocker, eight officers and 950 other ranks sailed for Le Havre on the *Empress Queen*. They remained on ship until dawn before marching through Le Havre to the camp where the advance party awaited them.

Plainly the problem of unfit men persisted in that two men were admitted to hospital in Le Havre and a further nine were directed to attend a Medical Board rather than moving off with the rest of the battalion on 30 October. This move was effected by train to Bailleul. The diary once more describes it in detail, "Battalion paraded in marching order, moved through Havre and arrived at Gare du Marchandise at 4pm when it entrained." Bailleul their destination is located close to the Belgian border about fifteen miles north west of Lille (then under German occupation) and five miles from the front line. The recent slaughter of the British army at Loos had occurred just eighteen miles away to the south-east.

When they arrived at Bailleul, and after the distribution of rations outside the station, the battalion was billeted across the town, with headquarters fixed at the Hotel de Fauchon. At this point the diary discloses that they were to be attached to the Canadian Corps. The attachment is unexplained in the diary but it was probably due to the Canadian nationality of the battalion commander.

Lieutenant-Colonel Arthur Cameron MacDonald, born in Nova Scotia and educated at the Royal Military College of Canada, had been a civil engineer for 30 years when he joined the RE as a Captain in July 1915. Within two months he was promoted to Lieutenant-Colonel and was given command of the 11th Labour Battalion.

After three days in Bailleul the battalion paraded in mass formation on the New Aviation Ground before Brigadier-General Armstrong who was the Chief Engineer attached to the Canadian Corps and as such was in charge of the entire Corps' engineering work. After inspecting the men General Armstrong welcomed them "and expressed the hope that they would make a good name for themselves in the country by their work and discipline." Armstrong was a native of Montreal and had been to the same Canadian military school as Colonel MacDonald. Thereafter he was a civil engineer specialising in Canadian railway surveying and construction. He had served for the three years of the Boer War and then remained in South Africa for the following eight years as a railway engineer before returning to Canada in 1911. In August 1914, when Britain brought Canada into the war, he was as a Lieutenant-Colonel given the role of Commander Royal Engineers 1st Canadian Contingent before promotion to Brigadier-General and Chief Engineer in September 1915.

Immediately after this parade the battalion split into its component four companies A, B, C and D, consisting of 240 non-commissioned officers and men, with two officers attached to each. Thomas Wilson along with Lieutenant Westlake was given C Company and proceeded to billets in the villages of Mont Noir and St Jans Cappel which were north and north-west of Bailleul respectively. Mont Noir was one of the 'mountains of Flanders' the ridge of hills which straddle the Franco-Belgian border at this point and form the highest land in Belgium. Although only 'mountains' in a Belgian context, with peaks no higher than 160 metres, riding up them on a horse would still have been a noticeable climb. The top of Mont Noir would have provided a relatively safe environment. The front line was about five miles to the east below. Even so the 'mountains' were an easy and obvious focus for enemy aircraft and the boom of the guns would still have been audible there.

The other companies went under canvas, with the officers in Armstrong huts, and the adjutant provides us with a description of the men's routine. The day started with reveille at 6.30am, breakfast 7.15, first parade 7.45, lunch on works 12 to 12.30pm, dinner 4.45, roll call 8.30 and lights out 9.15. Sundays varied the routine with a later reveille, first parade at 9am followed by 45 minutes of drill leading up to church parade which entailed a half hour out-door act of worship led by the Battalion padre. It was followed by another 45 minutes of drill before inspection of tents, billets and camp. Sunday lunch was followed by an afternoon off.

Attendance at church parade was compulsory but religious ceremonies only occurred when not on active operations or where conditions were not too dan-gerous for a large open air assembly.[282] Some soldiers complained about them – thinking they were just for officers. Others found the improvised altars and surpliced chaplains in tin hats a deeply moving sight. Most men enthusiastical-ly joined in the hymn singing. For Thomas Wilson, a devout Anglican and reg-ular church attender, they were an important feature of the week and an aid to coping with the awful sights, smells and sounds of warfare.

Initially C Company's work consisted of quarrying in the 'mountains' between Mont Noir and Westouter, just inside Belgium. The other companies were engaged on draining and repairing trenches and renewing the adjacent wire entanglements in the Belgian villages of La Clytte, Kemmel and Dranoutre. These trenches were not in the front line but in the third or reserve line. They were all within what was called the Ypres (or to the Tommy, 'Wipers') salient, a bulge which intruded into the German line forming the only unconquered part of Belgium. It was never to be conquered by the Germans and nearly every division of the British Army was to serve here. It remains to this day hallowed military ground littered with British military cemeteries and war memorials.

The day after the Bailleul parade General Armstrong and his staff visited the four companies and gave full instructions as to the work required of each. As to the conditions in the camps the diary gives some fascinating glimpses. Aside from this being November and not obviously easy Flanders camping weather it is quickly recorded that the ubiquitous feature of the Western Front, mud, made an early appearance. Also the shallow trenches dug between and under the tent walls so as to provide foundations became running streams. In consequence tent boards when received "added greatly to the comfort of the men." The tents were further improved by placing sandbags inside the tents and plastering the earth sod lower walls with clay to prevent water ingress. Later in the month the men were supplied with kerosene stoves and were

223

instructed to adapt biscuit tins as flues so as to provide them with some form of heating. Some of these problems seem to have been caused by delays and inadequacies in supplies and materials. Things seem to have improved slightly by the second week of November when the companies were erecting huts to serve as a recreation room, canteen, drying shed, stores and orderly room. A separate slightly smaller shed of twenty by eighteen feet was to serve as the officers' mess. The diary also supplies details of the camps' water supply, cooking arrangements and latrines. At the same time the adjutant describes the rations as "plentiful and fairly varied. Of good quality."

Thomas Wilson and the rest of C Company billeted on the local population almost certainly had a more comfortable existence than those in huts and tents: this was probably not coincidence but on account of his age. Most of his brother officers were far younger than him and his superiors did not ignore the fact when determining his accommodation.

Another Lieutenant who went to France in October 1915 was Raymond Asquith, the 36-year-old barrister son of the Prime Minister, Raymond Asquith, serving with Grenadier Guards. In a letter to his friend Lady Diana Manners he described his first billet with local people:

> *Two or three rather muddy officers in the parlour of a French cottage and a few faithful servants… playing with the women in broken French in the kitchen next door, being sweet to children and making terrible smells with onions: outside big guns booming at a safe distance.*[283]

In contrast the men's living conditions, along with the long hard physical work they were engaged in, had implications for their health. In the first week 35 men of the 11th Labour Battalion were admitted to hospital. There is no indication that any of these injuries were the result of enemy action although the first reference to the presence of shell fire resulted in the battalion commander and Lieutenant Ansell having to lie in a ditch on the road to Dikkebus. It is also evident that there was the fear of attack from the air and in consequence the tents were smeared with coloured paint to make them less conspicuous to aircraft. Another danger was the stormy November weather: thirteen men in A company were injured when the barn they were sheltering in was blown down.

At the end of the first week of November the battalion held its first court of enquiry. Pioneer Smith of C Company was accused of being absent without leave. The court decided that he had been absent since 13 October 1915 when the battalion was under formation in Southampton and forwarded the proceedings in triplicate to GHQ. Although unauthorised absence was a serious matter it is a common misconception about the Great War that all deserters were executed. In fact although many thousands were imprisoned no executions were carried out for desertion on British soil. A total of 346 executions took place during the war, of which 322 were carried out on the Western Front.[284] Of the total, 306 were shot for the military offences of desertion or cowardice and the remaining 40 for committing crimes such as murder or mutiny.[285] By the Armed Forces Act 2006 these 306 men have been granted a posthumous pardon. If Smith was caught and arrested it is likely that he was punished by imprisonment in England. By the end of November similar courts of the 11th Labour Battalion dealt with a further nine men similarly absent but like Smith they too had gone absent in England rather than the more serious of act of desertion from the theatre of war. Not until 19 April 1916 does the diary contain a reference to this more serious charge when Pioneer J Roach of A Company was tried by Field General Court Martial (FGCM) for "Deserting His Majesty's Service." FGCM was the most serious form of court martial and imposition of the death sentence was certainly open to it. However after two days the diary records the court's sentence of five years penal servitude. Perhaps in a sign that the term was hastily reduced by GHQ, when Roach was handed over to the Military Police on 26 April the sentence is recorded as being one of three years imprisonment.

As well as attending courts of enquiry the battalion's officers had a far more regular and onerous task in censoring the letters of the men. Communication with home was quickly recognised as an essential part of the maintenance of morale and the War Office established a network of post offices in France and Belgium. Censoring these letters for breaches of military secrecy imposed a significant workload on company officers. Lieutenant Asquith writing to his wife commented on this aspect of his duties in France:

The most laborious thing one does is reading through and censoring the soldier's letters. They are usually very long and very dull and full of formulae which hardly amount to idiom. The only things I ever scratch out are the expressions "hoping this finds you as it leaves me" and "now I must draw to a close." But God knows my own letters are very little better."[286]

On 14 November after less than two months in charge of the battalion Colonel MacDonald received instructions to return to England pending his posting "to the Near East" – in fact Salonika in Greece. He was instructed to nominate two officers to accompany him but in a sign that perhaps he was more of a civil engineer than a soldier, it is recorded that he was unable to decide who to nominate and decided to consult the War Office when in London. He handed over command to the adjutant and issued an order thanking all ranks for their keenness and attention to duty.

Just over a week later Colonel Charles Edward Hayes CB arrived to assume command. Hayes was a very experienced RE officer aged 60 who had entered the Royal Engineers as a subaltern in 1875 and proceeded upwards to full Colonel by 1907. After being made Companion of the Order of the Bath (CB) he had retired in 1912. During his service he had seen action against the Zulus in South Africa in 1879, for which he was twice mentioned in despatches, and in the Bechuanaland[287] Expedition of 1884-5. In 1915 the national emergency brought him out of retirement to command the 11th Labour Battalion where he was to remain in charge until its dissolution in 1917.

With the arrival of December and the onset of the Flanders winter it is obvious that inadequacies in the men's kit and clothing were of concern at battalion HQ in Bailleul. The adjutant Crocker, now Acting Captain, provides a wealth of detail in relation to this problem and its resolution. On 1 December an application was made for a second pair of boots for the men and by 3 December he records that anti-frostbite grease was being rubbed into the men's feet daily. A week later the men were issued with jerkins and fur waistcoats. On 15 December the men were issued with a second pair of boots and on the next day they received Mackintosh capes. The adjutant now records "they are now well supplied with warm and dry coverings." Less encouragingly the men were supplied with anti-gas tube helmets in the second week of December.

15 – PLUGSTREET

Thomas Wilson's C Company remained in Westouter Quarry until the beginning of the second week of December when instructions were received at the battalion's headquarters in Bailleul that both C and D companies were to relieve the 8th Labour Battalion to the south. This was in a different sector outside the area of the Canadian Corps but still within the 2nd Army area, under II Corps, 25th Division. The new camp was at Lampernesse 1.5 miles north-west of Neuve Eglise where D Company moved first. On the following day C Company, having paraded in marching order at the quarry, moved in motor lorries to Lampernesse. The day after, C Company commenced its new work in five different locations around Nieppe and Armentières. Four days later, and in order to replace Lieutenant Gibson who had left to join Colonel MacDonald in Salonika, Thomas Wilson joined D Company for duty in Ploegsteert Wood. On the day he joined the diary tells us that he accompanied Brigadier-General Charles Godby, Chief Engineer II Corps, on a tour of defensive works in the Wood. Godby, who was two years older than Thomas Wilson, had a record of long service as an RE Officer since 1882. Unsurprisingly for the time his previous active service had been in Africa, in the Sudan in 1885 at the time of General Gordon's death, and again in 1889.

This was the first of many encounters Thomas Wilson was to have with very senior Engineer officers as a result of his unit being attached to the chain of command at Corps level. Had he been attached to a field company he would have received his orders at battalion level from a colonel but because his unit was providing a wider range of engineering services for numerous battalions he was to meet many generals in France and Belgium. Most of them were a similar age to him and also had experience of Africa. Although the distinction in rank would not have been forgotten, they would have been conscious of the civilian engineering practice he had given up to be there, and would have accorded him far more respect and friendliness than to young inexperienced officers.

Ploegsteert Wood is about seven miles east of Bailleul and Mont Noir, but in terms of the adverse conditions it appeared much farther distant from the 'mountains of Flanders'. The British front line was just beyond the eastern edge of the wood and the opposing enemy trenches a few hundred yards further. Although the wood saw no great battles between 1914 and June 1917, and the area had a quiet reputation compared to many, the soldiers serving here suffered consistent if low casualties. Thomas Wilson would have seen there, probably for the first time since he arrived in France, stretcher and burial parties, dressing stations and of course burial plots marked with simple wooden crosses and inscriptions.

The British Army had been here since the autumn of 1914 and, as in many other locations where faced with unfamiliar and unpronounceable names, responded by simply dubbing it Plugstreet Wood. The battalions serving here, as elsewhere on the Western Front, christened the roads, tracks, paths and buildings with names associated with their component regiments. In the wood's case many of the names were selected by the London Rifle Brigade and as well as reflecting their humour also indicated the locations where they would rather have been. The Strand, Fleet Street, Oxford Circus, Hyde Park Corner and Piccadilly Circus now, slightly preposterously, appeared on official maps of this Belgian woodland.

The 600 acre wood formed part of the estate of the nearby Château de la Hutte which had been used as headquarters by the 1st Cavalry Brigade in November 1914 but within a year had been reduced to a pile of rubble by the enemy's artillery. As Thomas Wilson doubtless appreciated, the wood in its pre-war state had been no different from those within the Ingmire Estate, under the care and management of his brother, in far distant Westmorland.

The company's initial work here was the building of heavy gun emplacements on piles of concrete. The trees provided some cover which the artillery would utilise when these guns were commissioned, but many of them had already been reduced to the familiar stumps seen all along the front. However from contemporary accounts the wood was never entirely stripped of its foliage and continued to turn green in spring throughout the war.

Unsurprisingly the diary contains several references to their work coming under shell fire although at this time the majority of D Company's injuries resulted from accidents, which were frequently caused by slipping in the mud. The wood was sandwiched between the Rivers Douve and Warnave, both tributaries of the Lys and smaller streams traversed the wood ensuring a

Zillebeke Lake, 2008.

A Water Point, close to completion, Western Front, 1917.

Women of the WAAC, with two male helpers, sorting military clothing stores, Vendroux depot, Calais 1918.

The fruits of the Royal Engineers work in Calais; oats being mechanically sucked from canal barges, Vendroux depot, February 1918. Thomas Wilson is on the wharf (third from left).

A member of the Chinese Labour Corps filling sacks with oats, Vendroux depot, Calais, 1918.

The contents of one of the huge storage hangars, Vendroux depot, Calais, 1918.

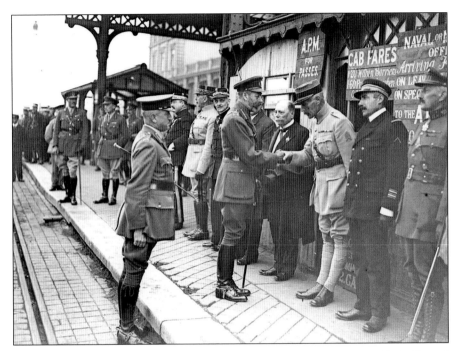

H.M. King George V meeting French officials on his arrival in Calais, 5 August 1918. General Radcliffe looks on. The signage indicates that Calais was firmly under English control.

Trench Art tea caddy made from the case of a 1916, 4.5 inch Howitzer shell and brought back to Rampson in 1918 by Thomas Wilson. Its engraving with Oriental plants and animals indicates it was bought from the Chinese Labour Corps based at Vendroux, Calais.

Thomas Wilson's Great War campaign medals presented 1920.

233

Part of the west window of St. Stephen's Church, Stainmore, consisting of fragments of glass brought back by Thomas Wilson from the ruined churches of France and Belgium, 1915-17.

Detail of the memorial window, St. Stephen's, Stainmore.

234

*Great War memorial window, St.
Stephen's Church, Stainmore,
with St. Michael and St. George,
commemorating the Alderson
cousins.*

235

Left to right, Erik, Mary and Betty, paddling in the Argill, summer 1918.

South Stainmore School photograph, summer 1919. Betty is in a sailor suit, third row from front, third from right.

Erik in his father's uniform, 1919.

Below, view of Barras Station taken by Robert in 1917. In testament to Stainmore's long winters there is heavy snow even on the final day of April.

Dorothy in Polam Hall school grounds following the summer theatricals, 1919.

Below, the Polam Hall girl guides in the Swiss Alps, 1919. Dorothy is centre front in white blouse.

Jack in his new Appleby Grammar School uniform, black stockings included, September 1919.

Below, Appleby Grammar School photograph, summer 1920. Robert seated extreme left; Jack second from right in the row behind.

Thomas Wilson, home to family and civilian life, Rampson, 1921. Shown with Polly, Erik (lower right), Betty (centre) and an unknown Stainmore friend (left).

Robert with Revd. Thomas Westgarth, Vicar of Stainmore, at Rampson, circa 1925.

Left, Betty on her confirmation day, 1925.

Below, Dorothy with Betty holding a favourite cat, Rampson, 1926.

Bottom left, Betty at Rampson on her 18th birthday, 10 November 1929.

Above, Thomas Wilson in his 60s, with Polly and Robert (wearing white spats) before his departure for the Argentine, summer 1927.

Robert's wife Edith (née Ewbank) and daughter, Sheila in M. Caseros, Argentina, November 1930. Sheila was also known as Celia in Spanish.

Jack with Polly on his 21st birthday, 7 May 1928.

Erik with his future brother-in-law, Stanley Cooper, watching birds on the grouse moor above Rampson, 1929.

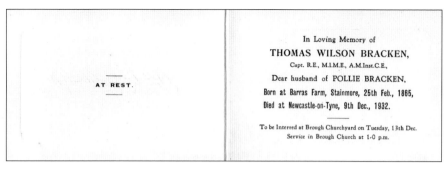

Thomas Wilson's funeral card.

Brough Church and churchyard, 1997. The tree in the foreground was planted to mark Thomas Wilson and Polly's otherwise unmarked grave.

244

quagmire state for a large part of the year. The men of D Company though had bigger concerns than liquid mud, for the diary now mentions the first gas alerts and much increased air activity from both sides. The entry for 19 December reads "many enemy aeroplanes about as well as our own. One duel occurred over the camp resulting in the German being driven off." On the same day B and C companies were affected by gas poisoning leading to a Pioneer's death in hospital three weeks later.

In the pre-Christmas period of 1915, Thomas Wilson started to collect Christmas and other greeting cards. They were widely available in British Army sectors and he probably purchased them on visits to headquarters in Bailleul. They consist of embroidered silk applied to French *cartes postales* and were made for use by the British Army. Several he collected have the year 1915 embroidered on them. One has the flags of Britain, France, Belgium, Italy, Imperial Russia and Serbia encased by laurel. Another carries the Red Ensign, the national flowers of England and Scotland, and the embroidered message 'Right is Might.'

Christmas Day was rewarded with a holiday for all companies, inter-platoon football matches in the morning and sports in the afternoon. Colonel Hayes visited each of the companies at dinner in the late afternoon. A sombre indication of how much alcohol flowed is demonstrated by the final entry for the day, "Pioneer Miell died at 7.30pm from suffocation caused by vomit passing into trachea." Miell belonged to B Company and while these events were unfolding in camp the eleven officers of the battalion were dining at headquarters in the Hotel de Fauchon in Bailleul. In our more egalitarian times this rigid and absolute distinction between officers and men may seem strange but officers at the time ate, slept and in part worked apart and in all three cases the pertaining conditions were very different from those of the men. The officers were looked after by orderlies and other mess servants and in addition they had their own individual servant or batman to look after their uniform, washing and other personal needs. The old joke that the British Army's sergeants really kept the military machine in business had much to it.

Four days after Christmas, Acting Corporal Smith of A company was severely wounded by a shell. He died the next day in hospital but the year ended, as the diary notes, with good progress on account of the better weather conditions. As 1916 opened the strength of Thomas Wilson's D Company is given at two officers[288] and 239 other ranks of which nine were in hospital.

New Year's Day was one of normal work and D Company continued in Ploegsteert Wood and at Touquet Berthe Farm to the south, due east of Ploegsteert village. Touquet Berthe was evidently not considered significant enough to be given a familiar name, although it served as an important supply base in the area and was where D Company drew its stores and materials.

On 4 January work was started on machine gun emplacements in the wood and General Godby visited Touquet Berthe and expressed his satisfaction with the work done. Each machine gun needed a deep dug-out to hold both the gun and crew during an enemy bombardment and these were what D Company was building. On the next day the officers held a court of enquiry into the Christmas Day death of Pioneer Miell: unfortunately no details of the outcome are provided in the diary except that they were forwarded to RE base records.

The diary records that the weather in these first weeks of January was good although this had its disadvantage, in that working parties in view of the enemy were put at risk of artillery fire. Two Pioneers in B Company were killed by a shell falling into a communication trench on the 19th and on the 23rd one of D Company's men was hit in the leg by a sniper's bullet. Also of concern was the threat of gas attack and all of the battalion's companies were thoroughly trained in the use of their gas helmets during January. Further machine gun emplacements were commenced by D Company to the south of Ploegsteert Wood to the east of the farm known locally as Maison 1875 (after its datestone) and just over 1,000 yards from the British front line. On the 21st General Godby instructed D Company to fortify Ploegsteert village about 3,000 yards back. Fortification included the building of dug-outs, barbed wiring and reinforced concrete works.

Plugstreet village was to the south-west of the wood. Before the war it was typical of many others in this part of Belgium but in the early months of 1916 it was crowded with troops moving up to the front line or retiring back into reserve, having been relieved. Many of those troops were billeted in its houses and it would have been crowded with transport carrying supplies to the dumps and stores, and ambulances evacuating the wounded from the village's dressing stations.

At this time this part of the forward line was in the care of the 2nd Battalion of the South Lancashires under the 25th Division but on 27 January the Division was relieved by the 9th (Scottish) Division. One of its components was the 6th Battalion of the Royal Scots Fusiliers commanded by

Lieutenant-Colonel Winston Churchill MP. Churchill remained in Ploegsteert for almost four months before resuming his political activities. He had arrived in France in November 1915 after resigning from the Government following one demotion too many from his former lofty position as First Lord of Admiralty. As First Lord he had been at least in part responsible for the Dardanelles debacle in which the Royal Navy had suffered its worst reverse since Trafalgar. As a result his star had considerably fallen: he was first demoted to the sinecure of Chancellor of the Duchy of Lancaster and later was removed from the War Council. At this point he resigned, telling Asquith in his resignation letter that he would rather serve in the army than continue "in well paid inactivity" in Whitehall.

The presence of Churchill in 1916 in the same Belgian village as Thomas Wilson lays open a wealth of published material about an otherwise small and obscure location. Prime among this material are Churchill's letters to his wife Clementine published and edited by their daughter.[289]

King's Regulations precluded correspondence with civilians on military matters as well as the keeping of a personal diary or journal. Thomas Wilson as a latecomer to soldiering doubtless followed the rules to the letter and his now lost missives home probably consisted of no more than regular reassurances of his health and safety, and inquiries about domestic matters at home. Churchill evidences a rather more cavalier attitude towards the rules in his own family correspondence.

In 1916 Plugstreet retained its civilian population, who had successfully petitioned the King of the Belgians to be allowed to stay when the British had tried to evacuate them in 1915.[290] It was a small village, centred on a crossroads, with a church at its centre on the corner of the village square. The church had a tall steeple and had been increasingly damaged by enemy shell fire through 1915. Also on the village square, facing each other across the crossroads, were two estaminets, Aux Trois Amis and Café au Lion d'Or. Both of these establishments continued to be run by their Belgian owners and were very popular with British troops in their limited leisure time.

On the south side of the village, on the road to Armentières, was a nunnery school for girls belonging to the Sisters of Charity. Churchill knew this as the Hospice and it was to be his Battalion Headquarters. In his first letter written from the Hospice[291] he provides an account of the village:

I am extremely well lodged here – with a fine bedroom looking out across the fields to the German lines 3,000 yards away. Two nuns remain here and keep up the little chapel which is part of the building. They received me most graciously when I marched in this morning, saying we had saved this little piece of Belgium from the Germans who were actually here for a week before being driven out. I have made the women at all the billets where I have stayed make their excellent soup for us – which they do most gladly – on the right and left the guns are booming, & behind us a British field piece barks like a spaniel at frequent intervals. But the women & children still inhabit the little town²⁹² & laugh at the shells which occasionally bluff into its old Church. It is very quiet on the front today, & really from your point of view this is an ideal part of the line. It is very unlikely to be the scene of a big attack by either side. It has no great concentration of German artillery opposite it. The trenches are good, well wired, with a broad interval between the lines. The houses have been little damaged. There are 2 bright red pigs rooting about among the shell holes of the meadow in front of this house. I think they must be Belgian Tamworths.

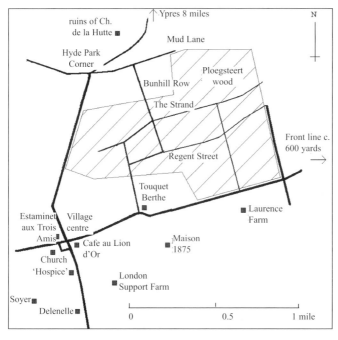

Sketch map of Ploegsteert

248

Churchill's companies while in reserve were lodged at three nearby farms, Soyer, Delennelle and Maison 1875 which was closest to the front line and near the machine gun posts which Thomas Wilson's D Company had just finished constructing. On the eve of Churchill's battalion moving into the front line Churchill advised his officers, "war is a game to be played with a smile. If you can't smile grin. If you can't grin keep out of the way till you can …"[293]

In the dark just before 6am on 27 January 1916 Churchill, his 29 officers and 700 men moved into front line position and relieved their predecessors. As they moved the men had feared that the Germans might have learnt that the former First Lord of the Admiralty was among them but no German bombardment greeted them. When Churchill was told of this fear he replied that if they had known the country would have been devastated for twenty square miles around. Churchill's battalion remained in the forward front line for just two days before moving back to Ploegsteert and the Hospice. On January 29 he wrote from there:

I got up at 4am (no rooster) and on coming in here about 7 we had breakfast and attended Mass in the little chapel. The old vicaire[294] was very gracious. His church is shattered, and the house in which he lives is freely shelled: but he sticks to his post & 'flies his flag' in the chapel of this hospice. The shelling yesterday evening which was very persistent was directed at a battery a few hundred yards away and was not aimed at any of these houses, though of course the projectiles passed very near them.

Later that day Churchill wrote to his mother:

There is a battery in the fields behind our house which the Germans try to hit; & this afternoon they put a dozen shells over us in search of it, which burst with loud explosions at no great distance. I had just had a splendid hot bath – the best for a month & was feeling quite deliciously clean, when suddenly a tremendous bang overhead, & I am covered with soot blown down the chimney by the concussion of a shell these careless Boches have fired too short & which exploded above our roof, smashing our windows and dirtying me!

After two days like this Churchill concluded that there was not much difference in safety between the trenches and the rest billets in Ploegsteert and so he returned to the front line on 1 February.

In Thomas Wilson's battalion diary, the arrival of the 9th Division in the area is accurately recorded on 28 January but there is no mention of Colonel Churchill in it. This is because although D Company was now geographically placed under the 9th Division, its engineering orders came from the higher Corps level and Chief Engineer General Godby. This also explains why Churchill's only recorded interaction with the Royal Engineers at Ploegsteert was with Major Hearn RE who commanded the RE element of the 9th Division and whom Churchill had known since 1898 when they were both in India.[295] However, Thomas Wilson, working on the defence of such a tiny village and with the inevitable mess gossip, was rapidly made aware of the celebrity politician in his midst. The likelihood of such gossip was increased yet further on 29 January and 6 February when Churchill brought his former government colleagues F. E. Smith and Lord Curzon respectively to Ploegsteert. Later Churchill ensured that the band of the 9th Division visited Ploegsteert so as to provide some musical entertainment. On 16 March he told his wife of this plan, "…on Sunday night I am going to give the men a concert, and have secured the Divisional band for the occasion." Furthermore Churchill's larger than life reputation was already well established and he further drew attention to himself by setting up his easel in the village to paint a view of the church with shells exploding over it.[296]

Exactly what Thomas Wilson made of Churchill's arrival in the village is unknown. As an active Conservative since the 1880s he would have been well aware of Churchill's Conservative pedigree and his perhaps opportunistic defection to the Liberals in 1904. That defection had been hugely controversial in Tory circles but the war had suspended party politics and in the Army camaraderie of 1916 Ploegsteert, he was probably viewed just as sympathetically as any other brother officer and for his ability to secure a rare bit of musical entertainment would have been much appreciated by all.

Churchill's battalion had been decimated at Loos the previous year and later in 1916 was to see action on the Somme. As such their posting to the Ploegsteert sector was a relatively easy one. However the Division G.O.C. (General Officer Commanding), Major-General Furse, was well aware of the sector's quiet reputation and was determined to stir things up with increased artillery action after his arrival there in January 1916. This desire would have been sanctioned by his superior the Corps Commander, General Sir Charles

Fergusson and from him via General Godby C.E. (Chief Engineer) would have come the consequent orders to Thomas Wilson's D Company to build gun emplacements and generally strengthen the defences around Ploegsteert in anticipation of the 9th Division's arrival. Of course increased action by the British Army led to a corresponding increase in shelling on the German side and this caused Churchill to move his battalion headquarters back 800 yards from the Hospice to Soyer Farm on 9 February.

On the following day he went with Brigadier-General Tudor G.O.C. Artillery of the 9th Division to Ploegsteert Wood to watch a British artillery bombardment. In a beautiful piece of synchronism the Labour Battalion diary records "D Company... parties working in Ploegsteert Wood moved out at 2pm when bombardment commenced." At this time the men of D Company were spread out in working parties at ten separate locations in Ploegsteert Wood and to the north and south of it and Thomas Wilson and his brother officer of the Company would have been kept busy conducting tours of inspection of these scattered locations from Company headquarters at Lampernesse Camp.

In a letter to his wife written on 10 February Churchill described the effects of the increased shelling on the village:

> *The shells hitting the church made enormous clouds of red brick dust which mingled gaily with their white smoke. Other black and white shrapnel burst over the street and struck the houses. Three of our men who were strolling in the town were hit – one fatally, & another sustained a shock from being near a shell from which he immediately died.*

Aided by their maps of the area the German artillery could easily and accurately target Ploegsteert Church tower and the busy crossroads beneath it as well as the surrounding houses. By 17 February Churchill determined on some very heavy retaliation. While he directed the operation by phone from his forward HQ at Laurence Farm, twelve inch naval guns mounted on an armoured train six miles away were fired on the German line which was at its closest just 80 yards away from the British.[297]

Far from quietening the Germans down this bombardment seems to have merely led to a further retaliation which finally felled the spire of Ploegsteert Church on 19 February and it is quite likely that the men of D Company were given the job of cleaning up the mess. It may have been at this point that

Thomas Wilson rescued from the mess some fragments of stained glass. It is equally likely that he had already visited the intact if damaged church and following a moment of contemplation and prayer picked up some broken glass. In total, he collected glass from three different ruined churches during the War, and these were later assembled into a window in St. Stephen's, Stainmore.

From this time on the church and village were gradually transformed into rubble and the civilian population increasingly departed to safety. In 1918 when Churchill revisited Ploegsteert he could not even decipher the position of the church amid the ruins.[298]

These relentless retaliatory bouts of artillery fire in the early months of 1916 were not without their effects on Thomas Wilson's D Company. Although their work continued with occasional inspections by General Godby, the battalion diary is full of references to its work in Ploegsteert village and Ploegsteert Wood being interrupted by enemy shell fire or British bombardment from the wood. On 6 March Pioneer Johnson was badly wounded by shrapnel in the village.

The diary entry for 17 March records "part of D Company now employed in placing Ploegsteert village in a state of defence: constructing wire entanglements, M.G. (machine gun) emplacements, Dug-Outs and defending houses." That this was being done in response to the increasing destruction caused by the enemy's shelling is made clear in Churchill's letter to his wife of 16 March, "All day the Germans have been shelling the little town. The hospice where I entertained F. E. [Smith] has been hit repeatedly, & the little chapel wrecked & all the houses around hit."[299] Five days later the battalion diary records another instance of severe shelling of the village and that the working parties sheltered in their dug-outs to avoid casualties. Thereafter for the rest of March, D Company's work was often interrupted by both enemy shelling and British bombardments. General Furse had certainly succeeded in stirring things up. The consequences of this are also reflected in D Company's strength which had been reduced by sixteen to 225 by the end of March.

At this point the diary gives eleven separate map references for the company's work on dug-outs, trenches, wiring and gun emplacements within a third of a square mile overlapping the tiny village. The Engineers were transforming Ploegsteert from a timeless Belgian village to a military fortress bristling with men and weaponry. Before the war Ploegsteert was not unlike

Killington or other Westmorland villages Thomas Wilson knew and loved. The only difference was that fate had decreed it as one of the places where two great armies met and fought. Doubtless its civilian population cared little about politics and the competing ambitions of empires but their presence in the village would have served as a reminder why the British Army was there.

In the first week of April Thomas Wilson's interaction with Ploegsteert's civilians increased when he conducted a survey of the cellars in the village prior to their planned conversion to dug-outs. In the same week screening was commenced to some of the trenches which were visible by aeroplane survey. Then without warning on 12 April D Company received orders from General Furse's 9th Divisional HQ that it was to be moved to Abancourt. The following day was spent on preparations and on 14 April D Company left Ploegsteert. Churchill's battalion was to remain in Ploegsteert for a further three weeks, when it was withdrawn and amalgamated with its brother 7th battalion of the Royal Scots. The erosion by casualties meant that these two battalions were no longer effective fighting units and so they were merged to become the 6/7 Battalion, Royal Scots Fusiliers. As the merged battalion was to be commanded by the Colonel of the old 7th Battalion, Churchill was set to be deprived of his front line employment and as a result he decided to return to Parliament and his political life for good.[300] His officers and men were not so fortunate: after the relative quiet of the Plugstreet sector they were despatched south to the Somme.

16 – THE DRUDGERY OF WAR

Great War diaries are riddled with cold statistics, map references, weather reports and other impersonal details. Personal details such as morale, optimism about the task in hand and other feelings are almost entirely absent. Into the former category come journey details: the company's rail journey to Abancourt is described in very great detail in the diary. From their camp the company travelled to Steenwerck and 'entrained'. Steenwerck is six miles from Ploegsteert across the French border. In a sign of the chaos and disruption the war had caused to French railways, they took four and a half hours to reach Calais where they remained in the train all night and into the early afternoon. That evening they reached Abbeville and at noon on the following day after two days in trains they reached their destination at Abancourt. Abancourt is between Rouen and Amiens and as such well outside the area of the armies and it would have been untouched by warfare. After the increasing despoilment and danger of Ploegsteert and the accompanying noise, smell and dirt, it must have come as a great relief to the officers and men of the company. The local towns and villages would have functioned as in pre-War days with well stocked patisseries and estaminets. Also the surrounding April countryside would have been in glorious contrast to the shell scarred and ruined landscape which existed in a great scar straddling the front line.

Abancourt was one of two new Royal Engineers store depots in France. These were created in the spring of 1916 because it became clear that large amounts of stores of all kinds needed to be kept in stock so as to enable them to be speedily transported to the army areas when new operations demanded and prior to the movement of large numbers of men and ammunition which clogged the railways and prevented the movement of goods. Abancourt was selected because it was close to an important railway junction enabling supplies from the ports of Le Havre, Rouen and Dieppe to be consolidated at the 32 acre depot[301] before being sent on when required to the southern area battlefields. A similar larger facility was constructed near Calais to serve the northern area.

As Abancourt was outside the BEF area it fell under the control of the Director of Works Major-General Sir Andrew Stuart RE and his staff. Stuart's role and the Works Directorate underwent a massive expansion during the four years up to the Armistice. This expansion was caused by its management of innumerable large construction projects encompassing depots and workshops such as that at Abancourt but also among other things aerodromes, port facilities such as docks, piers and wharves, hospitals, veterinary hospitals, schools for training, roads and tram-lines together with the associated French land acquisition and contracting.[302] Of course in August 1914 the War Office with its plan for rapid cavalry-dominated advance never envisaged any need to plan for construction needs, supply and storage of supplies and ammunition on this or any comparable scale.

It was also both bitter and bloody experience which eventually demonstrated that without new roads, railways and tramways at the front, the key and eventually winning component of massive and mobile artillery support could not be utilised in support of the infantry's advance. In their absence the awful deadlock haemorrhaging men's lives would continue.

On arrival D Company set up camp at Abancourt before commencing work on the construction of the depot with its huge ordnance storage facility. Details in the diary as to exactly what D Company's work at Abancourt are sketchy as Headquarters and the adjutant remained at Bailleul around 80 miles away. Such details as there are would have been provided daily by telephone calls from either Thomas Wilson or one of his brother officers.

On 25 April we are told that 50 men of D Company were engaged on concrete works and then just two days later they were informed that they would shortly depart from Abancourt. On the evening of the 29th they left Abancourt for Bailleul. Their return journey was far less protracted and took just seventeen and a half hours. While this brief trip to Abancourt was doubtless a welcome relief, just what it achieved and why it was ever ordered and then curtailed after just over a fortnight is not entirely clear. The relevant pages of the war diary of the Royal Engineer officer in charge at Abancourt in April 1916 are missing but the explanation probably relates to no more than the normal chaos and inefficiency of war.

D Company arrived back in Bailleul at 5pm on 30 April and luckily missed a severe gas attack which the Germans launched right along the Flanders front that morning. With a wind speed of nine miles an hour the gas blew behind the lines to a depth of 11,000 yards. Although the gas alarm was sounded any hesitation in fitting the respirator helmets was potentially fatal. All three other companies of the Labour Battalion were affected and the diary gives a full account of the attack, "we had no casualties from the attack. O.C. (officer commanding) B Co. states that the gas was not chlorine but smelt of 'rotten apples' horses and mules were not affected but several cows were killed." Elsewhere the British army was not so lucky: 89 soldiers were killed and over 500 incapacitated.[303]

Following this gas attack the officers of the battalion attended a lecture on poison gas and according to the diary obtained much useful information. A rather more mundane problem at the same time was the presence of castor oil beans in the animal feed and its consequence of equine diarrhoea for the battalion's horses and mules.

Perhaps in a sign that D Company's return was unexpected the company spent the first week of May exercising at drill before being given 3rd line trench repairs and road work under V Corps. On 19 May the Company's work was inspected by its new superiors, Major-General Glubb, Chief Engineer of the Second Army, Brigadier-General Petrie, Chief Engineer V Corps and Colonel Sinnott RE, officer in charge of roads. Glubb was another Boer War veteran who had won the DSO there, whereas Petrie had won his spurs in action in Burma in the 1880s and China in the 1890s. Sinnott on the other hand was not a professional soldier but had been a chartered civil engineer since 1886 and had joined the Royal Engineers as a territorial officer at the age of seventeen.

On 23 May Thomas Wilson had another meeting with General Petrie about a preliminary survey for a water pipeline from the River Lys to Kortepyp in Belgium (now spelt Kortepijp, due north of Nieppe in France). The scheme was to establish a reservoir on the higher ground there, with water points to the lower level below. Four days later General Petrie received Thomas Wilson's report and two days thereafter it was adopted with some variations relating to horse troughing. For the rest of D Company, work continued repairing roads and trenches in the vicinity of Nieppe. Their work is recorded as being hampered by very wet weather and a shortage of materials during the first two weeks of June.

By 27 June the D Company was engaged on road work near Neuve Eglise (now Nieuwekerke, three miles north west of Ploegsteert) and it was to remain in the area for several weeks. Neuve Eglise was a slightly larger village than Ploegsteert and sits on the crest of a hill. It is dominated by its large landmark church from which it derives its name. It is scarcely surprising that Neuve Eglise caught Thomas Wilson's eye as it had the enemy's artillery. During his visit he collected his second piece of stained glass from the damaged church. Although we do not have the benefit of Churchill's description, the village of Neuve Eglise was equally close to the front line and equally at the mercy of German artillery as Ploegsteert.

Although the diary refers to it as road work it was not the municipal form of road repair that we are familiar. These 'roads' were in fact tracks leading from the reserve positions to the front line and they were repaired by laying corduroy mats which were wired onto wooden bearers with splayed ends so that one fitted into another. The mats were only three feet six inches (just over a metre) wide and so provided what was effectively a walkway for soldiers passing to the front line. They were quick and easy to lay under cover of darkness thereby avoiding the enemy's shell fire. The diary tells us that over 2,000 tons of these mats were despatched to the battalion's working parties during the last week of June.

Although by no means glamorous work in engineering terms these matted tracks provided relief from the general sea of mud in which men and animals were known to drown. Also given the battle of the Somme commenced to the south on 1 July 1916 it is very unlikely that any of the battalion's men complained about the task in hand.

The Somme battle began with an artillery barrage so great it was audible on Hampstead Heath. As such it would have been very clear to the men of D Company that a very big battle was afoot. The barrage involved a quarter of a million shells fired at an average of 3,500 per minute. As soon as it was over the British and French attacked along a 25 mile front.[304] By preceding standards this artillery fire was most impressive but it was still insufficient to knock out the German defences.[305] In consequence when the infantry moved forward it was into machine-gun fire, intense shelling and uncut wire and as a result on the first day alone the British Army, in its blackest ever day, suffered 57,000 casualties of which 20,000 were fatal.[306] With the French still enduring Verdun and after almost two years of planning, the huge Somme campaign could not be hastily abandoned. Despite the planned breakthrough never occurring, the blood-letting was to continue until mid-November.

When the casualty lists were read at home in Britain, a stunned nation would never feel the same way about war again. So far as can be ascertained the allied casualties were 650,000 as against 400,000 Germans.[307] So much for Haig's dream that the Somme campaign would destroy the German defences and enable him to pour his beloved cavalry through the breach and restore a war of movement and accomplishment.

On 3 July in the relative quiet of the Ypres salient, 55 miles away, Thomas Wilson's D Company is recorded as being engaged in night work laying a mat roadway from the tramway at Neuve Eglise to Lindenhoek to the north. Later in the year there is a reference to D Company repairing a trench tramway at Trois Tilleuls. Tramways such as these were devised to solve the problem of moving large amounts of ammunition, rations, engineer stores and water from the nearest railhead to the front line often several miles away. Initially the army used a combination of lorries and carrying parties but the solid rubber tyres of the lorries were better at destroying roads than any enemy action and carrying parties were slow and limited in capacity.[308] The answer gradually provided was narrow gauge tramways.

Road repairs by the entire battalion in the south of the Ypres salient continued albeit subject to the weather and availability of materials up until the end of 1916. As the Flanders winter arrived and road materials became scarcer the companies of the battalion became more engaged in erecting road screens and flash screens around artillery pieces. This was done to prevent the enemy observing and positioning movements along the roads and locating the British artillery from its firing flashes. Assistance with the road work was provided to the Engineers by other British Army labour companies and Belgian civilians but the scale of the task is illustrated by the diary's statistic that 792 lorry loads of materials were sent out from La Clytte railway siding[309] during the final week of July. Not all of this road work was done at night and the dangers of the enemy's artillery fire are illustrated by the death of B Company's Sergeant Seymour on July 19th. In August D Company's materials dump at De Broeken was bombed from the air although without causing any injuries. Also the work was not solely repairing roads broken by transport and shell fire and laying corduroy matting walkways; in addition the battalion's work consisted of building metalled roads for heavy artillery.

Both major British battles of the war thus far, at Loos and the Somme, had demonstrated the necessity of free movement along adequately maintained roads and the need for even bigger concentrations of artillery fire in advance of any attack. As a tiny part in a huge military machine, this small aspect of the work of the Royal Engineers would play its part in the eventual achievement of an armistice, for it was to be slow unglamorous and incremental improvements in the Allies' position rather than the glorious cavalry charges longed for by the Commander in Chief which would result in the eventual victory.

By mid-August IX Corps had replaced V Corps in the area south of Ypres and General Scholfield Chief Engineer IX Corps called on the officers of D Company on 16 August. On the following day orders were received that any man in hospital for two weeks or more was to be struck off record of the battalion's strength. This reduced D Company's strength by seven men to 201 at the end of August 1916.[310] By October its strength fell below 200 and the final figure given while Thomas Wilson was involved was 183. This depletion was caused by both accidents and enemy shelling.

Shelling was particularly severe at a road junction to the north of Ploegsteert which the London Rifle Brigade had christened Hyde Park Corner on account of its congestion and which D Company were given the task of widening in October 1916. It was then a busy crossroads located on the Messines-Armentières road at the point where the road veers sharply to avoid the higher ground occupied by the Château de la Hutte. As it does so the Mud Lane turning to the south goes in the direction of Ploegsteert Wood and the Red Lodge Road turns off to the west. These turnings, now reverted to farm tracks, were crucial for the army transports, ambulances, ration and ammunition parties supplying the numerous army units in the wood to the south and those sheltering under the cover of Hill 63 to the west. As such the junction was unsurprisingly a favourite of the German artillery and its location is marked today by two nearby British military cemeteries and a memorial to the missing.

17 – ARRAS

In January 1917 the battalion's time in Belgium came to an end. Early in the morning of the 20th the entire battalion, its transport and stores, were moved with the aid of 46 motor lorries to Bailleul where they entrained in thick snow. At nine at night their train arrived at Doullens. Doullens is mid-way between Arras and Abbeville in Picardie and the battalion was despatched there to commence work on a new railway in the Authie Valley. Doullens, a significant railhead, was established as General Foch's HQ early in the War and was to be the scene of the great Allied conference of 26 March 1918. As such it was an army town, stuffed with all the facilities and services which attach to a great fighting force.

Geographically the valley of the river Authie proceeds in a south-easterly direction from Doullens towards the Somme battlefield and the new railway was intended to ease the severe rail congestion which the Somme campaign had revealed. On arrival at Doullens the initial problem facing the battalion were those caused by the severe winter weather. The diary records how cold the weather was and the absence of fuel. After three days, work on the railway was commenced on ground "frozen two feet deep." Things did not improve and at the end of the first week in one of the most negative reports in the entire diary it states "all supplies difficult to obtain therefore conditions very hard for the men."

Thomas Wilson's D Company was initially encamped at Authieule just outside Doullens but after six days they moved into billets in the town, presumably on account of the weather. The severe cold lasted throughout February necessitating explosive blasting of the frozen surface before it could be prepared for the railway. However Thomas Wilson experienced little of this because on 8 February he left the Labour Battalion and travelled 28 kilometres to join the 42nd Army Troop Company under VI Corps, British 3rd Army and based at Montenescourt just to the west of Arras.

This new posting taking him away from his great specialism of railway building seems odd. Perhaps in the mass of paperwork concerning officer administration at GHQ it was either unknown or overlooked, or perhaps it was felt his more general engineering skills would be of greater use in the new great push planned for spring 1917. His new posting would place him in the greatest danger he had yet encountered and test his skills as an officer as never before.

The 42nd Army Troop Company had only arrived in Montenescourt six days earlier having previously seen service near Béthune. It had a long and not undistinguished pedigree on the Western Front having been in France since 7 September 1914 as the 42nd Troop Co. RE, becoming the 42nd Army Troop Company when Army Troop Companies were created. When Thomas Wilson arrived parts of the company had been engaged in erecting Nissen huts and bunks for the officers' accommodation in camp in Montenescourt. While these mundane matters were under way and Thomas Wilson was settling into his new Company, the Germans started a huge tactical withdrawal from their Somme front line to their new, shorter and far stronger Hindenburg Line. This would become known to both Germans and the British Tommy as the Siegfried Line.

The British High Command was confused by this unexpected withdrawal. Conversely the British press was quick to categorise this move eastwards as weakness and one presaging ultimate victory. In fact it amounted to a brilliant tactical withdrawal, which reduced the length of the line which had to be defended by 25 miles and thereby released thirteen divisions into reserve,[311] behind a far more impregnable barrier. As to the territory which was now 'captured' the Germans had pursued a scorched earth policy systematically devastating it, so all that the Allies were to find were useless ruins. Furthermore booby-traps killed many soldiers advancing through it. In the town hall at Bapaume two French deputies were killed when the mines concealed in it by the Germans blew.[312]

As the German 'retreat' continued, and after just five days in Montenescourt, Thomas Wilson left the Company to attend a two week heavy bridging course at Aire-sur-la-Lys. The Royal Engineers had established this Bridging School in December 1916. Near St. Omer, Aire was well back from the war-devastated area and provided a pleasant and civilised environment in which to spend his 52nd birthday on 25 February. On the following day he returned to Arras and Montenescourt where the very severe winter of 1916-17 was finally thawing. On the softening ground, Army transport movements were restricted, hampering the Company's work.

Throughout March and into early April that work consisted of bringing improved water supplies to Montenescourt and the adjacent villages of Wanquetin, Lattre-St-Quentin, Hauteville, Gouves, Noyellette, Habarcq, Agnez and Duisans. In preparation for the next big offensive these villages just to the west of Arras were packed with British troops of the 3rd Army waiting for action. A large part of these troops consisted of cavalry and the Company diary makes several references to the provision of cavalry horse troughing.

Private Briggs of the Royal Warwickshire Regiment was in the village of Lattre-St-Quentin in early April 1917 while providing infantry support to the 153rd Field Company RE. He was delighted with his attachment, and the resulting armlet he wore with RE stamped on it in red, because he quickly found that the Engineers were provided with better billets and rations than the infantry. He also found that the Engineers' marching stride was longer and slower than that of his own regiment. He describes drawing his pay before the battle and spending his on fresh bread and chocolate but, unlike many, resisting the estaminets' wine. He provides a description of the village and his arrival there on Easter Saturday:

> *According to Dame Rumour we were again in for it, as we were to follow immediately in the wake of the infantry, several divisions of which were to make a push at Easter to attempt to dislodge the enemy beyond Arras... The march was a novelty to me as I had not hitherto seen a company of Royal Engineers on the march before. The quantity of transport which was embodied in this company was a revelation, consisting as it did of a pontoon section and a mule transport, so that we made quite a brave show. We marched to the village of L-St-Quentin where we were billeted for the night in comfortable billets. This village was a rest place for troops, several cinemas and innumerable estaminets catering for the pastime of the soldiers.*[313]

The Easter Monday campaign when it came would be known as the battle of Arras and it would be the first battle that Thomas Wilson would witness at close quarters. Before describing the events of it, it is important to establish the political context in which the battle was fought. In December 1916 following a Cabinet coup David Lloyd George replaced Asquith as Prime Minister.

Lloyd George, while utterly determined to win the war, brought with him a dislike of the Commander in Chief Sir Douglas Haig, who he considered, probably correctly, cold, unimaginative and callously wasteful of soldiers' lives. He was determined that the scale of sacrifice of British troops seen in 1916 would not recur under his watch. Also in late 1916 the French appointed the charismatic General Nivelle to be their new Commander following his successes at Verdun. Lloyd George was attracted to Nivelle on the questionable ground that French generals could win through where British ones could not. Nivelle's plan was for a huge French offensive on the Chemin des Dames, north of the Aisne, with a supporting British offensive out of Arras also under the overall command of Nivelle. As a result of the decision to adope Nivelle's plan Haig, who had been planning his own spring offensive in the Ypres salient, realised the attitude of his new political master and relations between them were to remain highly strained until the end of the war.[314]

Of the villages where Thomas Wilson's company were working and where the reserves of the 3rd Army were billeted and camped, Duisans was selected for the location of his company headquarters and officer's mess even though it was the closest to the German line just five kilometres away. On 6 April the mess was hit by a shell wounding a Lance Corporal in the head. On the same day the United States entered the war but it would be another year before US troops on the Western Front made a fighting contribution.

Prior to the battle on the ground the British attempted to rid the skies around Arras of German planes so as to conduct unimpeded reconnaissance work. As a result, during the preparatory period 75 British aircraft were shot down and nineteen pilots were killed; and by the battle's end the number of British planes lost was 131 and the Royal Flying Corps in France had lost a third of its strength.[315]

The ground attack from Arras commenced on Easter Monday 9 April at 05.30 and huge numbers of reserves poured forward along the Arras-St. Pol road from the villages where Thomas Wilson's company had been engaged in accommodating and watering them since February. As they travelled to the front line they passed and used lines of water bottle fillers which marked the end of the water pipeline laid by his company from the pumping station on the river Scarpe just to the north. The pipeline had only been brought into commission that morning by his Troop Company and its operation was policed by the company's men under Lieutenant Anderson and Second

Lieutenant Wise. Along with the many thousands of infantry and cavalry troops who moved that day was Thomas Wilson and a detachment of 25 Royal Engineers. Their initial destination was the basin of the Scarpe river just to the north of the centre of Arras rather than the deadly battleground which lay a tiny distance beyond.

Arras, the ancient regional capital of Artois, had been the scene of one of the great defensive sieges of the war. General Foch had arrived in Arras on 5 October 1914 (having been made Commander in Chief the previous evening) and forbade its evacuation. As a result of his order, the German front line was held at a point just to the west of the village of St.Laurent-Blangy from October 1914 until the great British attack of 1917 was launched. As the line barely moved an inch over 30 months, the Germans had ample time to construct a formidable triple line of defences from which to repulse any attack and each line of these defences would need to be over-run if the British were to break the long siege of Arras.

Back in October 1914 the German's retaliation for this unexpected defiance was a brutal bombardment throughout October 1914, which even the Kaiser watched over two days. On 21 October the 75 metre belfry of the Hôtel de Ville, which formed an excellent observation post and which had been the principal enemy target, was felled by a 21 centimetre shell. For centuries the top of the belfry had been adorned with Arras' ancient emblem, a golden lion: the symbolism of its loss was greatly felt in the city. In July 1915, the cathedral and the Saint-Vaast Palace behind it were badly damaged. However like Ypres, although increasingly ruined and 'martyred', Arras did not fall. The centre of the city was just two miles from the German front line and the French continued their defence of it until March 1916 when the British Third Army took it over.[316] The British remained in control until the end of the war and therefore Arras was, in effect, a British town from 1916 to 1918.

Just prior to the British take-over, in January 1916 President Poincaré visited Arras and later described it thus:

> *We went to Arras which is increasingly devastated. There scarcely remains one single undamaged house. We left our cars at the station which is terribly ravaged. We visited a nearby battery of 75s dug in behind the walls of a house. Then up a long communication trench paved with red bricks, we made our way to front-line trenches to the east of Arras.*[317]

264

Private Briggs describes his own arrival in the centre of Arras on the first day of the battle:

We came rather suddenly upon Arras which is a fairly considerable town. The first sight of the place realised my worst fears. It was a nightmare city from beginning to end... the first glimpse was of shattered houses, trees with branches lopped off by shell fire, gaping shell holes and these eloquent signs coupled to the sounds of war, for there was a continuous roar of artillery, were well calculated to unnerve anyone. As we marched into the city... the signs and havoc became much more pronounced. Large buildings partly demolished, many of them smoke blackened, roads littered with rubbish, barbed wire entanglements, camouflage netting stretched across dangerous roadways as a screen from enemy observation, danger notices and direction posts strung out one at each corner, ponderous guns belching forth messages of death and destruction from artfully hidden emplacements in the squares; ...We were halted for a short space under the shelter of a great municipal building and the sights that we had a short leisure to gaze upon absolutely beggared description. This roadway was crowded with soldiers steadily marching along and coming from the opposite direction was a continuous stream of wounded, blood bespotted humanity. The sights sickened me from their very persistence. Yet the most amazing feature of it was that these wounded appeared to be cheerful, as if glad to get out of the inferno beyond at such a price! As I gazed at this remarkable scene, a building at the end of the road was blown up by a German shell, the wreckage flying to a stupendous height and a pall of black smoke and falling debris obscured the end of the road for some minutes. The smoke had hardly cleared when another building further over to the left was blown up. All our nerves were in such a state by now that it was a positive relief to get the order to move on. We passed by the blown up building and came in view of the railway station. It presented an amazing sight of shattered glass, brickwork and ironwork, a glaring monument to the utter madness of warfare.

As his description testifies, by the spring of 1917 Arras, after enduring two and a half years of daily bombardment from the German-held higher ground to the east, had been increasingly reduced to rubble. It only continued to function as an underground city where a thousand civilians attempted to carry on normal life in the city's extensive caves and tunnels. The rest of the civilian population had been evacuated and those that remained were subject to a strict regime of British army security regulations. The reason they were not all removed was that some were required to run the bars and shops that, for the sake of military morale, had to be kept open.

One rule was that the shops and bars, largely located in the cellars of the Grand' and Petite Places, were only permitted to serve British soldiers for two hours from 19.00 and in attempt, doubtless futile, to keep them apart, French civilians were only permitted in the streets after 21.30 by when, in theory at least, the troops had retired to their billets in the city's ruined and abandoned houses and their cellars.

Arras was fortunate in having this subterranean world which had been dug out from its soft porous stone from the fourteenth century onwards. During the war the underground network was secretly extended and electrified to serve not only as accommodation, hospital and shelter but also a cover for 24,400 infantry soldiers who exited this shelter directly into the front line when the battle began.[318] Of this total, 13,000 were lodged in the caves of the city's centre. Private Briggs described this subterranean world thus:

At last we came to a dug-out into which we filed. To my great surprise this dug-out was the entrance to a series of underground caves of great dimensions and to my further surprise I found them electrically lighted. It was absolutely the greatest surprise I had struck since my arrival in France. Here we were snugly quartered under the city whilst enemy shells were pounding it mercilessly. No sounds of battle permeated down here and the only discomfort was the water which dripped from the chalk roof continuously making the floor very slippery. But we got our oil sheets out and made ourselves as comfortable as possible, smoking and chatting and we got to know how the battle was progressing from a R.A.M.C. Corporal who was dressing some wounded in one of the caves.

The first day of the battle went well: the German's front line trenches were swiftly over-run and the second line fell too within the first two hours of battle. This success was achieved in large part by the use of a new artillery device, the creeping barrage. This meant that the targets of the artillery moved steadily forward with the infantry following close behind to take advantage of the stunned defenders. The initial British success meant that the army achieved its greatest advance in a single day thus far in the war.

After the first day problems swiftly emerged. The artillery had difficulty getting their guns over the captured German trenches which was not something they had ever done before. The tanks which were supposed to precede the infantry got bogged down in the mud and suffered mechanical failure. Also the German third line of trenches was proving to be a far harder nut to crack than the first or second. By the third day, advancing in blizzard conditions the attackers were reaching the limit of their endurance just as the German reinforcements began to arrive. At Haig's insistence his beloved cavalry was thrown into the equation but they were soon halted by wire and machine guns. They were never to see action in such numbers again on the Western Front.[319] On 14 April three British generals defied military protocol and protested directly to Haig about the mounting casualties. On the following day offensive operations were called off after achieving a dent of four miles along ten miles of the old front line. Later in the month and up to 7 May more minor offensive operations were conducted in the Arras sector. Overall General Allenby, in command of the 3rd Army, was the clear victor but the cost is reflected in the British Army's memorial in Arras commemorating the 36,000 British soldiers without a known grave on the Arras battlefield.[320]German losses were approximately 80,000 but despite this enormous figure, the German army still managed to stabilise the front some ten kilometres from Arras along the line of the villages of Gavrelle, Fampoux, Roeux and Monchy-le-Preux.

The poet Siegfried Sassoon probably best encapsulates the attitude of the British Tommy to this 'victory':

> *'Good morning. Good morning!' the General said*
> *When we met him last week on our way to the line.*
> *Now the soldiers he smiled at are most of 'em dead,*
> *And we're cursing his staff for incompetent swine.*
> *'He's a cheery old card' grunted Harry to Jack*
> *As they slogged up to Arras with rifle and pack*
> *But he did for them both by his plan of attack.*

To the north the Canadians had taken the great strategic vantage point Vimy Ridge but at an appalling cost in dead and wounded, marked still by the huge memorial to the 11,500 Canadians who were killed in capturing it.

Thomas Wilson who had for the first time witnessed a great army moving

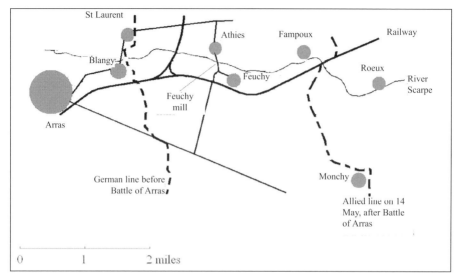

Battle fronts, Arras, April-May 1917.

into battle, would have known of the huge numbers of Harrys and Jacks he had seen marching up to Arras and who were never to return. Of course in accordance with Army convention, the War Diary which from 1 April is written in his own difficult pencil hand contains no emotive comment on casualties although they were most probably no less felt for that.

On the eve of battle while sleeping in a field surrounded by other infantrymen Private Briggs reflected on the following day's likely sacrifice:

> *I knew I was exempted from taking part in the actual fighting, yet I could not help thinking of those around me. How many would never see another night, how many would lose limbs on the morrow. That my own thoughts were common ones it was evident to see and I fear that very few slept that night in the open air.*

On moving into Arras on 9 April Thomas Wilson and his detachment of 25 men proceeded to the basin of the river Scarpe where until that morning the British front line had been. Here they erected further troughing for the cavalry and a night party laid an auxiliary drinking water pipe. After three hours in the caves Private Briggs and his RE Company were ordered forward into what was newly captured territory:

We filed out into the open trench and then we followed a road littered with rubbish of all kinds. We reached a village a short way further on, or rather I should say a collection of rubbish, for the place had been pounded out of recognition. There was a great crowd of transport on this road and an amazing lot of soldiers were clearing litter away, repairing tracks, laying wooden roads, etc. We continued our march to another village further on. This had only been captured a few hours before and in the trenches close to this village, I saw the first German dead.

Thomas Wilson made a similar journey at 4.30pm on the first day of the battle when he led a reconnaissance party of five other ranks into what had been enemy territory since October 1914. With their horses they proceded easterly by road out of Arras via St. Nicolas and the newly liberated villages of St. Laurent-Blangy and Athies. Blangy had been taken at around 9am but it was mid-afternoon before Athies fell into British hands. As such their journey was made only just outside the full heat of battle and they witnessed scenes of utter devastation. The dead and dying were still where they fell and from the timings given, the congestion and detritus of battle seriously impeded their progress. As well as British troops and artillery moving forward along the roads, a large number of enemy prisoners and the wounded needed to be brought out in the opposite direction. The number of prisoners taken was considerable, with 5,000 men of two German divisions captured in St. Laurent-Blangy alone.[321]

Thomas Wilson's destination was about three miles away, a weir on the Scarpe, located between Athies and Feuchy. The German second line of defences had been located there. It had consisted of a powerfully fortified system linking the two villages and of which the weir and accompanying mill formed a part. Their purpose was to inspect the German water pumping plant there and report to the officer in charge of water services VI Corps on the practicality of moving this plant by road nearer to Arras and re-commissioning it in the river for British army use.

The adventure is best described in Thomas Wilson's own words:

The party reached Athies Crossroads about 6.30pm at the same time as the first field guns. The bridge over the Scarpe was found intact but prepared for demolition, with a cradle sling underneath and earth for tamping in readiness on the bottom flanges of the bridge girders. Trenches had

269

been dug behind the lock walls near this bridge and preparation made for blowing these walls in but they were found intact also the lock gates and operating gears except slight damage to two of the latter apparently by shell fire. The lock appeared to have been in recent use also an iron canal barge in the canal just below it. Although Athies village was found to be entirely smashed, a mill and buildings south of the bridge and lock were not seriously damaged. A 25 foot diameter water wheel was still working, a dynamo of about 35 H.P. running and the electric light still on in the cellars and basement of the mill of which a party of Camerons[322] were then in possession. This locality bore marked evidence of the enemy's unexpected and hurried departure. At 8.30pm a report was sent back by runner that with four hours work repairing the road through Athies village to the Scarpe it would be practicable to convey pontoon wall and pumping plant by road… and place it in the river Scarpe… the reconnaissance party returned to Arras.

On the next day at 1pm he led the same reconnaissance party this time on a southwards approach to the weir. They went via Blangy and the railway arches of the Arras-Lens Railway, along Feuchy Lane before turning north to the weir. The scale of the congestion along these roads and the difficult riding conditions is again signified by it taking until 6.30pm before Thomas Wilson could despatch a runner to confirm that the northern approach was to be preferred. The second reconnaissance mission was not entirely in vain though as it discovered "a copious spring of good water from the chalk" just off Feuchy Lane. Subsequently the company utilised this spring as a water bottling point and horse troughing for the advancing infantry and cavalry.

His billet in Arras was at 12 Rue de la Coignée and he remained there from 9 April until his company left Arras in June 1917. Rue de la Coignée was just outside the completely devastated central area but still within easy range of the enemy's artillery. Arras was described in *The Blue Guide to North Eastern France* of 1922 with the words, "shattered by four years of bombardment at close range, Arras holds a place second only to Rheims among the 'martyred towns' of France. The former division between Cite and Ville (upper and lower town) has largely disappeared."

His billet was close to the cathedral which he obviously knew and visited because from the ruins of it he obtained his third and final piece of stained glass. He also retrieved from the cathedral a small panel of carved wood which had originally formed part of a screen, the choir or a door. This he also eventually took back to England and gave to his brother Robert. Again the 1922 *Blue Guide* describes the cathedral's devastation "…the shattered Cathedral built in the classic style… the façade… is largely intact but the interior… has been laid waste." The state of the interior in 1916 is detailed in one of army padre Julian Bickersteth's letters:[323]

> *The roof was almost entirely gone and lies a heap of masonry, bricks, mortar and dust in ugly heaps. The windows are all destroyed – the stalls broken down – in fact, the whole place is a scene of absolute desolation. The High Altar is cracked in two – the cavity for the relics laid bare. The chandeliers are smashed to atoms and the tombs and side chapels hardly recognisable. The central tower has fallen through the nave and has left a heap of masonry thirty feet high. I picked up two or three small pieces of mosaic as mementos.*

Evidently Thomas Wilson was not alone in retaining bits of the cathedral from his visit. Formerly Arras would have been just the sort of historic city he would have loved to visit and, as may well have occurred to him, not unlike the ancient English cathedral cities of Carlisle and Durham which he knew so well.

For the remainder of April the company's work continued to be associated with the provision and improvement of water supplies. The water supply on the St. Pol-Arras road had to be maintained and an additional 240 feet of horse troughs were installed there for the cavalry on 10 April. In Arras itself day and night parties of the company worked on the new supply from the Scarpe Basin just to the north of the city and which from 11 April was pumped with the aid of an improvised fire engine. To the east of Arras and across the old front line pipes were laid to carry clean water closer to what was now the front: for as the Army moved, its water supply had to move too. In addition to the above, in the centre of Arras the water tower and its associated pumping plant which had been improved by the French Army was repaired and improved further by Thomas Wilson's company, by adding an auxiliary pump. This item of work is specifically referred to in the official regimental history.[324]

At Athies Mill an RE guard was posted on the power plant which in the event was not moved but was utilised in position for horse troughing and, once the advance was halted on 15 April, for a water pipe from there to the artillery position known as Battery Valley beyond Feuchy village near Fampoux.

On 16 April, Thomas Wilson's commanding officer Captain P. M. Cooper left the company and Thomas Wilson as the most senior officer assumed command. Cooper had joined the Royal Engineers from Jamaica and after the war he was to have a distinguished civil engineering and public service career there. He was 30 years old in April 1917 and was evidently quite content to allow Thomas Wilson to keep the company's war diary which, given he was in charge, contains surprisingly few references to him. One of the few tells us that on 12 April he went with Lieutenant Anderson to Athies to inspect the electric plant at the mill. Anderson was Thomas Wilson's junior officer because he had received his commission as a Second Lieutenant on 5 December 1915 and had only been promoted to Lieutenant in January 1917.

As a result of Captain Cooper's departure and the relative success of the battle the Company's HQ was moved on April 19 from Duisans to 20 Rue du Crinchon in Arras. As such Thomas Wilson's headquarters were very convenient to his billet in Rue de la Coignée. However unlike his earlier and later HQs and billets he was here exposed to significant danger. His company with its considerable technical ability and transport was too valuable to be normally housed very close to the front line but in the urban environment of Arras, the benefit of proximity to the tasks in hand outweighed the danger it imposed.

After nine days in charge Major N. W. Benton joined the Troop Company and took command. Benton was a career soldier who had been an officer in the Royal Engineers since 1900. After three years as a subaltern he was promoted Lieutenant and then Captain in 1910. In 1916 he was promoted to Major at which rank he stuck for the rest of his military career.

In April as the German line was pushed back, conditions in the city improved. For instance some of the city's shops which had been operating underground re-opened in the Grand' and Petite Places and at one of these Thomas Wilson bought a brass match box cover embossed with the city's name and crest. Arras still remained within range of the larger German guns and casualties from shelling continued to be suffered. Among the injured from this shelling was Major-General Kenyon, Chief Engineer, 3rd Army[325] who was hit while in the Place de la Gare. The station area on the south-eastern side of the city continued to be hit until July 1917.

On the other side of the city was Thomas Wilson's billet and it, along with those of the rest of the Company, were shelled over an hour and a half on the evening of 3 May. He describes the effect of this shelling as "one shell fell in the garden of billet and another removed the roof of Riders Stable."

On the evening of the next day enemy shelling caused a fire in an ammunition dump on the northern edge of the city close to where the Company's horses were stabled. As the enemy artillery saw the fire and explosions they realised they were onto something and commenced heavier shelling of the location with 3 and 4.5 inch shells falling rapidly. At 1.30am when the shelling lapsed the men of the Company decommissioned and used the fire engine which they had installed as a water pump nearby to fight the fire. After it was extinguished Thomas Wilson inspected the damage and reported in the diary:

> *It was found that of the Company's horses, all stabled close to where the fire originated, one had been got away unharmed, three were wounded (one since shot) and the rest killed. Many pieces of shell came through the roofs and the windows of billets whilst dump was burning. No casualties occurred to personnel.*

On 13 May, Thomas Wilson records the departure of Sapper Cropper from the company to the Reserve Training Centre at Chatham as an officer cadet awaiting commission. Prior to 1916 such a promotion from the ranks, unless made in the field on account of casualties, was impossible and it illustrates the changes which the war had forced in the officer class of the British army.

Towards the end of the month the area of the company's billets were shelled again and a fire in the Citadel at Arras was extinguished by a company party. As the main British Arras offensive was ended the French or Nivelle offensive opened on the Aisne on 16 April. Nivelle's grand plan was to advance six miles: in fact he got no further than 600 yards. He anticipated 15,000 casualties whereas 100,000 occurred.[326] This dashing of heightened expectations proved fatal to Nivelle's career: he was removed from his command and despatched to North Africa. More seriously it led to substantial mutinies across the French army. Fortunately a bad situation was not made worse by the severe punishment of the mutineers. Petain who had replaced Nivelle organised immediate improvements in conditions and remarkably few soldiers were punished with executions.[327] However for the remainder of 1917 the French launched no independent attacks and merely kept to holding their part of the line. Lloyd George's attempt to bypass Haig by using Nivelle was in tatters and Haig's original plan to attack in Belgium was now to prove unstoppable.

Haig wasted no time and on 7 May at Doullens he informed the British army commanders that the main theatre of British military operations would now be Belgian Flanders. As he did so Lloyd George, hardly chastened, failed to answer Churchill's Commons question of 10 May why the Allies could not just sit tight and await the arrival of the Americans.[328]   While the British Government kept its counsel on Churchill's question, Haig, bruised by the Somme and the following political and military criticism, was determined to demonstrate his abilities as a commander and win the war using the British army in Belgium. The consequence was what was to become known as Third Ypres or by the name of what was merely its initial objective, Passchendaele.

18 – THE MOUTH OF HELL

In preparation for this new Flanders offensive, Thomas Wilson and the 42nd Army Troop Company of four officers and 129 other ranks left Arras on 7 June for Belgium. They were not the only RE unit to be sent to Belgium that summer as by now it was almost universally acknowledged that a huge amount of bridge and dug-out construction needed to be done in preparation for the attack as well as building tank causeways, dressing stations, observation posts and subways.

As Thomas Wilson's RE Company left the city in June the Mayor and corporation of Arras returned, followed by the evacuated civilians. In September the railway station re-opened to civilian traffic and in October 1917 the Paris-Arras line came back into service after a three year interruption.[329] The great battle and its many British Army victims had at least improved the position of the people they were fighting for.

In the usual way the war diary contains much detail of their journey to Belgium. In order to avoid the congestion and dangers of the area to the north of Arras, the Company proceeded west out of Arras on the St. Pol road. Thomas Wilson, almost certainly on account of his age, was put in charge of motor lorries, Lieutenant Anderson the company's horses, and the men with Major Benton and 2nd Lieutenant Wise marched ten miles to Savy Berlette where they were billeted for the night. In a sign of the gradual motorisation of the British Army, on the way a message was received from the Mayor of Aubigny that buses would be supplied for the second day to take them to Hurionville, a village just outside the town of Lillers. After reaching Hurionville, Thomas Wilson went into Lillers and was photographed there. On the back of this photograph he later wrote "Lillers – photographed when en route… from Arras to Ypres." Being in charge of the Company's motor lorries he would most certainly have arrived first with plenty of time to visit the army photographer in Lillers. The Dennis 3-ton lorry which he was travelling in was capable of up to 55 mph and he, as officer in charge, would have been driven in the first vehicle at the head of the convoy. Throughout the War

RE Field Companies coveted the Troop Companies mechanical transport which they were denied[330] but given the Field Companies were always tied to the infantry its not difficult to see why this was so.

Lillers had been chosen by the Commander in Chief as the BEF's forward headquarters in 1915 and by June 1917 it had become a British Army town with all of the associated services which the general headquarters of a military force attracted. As such, it is not surprising that here on 9 June Thomas Wilson had his officer portrait taken and waited for it to be printed before sending it home to his family. As well as sending it and a letter home, he also took the opportunity to write to the ICE in London and let them know his whereabouts. In the ICE 1917 Member's address book, against his printed entry and address in Grey Street, Newcastle a clerk has written in red ink "c/o 42nd Army Troops RE BEF France" and the date of annotation "18.6.17."

On the following day the journey continued to Morbecque and on 10 June they crossed into Belgium and arrived at Peselhoek six miles from the devastated city of Ypres. On the same day as Thomas Wilson left Arras, in Belgium on the Messines-Wytschaete ridge the RE tunnelling companies exploded a million pounds of TNT under the German lines.[331] The most southerly of the component mines was laid under and obliterated the well fortified German strongpoint which the British knew as Factory Farm. Its location opposite Plugstreet Wood, together with the highly significant involvement of his own regiment, probably ensured that Thomas Wilson followed the brief battle of Messines, as it came to be known, very closely.

He may also have heard the explosion which caused panic in German occupied Lille fifteen miles away. Possibly as many as 10,000 German soldiers were either killed outright or buried alive by the explosion and the result of it plus the follow-up surface operation was a German withdrawal from the ridge to a new line further east.[332] Haig, having accomplished this preliminary victory, was even more confident that with one more mass attack the German will to resist would be broken forever. On 19 June he expressed his usual religious certainty in outright victory directly to the War Cabinet who, with varying degrees of enthusiasm, eventually agreed to permit the attack timed for 31 July.

Messines certainly ensured that some of the higher ground overlooking the Ypres salient was taken from the Germans and meant they were unable to fully observe battle preparations for the next phase of British operations; but the higher ground to the east of Ypres which formed the Gheluvelt Plateau remained in German hands and left them with a clear view of what the British army was up to on the plain below. The ever increasing activity there swiftly indicated to the enemy that Messines was only the first part of the offensive.

Peselhoek where Thomas Wilson's company arrived on 10 June was the headquarters of VIII Corps, then in reserve and attached to the British 5th Army. Just a few miles away at Louvie Chateau, Sir Hubert Gough was establishing 5th Army headquarters from where he would command the attack. Thomas Wilson's company remained there for just five days before leaving for Dickebusch (now Dikkebus) about five miles away to the southeast. The men marched these five miles before being billeted in the village for the night. On the following morning of 16 June they moved, again on foot, just over a mile north to Andes Farm where they were to be billeted for the coming months. It was approximately three miles west of Ypres. The company's HQ was a short distance away to the west of the farm by a small lake and was probably located in a barn or other outbuilding. They would remain there until after the battle began at the end of July. Looking east from Andes Farm they had a perfect view of the ruins of Ypres.

Their work was to be under II Corps, and in the 8th Division front line area beyond the Ypres-Comines canal and just south of the shattered city. This area lies in front of the Gheluvelt Plateau and the enemy hidden among the trees on its western ridge were watching II Corps' every move.

On their first full day in the area the four officers of the company made a reconnaissance of the area east of the canal to investigate the options for building dug-out accommodation which was needed to house the assembling troops out of sight of the enemy and its artillery before the battle commenced. Their joint report survives and over three pages it neatly summarises the problems of launching a surprise attack from so flat and low-lying an area. It was addressed to their regimental superior Chief Engineer VIII Corps that evening.

The potential problems they identified of poor drainage, easy enemy observation, previous damage by shell fire and lack of cover (save for the rather obvious ones provided by the canal with its banks and locks and the two embanked local railway lines[333]) might, when repeated across the whole Ypres area, have served as a reasonable excuse to call off the attack but minds at GHQ were fixed and the Company's building and repairing of dug-outs along the canal and railways began next day.

Captain Ferrie of the 196th Machine Gun Co. described his dug-out near Ypres in 1917:

> *I suppose I may say that my dug-out is not a dug-out at all. It is a commodious modern residence on the reverse slope of a great earthwork or artificial bank. It is built of iron arches covered with sandbags, bricks and earth to the depth of six feet all round. It is large enough to stand up in, which is a great blessing. It is lit with electric light. It has a stove and a chimney. The only luxury that is wanting is a window; and as you will gather that the view is not a very cheerful one you will see that this is easily dispensed with.*[334]

Within five days of the dug-out work commencing the predicted problems of mud and poor drainage were noted. Also owing to the risk of enemy observation all the work had to be camouflaged and the numbers working had to be reduced, leading to the implementation of shift work between 4am and 9pm. All materials were moved at night in a further precaution against the

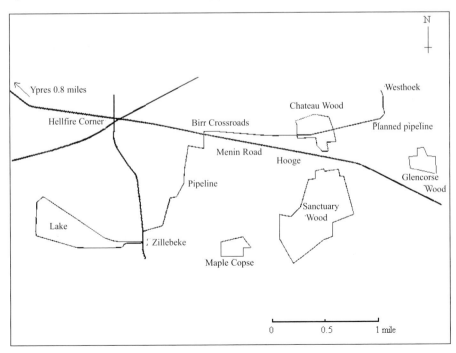

enemy discovering and then shelling the dug-outs' locations. Despite all of these steps the railway dug-outs were reported as being "much shelled" on 23 June. On the same day 2nd Lieutenant Wise was admitted to hospital with muscular rheumatism, thereby reducing the officer strength to three.

Wise's 'muscular rheumatism' was in fact a considerable euphemism, as his officer file discloses. In fact he was suffering from a urethral stricture or difficulty in passing urine which had first occurred ten years earlier following gonorrhoea in his mid-twenties. When he volunteered at Westminster in September 1914 he omitted to mention this condition on his army medical form; he was similarly silent on the topic when he left the Royal Fusiliers when awarded his RE commission in February 1916. Notwithstanding these omissions the army evacuated him from Ypres in early July, hospitalised him in England and on release from hospital sent him for relatively light duty at the RE training centre in Newark rather than back to France.

Two days after Wise was hospitalised, on 25 June the Company's officer strength was reduced to just two when Lieutenant Anderson was given special home leave of ten days to get married. Presumably Major Benton and Thomas Wilson organised a small celebration for him in the officers' mess at Andes Farm on the eve of his departure.

As June turned to July and the dug-outs were increasingly completed and fitted with infantry bunking, orders were received to commence work on the provision of drinking water for the battle. Although Flanders seemed to contain little else but rivers, streams, ponds, lakes and canals this did not mean that any of this ubiquitous water was safe for drinking: the provision of safe drinking water was an important aspect of the army's engineering needs.

With these in mind a pumping house was erected on the southern side of Zillebeke Lake with a coal-driven engine used to pump a supply by pipeline along the lake's shore to its eastern tip where it was closest to the road. At this point accumulator tanks were erected with watering points for water bottles and jerry cans so that on the day of battle as the infantry reached here from their dug-outs on the canal they could replenish their water supplies before moving forward. To the company this was known as FWP (Forward Water Point) Zillebeke. The pipeline was to be continued with just over a mile of four inch pipe to Birr Crossroads on the Menin Road where a second FWP would be provided. Today the site of Birr Crossroads is marked by a military cemetery containing the graves of 660 British soldiers.

The pipeline was a big project for one RE Company to undertake and as a result they were given infantry support to act as carriers and unskilled labour. The company's weekly progress reports quickly refer to problems in the supply of pipe fittings, transport failing to get through, shell fire, insufficient infantry and casualties but nonetheless 1,198 yards of pipe had been laid by 13 July with 650 yards required to complete the job. The difficulty with this final section was that it was being laid within the enemy's view and the working parties were deliberately targeted. The first 700 yards from Zillebeke were laid uphill and so out of sight but after the crest of the hill was reached they were exposed to specific rather than random enemy fire.

Given this landscape it is unsurprising that the diary records increasingly heavy shell fire at and close to the crossroads. In any event Birr was a favourite enemy target because just beyond it, up the Menin-Ypres Road, was the enemy-held village of Hooge. The straight descending road between the two gave the German artillery spotters a clear view of the company's work of assembling accumulator tanks, bottle filler taps and water troughing. Even night working did not entirely solve the problem because knowing exactly where the busy transport nodes of Hellfire Corner and the Birr Crossroads were, German artillery could fire blind in the dark and still be fairly confident of hitting a target of some kind.

Hooge and the Menin Road was to be at the very centre of the planned attack by II Corps along with the other four Corps comprising the forward units of Gough's 5th Army which was intended to drive the Germans back towards Bruges. Then, if it continued to work, Haig and Gough's plan was that the Belgian coast would be taken, depriving the enemy of the submarine bases which were devastating British shipping. From Hooge, II Corps were to advance to the vital Gheluvelt plateau which formed part of the strategic initial target, the Passchendaele Ridge. As such the provision of a water supply to sustain this part of the 5th Army's advance was a key part of the preparation and this work and the difficulties it entailed is specifically mentioned in the official regimental history of the war.[335]

Lieutenant Raymond Asquith was briefly in the line opposite Hooge in June 1916 prior to his death on the Somme two months later. He described Maple Copse and Sanctuary Wood just beyond the Birr Crossroads as not having a leaf or blade of grass that summer. In a letter to Lady Diana Manners he did not remotely hide the awfulness of the place describing it as:

the most accursed unholy and abominable place I have ever seen, the ugliest filthiest most putrid and most desolate – a wood where all the trees have been cut off by the shells... nothing remained but black stumps... craters swimming in blood and dirt, rotting and smelling bodies and rats like shadows, fattened for the market and moving cunningly and liquorishly among them, limbs and bowels nestling in the hedges, and over all the most supernaturally shocking scent of death and corruption that ever breathed o'er Eden. The place simply stank of sin and all Floris could not have made it sweet.[336]

He was rather more complimentary about Zillebeke Lake which he saw when in reserve on 16 June:

We have a line of dug-outs behind a lake. It is about as big as Rydal Water and is fringed with poplars. Last night under the full moon it was really quite beautiful.

By mid-July the war diary refers to a new danger, mustard gas shells, which the Germans used for the first time in the Ypres salient on 12 July.[337] From then until 10 November 1917 the British Army suffered 40,000 gas casualties in the Ypres area.

Mustard gas or Yperite as it was named in commemoration of its first use was the most dangerous poisonous chemical used during the war. Its chemical name is dichlorethyl sulphide. It is odourless and of yellow-brown appearance (but otherwise unrelated to culinary mustard) and is slow to take effect. Its usually unaware victims are struck by severe blistering to the skin, conjunctivitis leading to often permanent blindness and, if inhaled, internal bleeding and blistering of the respiratory system leading to a slow and agonising death within four to five weeks. Soldiers in the First World War who inhaled the gas often had to be tied down in their hospital beds to prevent them writhing in agony. Even those who avoided inhalation or blindness would still be hospitalised for many weeks with skin damage which, in advance of the invention of protective clothing, could not be safeguarded against. Twenty of the men of Thomas Wilson's company, amounting to one sixth of its strength, were hospitalised by mustard gas up to 21 July and a further four gas casualties occurred before the end of the month. Because of the time taken before they either died or were discharged it cannot be said how many of the 24 died or were permanently blinded but almost certainly some of them were. Those men unaffected who helped the injured into ambulances may have shared Wilfred Owen's famous sentiments:

> *If in some smothering dreams, you too could pace*
> *Behind the wagon that we flung him in,*
> *And watch the white eyes writhing in his face,*
> *His hanging face, like a devil's sick of sin;*
> *If you could hear at every jolt the blood*
> *Come gurgling from the froth corrupted lungs,*
> *Obscene as cancer, bitter as the cud*
> *Of vile, incurable sores on innocent tongues, –*
> *My friend, you would not tell with such high zest*
> *The old Lie: Dulce et decorum est*
> *Pro patria mori.*

Avoiding the effects of gas meant the wearing of cumbersome and uncomfortable gas masks while the sappers and their officers carried out their already demanding duties. Captain Frayling RE of the 171st Tunnelling Co. described working in a gas mask as follows:

> *For hour after hour, mile after mile, night after night it meant getting round the job in a gas mask. The donning of a gas mask seemed to take away a third of a soldier's efficiency. If the design of gas masks had evolved with the care given say to the design of machine-guns, it could have been a contribution to the winning of the war... It was dinned into us that gas casualties were unsoldierly slobs who had not used their gas masks.*[338]

Aside from continuous shelling and the mustard gas, which remained active for several days in the ground in which the water pipeline was being laid, their work in the final days leading to the battle had to be done at night so that it avoided shell fire and was concealed from the enemy's reconnaissance balloons and aircraft which might have revealed the date and timing of the now imminent attack. It is little wonder that in a very rare instance of recording any low morale the entry for 28 July records "work difficult owing to gas and shells. Men almost done up." One of the problems for morale was that as an aspect of work on the pipeline and storage tanks was finished it could subsequently be damaged by shell fire. For instance two large storage tanks at FWP Zillebeke were "hopelessly holed by shell fire" on 28 July. This led to a need for rolling repairs to the pipeline in addition to the completion of the as yet unfinished FWP Birr Crossroads. With the company enduring significant casualties some relief was given by the arrival the 133rd Army Troop Co. RE who were given responsibility for the pipeline along Zillebeke lake; but even there they sustained five dead and thirteen wounded from shell fire in the second half of July.

Even in these hopeless conditions there was no option of giving up on the water project at Birr Crossroads and on Saturday 28th July the diary records that Lieutenant Bracken led a pipe-laying party which succeeded in completing the 5,000 feet of new pipeline under shell fire. Of course in the last analysis this was why he had been given his commission – to exhibit bravery by leading his men through appalling danger in order to get the job done. On the following day the diary in an unprecedented entry records "reported Company tired out. Company rested."

In 1929 in a letter to *The Penrith Observer*, Thomas Wilson described how the men kept up their morale in Flanders by singing songs and in particular the song of his hero the huntsman John Peel which he described as being:

> *Sung in snatches by relief parties in the dark, marching shoe-top deep in Flanders mud towards the front line and by relieved coming out, sandwiched with "Cock Robin" between bits of music hall ditties and Sunday school hymns.*

It seems safe to assume that this collective singing encompassed the widely known words of the John Peel chorus:

> *D'ye ken John Peel with his coat so gray?*
> *D'ye ken John Peel at the break o' the day?*
> *D'ye ken John Peel go far, far away?*
> *With his hounds and his horn in a morning.*

But whether it encompassed some of the later verses referring to the human fellowship of the hunt, amid the gloriously unchanged English countryside, the timeless companionship of Man's Best Friend and its final sentiment of never giving up, seems more doubtful; although certainly Thomas Wilson had known all the verses since his boyhood and more recently from singing them at the close of meetings of the Tyneside Cumberland and

Westmorland Association:

D'ye join John Peel both oft and far,
O'er rasper fence and the gate and the bar,
From Low Denton Holme up to Scrathmere Scar,
When you strove for the brush in a morning?

D'ye ken that hound, whose tongue was death?
D'ye ken her sons of peerless faith?
D'ye ken that a fox, with his last breath,
Curs'd them as he died in a morning?

Here's to John Peel, with my heart and my soul,
Come fill, o fill to him another bowl,
And we'll follow John Peel thro' fair and foul,
While we're waked by his horn in a morning?

Yet another impediment to the company's work which could not be helped and which the diary does not elaborate on was the waterlogged ground caused both by shell-damaged drainage and the increasingly wet late-July weather. The combined effect was to turn the ground over which the pipeline was being laid into a quagmire. The Flanders rainfall in July and August 1917 was the heaviest in 30 years. Sapper Albert Martin RE, also serving with the 5th Army but with a different unit, recorded the conditions:

> *For eight days our men have been in the trenches under the worst possible conditions regarding weather and shell-fire and to expect them to make a successful advance now is asking too much. The state of the country is indescribable owing to the recent rains and the naturally marshy nature of the ground churned up into a filthy sloppy mass by all manner of shells. Rifles and machine guns are choked up with mud and are unusable.*[339]

The last day of July was day zero or 'Z Day' as the diary terms it and hour zero of day zero was fixed at 3.50am when it was supposed to be dawn. However due to the cloud and drizzle the first half hour of the attack was fought in darkness. Many who were there recalled the silence which preceded the great battle as the officers calmly gave the men pep talks and tots of rum were dispensed. It was broken by the awful sound of the artillery barrage and then the whistles as thousands climbed up ladders and over the top. The

Somme's legacy of death and injury meant that this time the participants knew it would be no easy march to victory. Few, however, can have imagined the extent of the horrors which awaited them and which Siegfried Sassoon summarised as "I died in Hell (they called it Passchendaele)."

They had been ordered to move fast as soon as they saw the protective barrage ahead of them was in place and keeping enemy heads down. They were to follow the barrage of shells as close 'as a horse following a nosebag' at a pre-determined steady rate of 100 metres per four minutes.[340]

The plan may have been brilliant in theory and the artillery hugely impressive to be even capable of it but as 8th Division advanced along and to the north of the Menin Road and into Hooge and Bellewaerde they were delayed by the shattered conditions in Chateau Wood. With both poor visibility and communications the barrage, unaware of the delay, continued to move ahead and lose the infantry. The enemy freed of the shrapnel raining down on them moved out of their undamaged concrete shelters and commenced heavy fire from Glencorse Wood. In heavy rain and suffering increasing casualties the Division consolidated under Westhoek ridge just short of the hamlet of Westhoek. This was short of their second objective which was to get beyond Westhoek. Their fourth and final objective for the day – to get beyond Zonnebeke and more than half way to Passchendaele – remained a distant dream of Army HQ.[341]

Other parts of the 5th Army had done rather better on day zero and as a whole the attack over a fifteen mile front led in the first two days to more ground being taken than in any previous Western Front offensive. However this initial success was to prove deceptive: Passchendaele, only the initial objective in the plan to clear the Belgian coast and just four and a half miles in, was to take sixteen weeks to take and cost the British army almost 245,000 casualties of which 66,000 were killed.[342] Yet again the army commanders had set overly-ambitious objectives and under-estimated their enemy's resilience. In the weather Gough may have felt unlucky but wet summers were not unknown and once the results of days of heavy rain became obvious to all, the further offensive could have been called off. No wonder the British Tommy re-christened the battle Passion Dale.

Thomas Wilson's Company did not move forward at 3.50am but remained in their billets and at their HQ awaiting orders. These came by telegram at 7.50am when the Chief Engineer II Corps instructed Major Benton to "move your men on to site of work as soon as possible and commence work." The nature of the 'work' is set out in the Orders for Z Day which have also survived with the diary. Like the orders for the infantry of II Corps they were not unambitious. Not only was the water supply to be repaired and maintained at the two FWPs of Zillebeke and Birr Crossroads but a line was to be laid out and pipes installed in the newly captured territory beyond Birr Crossroads and all the way to Westhoek. Lance Corporal Tonks drew a map of the proposed line. It was to go on the north side of the Menin Road past Hooge Chateau and right through Chateau Wood which lay behind, where even the infantry of 8th Division struggled to get through, before curving northwards into Westhoek. Like so much else on 31 July it was to remain just a paper plan.

Hugely ambitious as these orders were their importance meant that they were allocated an impressive amount of manpower. Two whole companies totalling 225 men of the 2nd Battalion the Royal Irish Rifles were ordered to assist the Royal Engineer Company. An agreed number of R.I. Rifles were allocated to each sapper party and the transport in the form of pontoon wagons, sappers and infantry met at a place of assembly near Zillebeke village. Initially Major Benton remained at Company HQ but Lieutenants Bracken and Anderson went to the point of assembly and supervised the despatch of parties as the pipeline route was followed. Thomas Wilson was put in charge of repairing parties between Zillebeke and the crossroads while the just-married Anderson was put in charge of pipe laying thereafter. The orders envisaged that once all breaks were repaired the entire company together with infantry would move forward from the Birr Crossroads along the evolving new pipeline to Westhoek completing it as they went.

As in so many battles both before and since the planning of headquarters and what happened on the ground were worlds apart. Perhaps the Corps Chief Engineer still believed the old myth that the enemy artillery would have been destroyed by the British barrage or that the Germans would be too busy retreating to fire on the sappers and the water pipeline. In the event once the attack got underway with a British artillery barrage this was answered by a German counter-barrage. With these enemy shells raining down on them Thomas Wilson's parties attempted to repair the existing and increasing breaks in the pipe and the damage done to FWP Zillebeke. The record of events in the diary does not attempt to mask the situation on the ground. The shell fire is described as "very heavy" and the pipeline beyond Zillebeke is described as "completely damaged and hopelessly smashed." At Birr Crossroads when he got there Major Benton found the FWP "hopelessly broken up."

Unsurprisingly given this situation, and aside from the fact that Weskhoek remained under the enemy, he still bothered to inform Corps HQ that no attempt was being made to work beyond the crossroads. Benton issued orders for the recovering of valuable materials assembled for taking the pipe forward before it was lost to the mud and shell holes but even though he used the word 'hopeless' more than once in his report the sappers continued to repair the breaks and overnight on 31 July-1 August water was got through again.

The company's near superhuman efforts did not go unrecognised and the official Royal Engineers history of the war records their difficulty in laying and maintaining the water supply and the significance of the FWP at Zillebeke:

> *The line from Zillebeke Lake was taken almost to Birr crossroads, but was completely destroyed during the night preceding the attack. The intense and continuous shelling made it impossible, both during the preparatory period and during the battle, to maintain water-cart points or pipe lines within about 5,000 yards of the line. The furthest forward water-cart points supplied by pipe which could be maintained were situated at... Zillebeke.*[343]

For Thomas Wilson's company day zero was followed by two days of rest and baths followed by 'back area work' during the first week of August. One major task was to clean the ubiquitous mud from their uniforms, tools and equipment. The diary for this week contains a long list of men who were granted an unusual two weeks home leave as a reward for their efforts. The reward was not an isolated piece of army generosity but reflected the appalling casualties and conditions they had endured on the first day of the great battle.

Thomas Wilson's reward was to be a transfer to a staff job outside the area of the Armies or conflict zone and in the relative safety and civilisation of Calais. A delphic diary entry for 8 August records his departure for his fresh posting: "Lt. T. W. Bracken RE left unit to report to D. of W. L. of C."

On 10 August, having endured rain on every day bar two since 31 July the 5th Army renewed its attack. In dreadful ground conditions Gough required them to advance by 800 metres and establish a firm presence on the Gheluvelt Plateau. The maximum advance achieved was only 400 metres and the only joy was the capture of Westhoek.[344]

By a piece of irony probably not lost on them at the time the 2nd Battalion of the Royal Irish Rifles who had been meant to enter Westhoek on 31 July in a supporting role with the pipe laying 42nd Army Troop Co. RE were now to do so, in the front line as part of 25th Division. Second Lieutenant John Lucy 2nd RIR who may well have met Thomas Wilson on 31 July described zero hour on 10 August as:

The sergeant roused everyone an hour before zero and repeated orders to sections. Rum was issued. I went along to inspect the men. Bayonets were fixed, cartridge clips and grenade pins loosened. Some men had collected boxes, others had dug holes in the trench side, or placed small ladders to help them clamber out. They stood facing the parapet, jaw muscles rigid, bayonet-points under cover – waiting. At two minutes to zero I took a good swig of neat whisky, saw the nearest men all tensed ready to climb out, and put my whistle to my lips. My heart thumped heavily. Exactly to the second pandemonium broke loose. I blew my whistle and was up and over, looking back to see my trench rapidly emptying... I broke forward into a trot... My boots struck hard on road metal – part of Westhoek, and I did not know it. There was not a brick left upon a brick.[345]

19 – RESPITE

'D. of W. L. of C.'? L of C meant Lines of Communication the area of northern France behind and outside the areas of the five British armies where support services were located and supplies were stored and brought up. D of W, although normally abbreviated by the Royal Engineers to DW, referred to Director of Works, Major-General Stuart RE who Thomas Wilson had probably already encountered during his brief 1916 visit to Abancourt.

Stuart's office, the headquarters of the huge Works Directorate, was in Amiens. His deputy was based in Boulogne and under the Deputy Director came the Engineer Districts each of which was headed by a CRE (Commander Royal Engineers) usually with the rank of Lieutenant-Colonel. Under the CRE came Division Officers who normally held the rank of Captain.

Within the Works Directorate War Diaries were maintained at CRE level and above and in the CRE diary for Calais appears the typed entry for 10 August 1917, "Lieutenant T. W. Bracken arrived for duty under me." The neatly typed entry recording his arrival in Calais serves as a useful metaphor for his changed army life. Gone were the days of pencil scribbled diaries written in the mess under flickering electric light after a long hard day in the field and to the accompaniment of relentless artillery fire. Aside from occasional aerial bombardment and the presence of the military, Calais was unaffected by the war and Thomas Wilson would have enjoyed convivial company, good food, a comfortable billet, secretarial staff and more army servants to ease his day at both ends. Calais's location ensured a succession of VIP, presidential and even royal visits, as well as various official delegations and what was in effect Great War tourism. A further consequence of Calais being the closest port of embarkation for England was that the British Army accorded it the status of a military base during the First World War and as a result it was given a Base Commandant with the accompanying rank of Brigadier-General: his war diary also provides a fascinating record of life in a bustling military town between 1917 and 1918.

A staff job at 52 and after almost two years of service was probably an appropriate reward for Thomas Wilson. Although his first eighteen months of army life had been relatively quiet, if not without danger, during the next six months he had witnessed at close quarters both great British battles of 1917. His engineering contribution to each, recognised as it was to be in the regiment's history, clearly did not go unremarked at the time. Sadly his file, like all other Officer Confidential Reports, was destroyed by a German bombing raid over London in September 1940. As a result there is no material regarding his transfer from the Western Front to become a staff officer well back behind the lines. However it seems reasonably likely that his regimental superiors and those in GHQ recognised that both by his experience in the field and on account of his age he had earned the privileges of an RE staff appointment well away from the omnipresent stench of death and the appalling physical destruction.

The caricature of red-tabbed GHQ staff officers, in *Oh! What a Lovely War* and *Blackadder Goes Forth*, as chinless, over-privileged and entirely unaware of the horrors of the trenches has been much overdone. Haig and his senior officers paid frequent visits to the front line and were not cosseted away from the horrors of the trenches. Also they worked long hours on vital work and many like Thomas Wilson had experience of front line warfare. Furthermore, while he was to enjoy life in a stereotypical French château, on the down side, after growing used to considerable autonomy and freedom of manoeuvre in the field, from now on he would be under the relentless watch of his superiors in Calais.

The superior whose staff he joined, in army-speak the CRE Calais, was Lieutenant-Colonel Philip J. J. Radcliffe. Radcliffe was 54-years-old and married to the daughter of Sir Frederick Weld, a significant explorer of New Zealand where he was briefly premier 1864-5 during the Maori War.[346] His own father was a baronet with estates of 3,500 acres in Lancashire and Yorkshire but as a younger son he had joined the Engineers in 1886, ascending to Lieutenant-Colonel in 1911.

Regrettably we do not know Thomas Wilson's reaction to this new posting although his batman and the other servants at Andes Farm must have had a considerable job in cleaning his uniform in preparation for the critical eye of Major-General Stuart in fairly pristine Amiens.[347] Given the two day gap between his departure from Belgium and arrival in Calais it seems likely that he had a night's rest in Amiens before reporting to the CRE headquarters in

Calais. CRE HQ was on the Boulevard International (since renamed Boulevard des Alliés) which along with three-quarters of Calais was entirely destroyed in the bombing of World War Two. From old photographs it was, like most of 'old' Calais, an attractive street of harbour-front houses. It looked directly onto the old harbour, with a view to the left of Calais's old fort. Just behind it was the city's main square, the Place d'Armes. His most likely reaction was surely one of exhausted relief at being in a relatively safe, civilised and unaltered French city, after witnessing at close quarters the mud and horrors of the Ypres sector.

His exhaustion may be reflected in the diary's next reference to him after 10 August, being his return from leave on 19 September. The diary does not record when this period of leave commenced, although as the previous two war diaries in which he appears make no mention of his taking leave not much complaint can be made of the omission. Family anecdote states that he took some of his earlier leave in Paris from where dolls and other presents were despatched to Stainmore but how much home leave he actually made use of prior to his arrival in Calais cannot be ascertained. Only from this period onward when he was adjacent to regular ferries to Dover and fast onward trains to London and Westmorland can it be said with certainty that he travelled back to his family in England. Officers were granted home leave approximately every six months. The period of leave depended upon what their units were engaged upon. If they were with a regiment of the line, leave could be as short as a week; if not it was usually ten days and very rarely more than a fortnight. As to what an officer did with his leave, it was a matter for him and it did not have to be taken in England, although unless impractical it usually was. Also when conditions allowed officers were additionally granted short periods of leave of a couple of days and during these short breaks many officers travelled south to Paris.

On 3 September, just before Thomas Wilson probably went on leave, both Calais itself and outlying RE facilities at Vendroux and Les Attaques were heavily bombed by German planes. Further large raids occurred at the end of the month and the increasing range and accuracy of German bombing raids led to the first adoption of serious anti-aircraft measures in Calais. Searchlights and anti-aircraft guns were installed for use but it seems doubtful that they were very effective as the Calais war diaries refer to bombing as late as September 1918.

Accounts of these raids appear not just in the Calais Royal Engineers diary but also that of the Calais Base Commandant, Brigadier-General F. W. Radcliffe. It seems surprising that both of the most senior British Army officers in Calais at this period were called Radcliffe but they were not related. General Radcliffe, himself the son of a General, had a far more distinguished service record than Colonel Radcliffe RE. Prior to his arrival in Calais General Radcliffe had commanded the 2nd Battalion of the Dorset Regiment in Mesopotamia (modern Iraq) where he led the landing on the Fao peninsula in 1914. Thereafter he was deputy military governor of Basra until he was severely wounded on operations in 1915. After this he was given a desk job at home before taking charge in Calais in 1917.

During the first two months of Thomas Wilson's service in Calais it is clear that by far the largest project the Calais engineer district was concerned with was the continuing construction and enlargement of the Vendroux Depot. Vendroux was located just three miles south-east of Calais. It was named after the Château de Vendroux at its western edge which served as the RE headquarters and officers' mess. Before the war the Château was the home of Jacques Vendroux, a Calais biscuit manufacturer and the father of Yvonne (born 22 May 1900). In April 1921 Yvonne Vendroux married Charles de Gaulle.

A part of the Château's estate had been first developed as an RE depot and workshop, named Les Attaques, in early 1916 in order to relieve the wharves and storage at Calais port; it originally covered 50 acres. Its location between the railway and the Calais-St Omer canal was ideal in that cross Channel barges could come into the depot and unload before materials were sent onward by rail.[348]

From April 1917 the original facility was greatly extended westwards and this extension was named Vendroux after the family estate upon which it was built. From the original 50 acres the site was increased and eventually extended over 800 acres by 1918-1919.[349] It encompassed four huge hangars for ordnance, stores, hay and oats. Its scale is evident from a descriptive memorandum attached to the CRE Calais war diary. Sixteen miles of drainage ditches were dug to keep the low-lying site dry, 170,000 tons of sand was used in levelling it, seven and a half acres of concrete flooring was laid for the sheds and the base contained over five miles of concrete or flagstone walkways. Two miles of road were built and the oats and hay depots had a capacity of 30,000 tons each. Forty-five miles of broad gauge railway was laid in sidings within the depot area and four miles of metre gauge track was built to enable movement of stores within and about the hangars. The Vendroux facility well illustrates that the old army amateurism was entirely gone. This was total warfare on an industrial scale with huge financial and human resources utilised to ensure Allied victory.

Some of the physical labour this massive construction project demanded was provided by British Army Labour Companies but with increasing casualties at the front during 1916-17 all available British manpower was required for front line duties. Therefore the War Office in concert with the Foreign Office began to look for a new source of cheap contract labour. In 1916 the French had started recruiting civilian labour in China and in October that year Britain followed their example. The first labourers arrived in France in the spring of 1917. From the files in the National Archives it is clear that this recruitment quickly aroused tensions between the War and Foreign Offices. The latter wanted the accompanying interpreters to be accorded the status of officers but the War Office was adamant that the British Army's officers should not be demeaned by according what they called 'coolies' officer status.

A further difficulty was that the German legation in China whipped up anti-British feeling by planting scare stories that once in France they would be forced to fight. In fact all of the 100,000 Chinese in France at the end of the war were excluded from combat duties. They worked behind the armies in the zone of the lines of communication although they did face the danger of aerial bombardment and some were killed in this way. All of them were recruited by the British Government's agents in Weihaiwei[350] with most recruits coming from the northern province of Shantung.[351] Their contracts were for three years terminable after one, with six months notice and then free transportation home. While under contract they were fed, housed and clothed (in a specially designed dark blue uniform), and given fuel and medical services by the British government.

On signing the contract with Britain they were paid a twenty dollar bonus. Thereafter their pay was in two forms: a rate of pay per day in French francs and family pay paid monthly in Chinese dollars to their families. The rates varied depending on their skill and class of labourer. At the lowest they were paid a franc a day plus ten dollars per month. At the highest the Class I interpreters were paid five francs per day plus 60 dollars per month.[352] In addition they were paid sick pay and a fixed amount of compensation was payable for death or injury.

A contemporary military document comments on these terms thus: "so it can be seen that every Chinaman joins on a long contract, is liberally paid, is looked after in every respect free by the Government, and that his family is provided for on equally liberal terms."

Chinese labour was increasingly present at Vendroux from April 1917 and special camps were constructed for their use. From the Calais Base Commandant's diary it is clear that a common problem was their breaking out of their camps at night – often following air raids. As the Chinese labour battalions were subject to Military Law under section 176 (9) of the Army Act and were commanded by British officers, the authorities could not ignore such breaches of discipline. Nonetheless the officer commanding them at Corps level addressed a paper to GHQ in December 1917 seeking a greater understanding of them and the need to avoid imposing the same punishment as those imposed on British soldiers who breached military law.

The expansion of Chinese labour at Vendroux was gathering pace by the autumn of 1917 and from the diary it is clear that in the second week of October 1917, the Royal Engineers in Calais were working on the design and supervising the construction of three new Chinese labour camps there. The RE officer in charge at Vendroux was Lieutenant Alderson who had been there since April. The diary tells us that on 13 October he went on leave and Colonel Radcliffe sent Thomas Wilson from the Calais HQ to Vendroux to cover for his absence. As it turned out Thomas Wilson would remain at Vendroux long after Alderson's return from leave and would eventually replace him in charge as Divisional Officer there. Alderson, like Thomas Wilson, had been a civil engineer in civilian life. Born in Harrogate, Yorkshire in 1870, he practised there and lived in the town at Dragon Parade.

During Thomas Wilson's first week in charge he had the drama and inevitable fuss associated with a royal visit. HRH the Duke of Connaught,[353] together with his entourage, arrived in Calais on 19 October and visited Vendroux. Apart from this reference in General Radcliffe's diary there are no further details of this visit but as Vendroux was an RE facility it is most likely that Colonel Radcliffe would have conducted the Duke round Vendroux; Thomas Wilson as acting Divisional Officer there would have met him.

From General Radcliffe's diary for 1917-18 it is clear that Calais was a popular destination for VIP visits. It is not hard to see why: it was easily accessible from England, behind the combat zone and relatively safe, while also being under military occupation. With things to see and visit it was plainly thought to be an appropriate destination by the British authorities. Two weeks after the royal visit, a party of Glasgow city magnates visited Calais and drove to Vendroux; earlier in October a British parliamentary delegation had visited. In the following month eight US congressmen are recorded there. The Duke of Connaught was back at Vendroux in January 1918 and was followed by a party of newspaper proprietors. Although such visits stopped with the launch of the great German offensive of spring 1918, once the Allies' fortunes turned the visits continued right up to the Armistice.

By November 1917 the RE work at Vendroux was changing from building facilities for the Chinese, to facilities for the prisoners of war who formed the second component part of the workforce at Vendroux. There were five prisoner of war companies at Vendroux during 1917-18 and they were put to work under guard as both construction labourers and in the workshop at Vendroux. Although the prisoners were left under canvas for the entire year, by 20 November winter hutting was being supplied for the Chinese labourers and the prison guards.

On the same day as the hutting supplies arrived, 20 November 1917, Britain launched its third major offensive of the year with the objective being the French city of Cambrai and the territory beyond it. For the first time tanks played a prominent part in the initial attack and as a result real gains of territory were made on the first day. However on the second the story becomes a more familiar Western Front one in that German reinforcements were rushed up preventing yet again the planned use of British cavalry. Doubtless to boost morale at home news of the initial breakthrough was released and bells were rung in response across the country; but these celebrations were premature. On the very day the church bells rang out the advance was halted at Bourlon Wood. After a week the attack was called off: taking Cambrai and using cavalry to do so remained only a GHQ dream.[354] Until the spring, as in former years, winter was now in charge of the battlefield.

In the run up to Christmas the RE diary records that severe frost was hampering the concrete works at Vendroux. Snow fell on Christmas day and in the following week and this caused the Vendroux power generation plant to cut out because of over-load. As a result the French Governor of Calais, who remained to represent the interests of the French state in what was a British army town, was asked to ensure that the military need for electricity took precedence over that of French civilians.

As 1918 opened the RE reported good progress in the construction of the huge ordnance depot but delays with the railway sidings adjacent to the oats depot. In mid-January Thomas Wilson took his second period of home leave from Calais. Since his last home leave to Westmorland his brother had died[355] at Bowersyke of a chronic stomach disorder. Aged just 49, he died on the day of his seventh wedding anniversary. From his *Westmorland Gazette* obituary of 29 December 1917 it is clear that his condition was undiagnosed while he lived. He continued working until just two days before he died and doubtless the struggle to maximise the estate's timber production for the war effort while enduring labour shortages caused by the call to arms contributed to his condition. In Thomas Wilson's absence, the squire of Ingmire Major Upton, who had been commissioned into the local Westmorland and Cumberland Yeomanry on the war's outbreak, led the mourners at Killington as Robert was buried next to his mother. He left a young widow and two infant children and family anecdote states that Thomas Wilson helped them financially after his brother's death. He was now at 52 the sole survivor of his siblings and it must have felt that death stalked him even when on leave.

Back in France by 6 February the steel tower elevators in the oats depot were ready for testing. They were driven by electricity and when commissioned for use, were capable of sucking the oats directly from the barges which had sailed across the Channel from Kent. In this way 3,520 sacks of oats per hour were filled. Five days later was the Chinese New Year and General Radcliffe visited each of the Chinese labour camps in the Calais area.

On 23 February Lieutenant Alderson went on home leave and once again Thomas Wilson took acting command as Divisional Officer, Vendroux. In a sign of just how congested Calais was, the diary tells us that Alderson's leave was delayed by a day due to the Dover steamers being full. During Henry Alderson's leave momentous events in the war's history were occurring on the Eastern front. On 3 March 1918 the Russo-German peace treaty was signed at Brest-Litovsk. By this treaty the Bolshevik Government gave up and Germany acquired the Baltic Provinces, Finland, Poland, Belarus, Bessarabia, the Ukraine and the Caucasus. This loss of territory amounted to a third of Russia's population, a third of its most productive land and almost all of its coalfields. In signing to save St Petersburg from the Germans, Lenin relinquished two centuries of Tsarist territorial gains.[356] This significant shift in the European balance of power only stiffened the Allies' determination to defeat German aggression and expansion.

The treaty was to have profound effect on the Western front. Freed at last from the nightmare of war on two fronts, and aided by its eastern divisions and captured Russian guns, Germany launched its last gamble on the Western Front, Ludendorff's great March offensive. A day before the German infantry attack was launched, Vendroux and Calais suffered a significant aerial bombardment involving fifteen planes and 60 bombs. Sixteen Chinese were killed and 34 Chinese and three British soldiers were wounded.

The German attack was launched on 21 March on the British line between St Quentin and Arras. The initial advances and numbers of prisoners taken were huge. Winston Churchill, who was visiting front-line headquarters, had a narrow escape. On 23 March the civilian population of Arras was evacuated, followed three days later by the civil administration. In a week the German advance was 40 miles on a 50 mile front and the key strategic target of Amiens was threatened for the first time since 1914. If Amiens fell its effect would be to divide the British and French armies and deprive the British of the exit route ports of Rouen and Le Havre. Facing a crisis without parallel since 1914 the Allies agreed to a unified command under Foch. For Haig this was a remarkable *volte face* which he had long resisted and self interest on his part cannot be ruled out. He may well have preferred to shuffle the blame onto Foch than be remembered by history as the Commander who lost the War.[357]

But the War was not to be lost; the British 5th Army held the line in front of Amiens and the Americans, still a minor partner in terms of troop numbers, agreed to permit some of their troops to join the British and French in small formations rather than waiting in reserve to form US armies of their own[358] as had previously been insisted on.

In Calais all leave was cancelled. On 28 March the King passed through the city en route to the front in order to steady nerves and stiffen morale. In three days he travelled 315 miles visiting British and Empire units.[359] On the German side, denied Amiens, the advancing Germans were exhausted and riddled with casualties. In another blind gamble to achieve a knock-out before the arriving Americans tipped the numerical balance, Ludendorff turned his attention northwards to the southern part of the Ypres sector around the river Lys. His ultimate objective was Calais and Boulogne in order to deny the British these evacuation routes from Flanders. The attack here began on 9 April and once again the Germans made significant advances. Ploegsteert, Neuve Eglise and the areas of the Franco-Belgian border where Thomas Wilson had seen service from 1915 to 1917 were completely over-run. The towns of Armentières and Bailleul fell but the significant railway town of Hazebrouck was held.[360]

On 11 April Haig issued his Special Order of the Day to all ranks:

There is no other course open to us but to fight it out. Every position must be held to the last man: there must be no retirement. With our backs to the wall and believing in the justice of our cause, each one of us must fight to the end. The safety of our homes and the Freedom of mankind alike depend upon the conduct of each one of us at this critical moment.

The order would have been received in Calais and forwarded on to Vendroux. Precisely what the officers in charge, Lieutenants Alderson and Bracken, made of the situation is not recorded, but on 15 April when the Passchendaele ridge, won at such cost, was evacuated Thomas Wilson must surely have felt like most of Britain, that the deaths of tens of thousands in 1917 had been in vain.

However, more positively, 2,000 American troops of the 77th Division disembarked in Calais in mid-April and the G.O.C. General Johnson was given lunch in a show of Allied unity by the Governor of Calais and General Radcliffe. On 21 April the band of the 307th US Infantry played in the Place Richelieu and on 29 April a further 4,000 US troops disembarked in Calais.

Even at the depths of the military emergency of March/April, Calais was never directly threatened and was never in range of German artillery fire. Even if the worst had happened and the remnant British army had had to be evacuated from France, the officers in Calais would probably have had both an early and orderly evacuation to Dover. This is why military life in Calais was not seriously disturbed by General Ludendorff's 1918 offensives. For instance on 28 April General Radcliffe visited Vendroux and stayed for lunch in the officers' mess; on 1 May the Officers Club in Calais opened in the former Grand Hotel.

On the other side, denied a real breakthrough to the Channel and knowing that time and the arriving Americans were against them, Germany's troops were becoming increasingly demoralised and their armaments exhausted.

Ludendorff called off his Ypres offensive and seemingly almost punch drunk, now attacked the French on the Aisne in a drive towards Paris. As Germany prepared for this, its third offensive of 1918 in as many months the Allies argued about how the American forces were best to be utilised and commanded. When the attack broke the first serious American engagement with the enemy took place at Cantigny, on the Somme. Despite this first US success the German advance continued to the river Marne and by 1 June they were within 40 miles of Paris.

Once again though the German army had over-extended itself and, as in the two earlier offensives, fell victim to exhaustion and over-stretched supply lines. At the same time significant numbers of American troops entered the battle zone under French and British corps, stabilising the Allies' front line in advance of the inevitable counter-attack. By May 1918 the American Army also became involved at Vendroux and huge storage hangars similar to those recently constructed for British use were planned for them. On 29 May General Radcliffe and the US General Herbert inspected the site of these hangars before welcoming another 2,500 US troops at the port of Calais.

Air raids continued to be a significant problem at Calais and Vendroux. On 15 May seven were killed and twenty wounded, and considerable damage was caused both to several sites at Vendroux and to the port area in Calais. On 6 June following an air raid a fire broke out in the hay depot at Vendroux and burned for 24 hours destroying over 20,000 tons of forage. Despite these setbacks the relentless expansion of the facility continued. By the end of May 1918 a camp for the Women's Auxiliary Army Corps was under construction. The formation of the WAAC was authorised in July 1917 and it meant women were put in uniform and sent to France for the first time as clerks, telephonists, waitresses and cooks. This change, along with their war-winning work in Britain's armaments factories, marked an important step on the road towards political and social equality for women. In a sign of how rapidly this trend developed, by September 1918 women police were put on duty in Calais for the first time.

Miss Dalgleish of the WAAC in Calais wrote the following account of an air raid in 1918:

Obtaining possession of our coats and shoes and keeping them within easy reach we returned to bed to await what was to most of us a new experience. The guns came into action all around but in the intervals we could distinctly hear the noise of the unwelcome visitors. For a time pandemo-nium reigned; shells bursting, shrapnel falling and the rattle and roar of the guns. We could not distinguish the different noises: had no idea whether bombs contributed to the noise or not but we kept our spirits by attributing most of it to our own guns.

Through it all our lady officers walked up and down, looking in at intervals, talking and advising without betraying the slightest anxiety. It was impossible to feel anything but stimulated by their demeanour, a feel-ing amounting almost to absolute trust and whatever our individual feel-ings might be one and all seemed determined to show themselves not unworthy of the example the officers set.

Next day we saw plenty of evidence of the night's experience in the quantities of glass lying about the streets, the holes made in the walls and windows by shrapnel and in the ruined houses. The number of casualties was considerable but by a curious turn of fate the larger number were German prisoners.[361]

The Allies' counter-attack started in the French sector on the Marne on 18 July 1918. The Germans, by now outnumbered three to one, ordered an immediate retreat and by 7 August they were back on the Aisne. On the next day the British countered from Amiens. By the end of the day the British and Commonwealth troops had advanced eight miles along a nine mile front: but instead of copying the Germans' and their own earlier tactics, the advance was halted in what became known as a bite and hold strategy. Bite and hold was then pursued in stages along the British lines, seriously wrong-footing the enemy.[362]

Back in Calais, promoting Allied unity was the major task in hand. On 4 July US Independence Day was celebrated with a lunch for Allied Officers at the Hotel Sauvage and ten days later 1,000 Allied troops took part in an International Review. On 21 July Belgian National Fete Day was celebrated with sports but on a less concordant note that evening 200 Scottish troops broke into the town and demonstrated against the Military Police. On the next day the situation worsened and the police billets in Rue Amsterdam were loot-ed. In response, half a battalion of the East Lancashire regiment were posted in the town bringing the disturbances to a swift end: after five nights on patrol the East Lancs were called off.

The restoration of order in Calais was extremely timely. On 4 August the

British military in Calais held church services to commemorate the fourth anniversary of the War's commencement and on the following day the King made what was to be his fifth and last visit to France during the War.[363] He arrived in Calais at 12.30pm and proceeded to lunch in the Officers Club in the old Grand Hotel. After lunch he motored to Vendroux and inspected the facility before leaving to visit General Plumer at British 2nd Army HQ. Amusingly there is only an account of the King's visit in General Plumer's diary; the corresponding entry in Colonel Radcliffe's diary merely consists of a line of stars. Perhaps he wanted to avoid telling GHQ that the Royal Engineer officers in Calais had a day off work on account of it.

Regrettably the omission robs us of knowing exactly what role Colonel Radcliffe and Lieutenants Bracken and Alderson played in the royal visit. However they would certainly have been in charge of the Vendroux part of the visit and it is likely that all of them met the King that day. Whether they managed to attend the lunch in Calais before racing to get to Vendroux before the King is doubtful but they would have known the Officers Club well.

The King's diary for that day reads:

At 2.15 motored to Vendroux where I visited the huge sheds containing stores belonging to the Inland Water Transport, Ordnance Depot, Supply Depot & RE Stores which cover 500 acres & have been created a few months ago.

Following the royal visit to Vendroux a shortage of prison guards is recorded as causing delays in completion of both the ordnance depot and the American stores, although these were in fact completed on 16 August. By 28 August Alderson, now promoted to Captain, was granted one month's special home leave and within ten days Thomas Wilson is referred to as Captain Bracken[364] and promoted in his place as Divisional Officer at Vendroux. The diary then records "Captain Alderson is to go to Zeneghem on termination of leave." In fact when Alderson returned from leave on 26 September he was posted to Ardres, just a few miles away to the south-east.

The sudden turn of events is explained by Alderson's officer file which contains several letters from his doctor relating to this period. These inform both the War Office and Colonel Radcliffe that Alderson needed to receive a course of treatment for what he called "anxiety, nervousness and insomnia." In modern medical terms Alderson was probably suffering from stress and possibly post-traumatic stress disorder. Seemingly his unsympathetic commanding officer thought this was not a valid medical condition and downgraded his role by transferring him away from Vendroux.

Thomas Wilson was doubtless pleased by his promotion to Captain after three years of service but how he felt about being put in charge at Vendroux and losing Alderson as his fellow officer there is far harder to guess. The two of them had worked together there for almost a year. Captain Alderson, who obviously recovered, ended his service as a Major in December 1919 following a final posting in March 1919 to the remnant HQ of British troops in France.

Soon after this promotion, in mid-September, Thomas Wilson went on home leave and during this late September fortnight he and his wife were photographed in the garden at Rampson. He is wearing his new captain's uniform but he has noticeably aged since the summer of 1917 when he was photographed at Lillers.

On the very day that Thomas Wilson returned to Calais, 29 September 1918, the war reached its climax as the Germans were attacked along almost the entire Western Front by each of the Allied armies. As they did so Ludendorff, without reserves and facing a collapsing German armaments industry, warned the Kaiser the war was lost and advised him to seek an immediate armistice. Within days the formidable Hindenburg system of defences was breached, and by 9 October when Cambrai was taken, the Allies were through it in its entirety and into the open country beyond.[365] The German high command opened armistice negotiations as their army retreated through France and Belgium. On 17 October British troops occupied Lille without a shot being fired. By the end of the month the British army reached the River Scheldt.

On 7 November the German armistice delegation was allowed to enter French territory. This sparked world-wide false rumours that the armistice was signed. General Radcliffe in Calais refers to this rumour in his diary entry for this day: in the US, erroneous newspaper headlines were printed on 7 November.

As the Kaiser abdicated, the Canadians entered Mons on the 10 November, the very place where over four years earlier the British Expeditionary Force had first engaged the enemy. That evening the German Government accepted the armistice terms and at 5.10am the German delegates signed.[366] Once they had done so Foch sent a telegram to all allied commanders and his words were transmitted on to both Calais and Vendroux. After such a titanic struggle pursued at almost unimaginable costs the diary references are masterful examples of understatement. General Radcliffe wrote "Armistice signed and hostilities ceased 11am. Town fairly quiet except for French boys." Colonel Radcliffe RE wrote "Order received that all hostilities are to cease at 11am this day."

One reason for the understatement may have been the prevalent feeling within the Allied armies that this was a suspension of rather than end to hostilities. It was a common fear in November 1918 that the Germans had merely obtained a breathing space from which they could regroup and rearm before going on the attack in the spring of 1919 just as they had in previous years. In general the Allies were stunned by the suddenness of the German collapse: their planners had not expected victory until late 1919.

Perhaps surprisingly, in Calais the unexpected suddenness of victory seems to have engendered some resentment among the RE officers that they had been robbed of their huge and still unfinished task of developing the mammoth Vendroux facility. In a letter to his friend the editor of *The Penrith Observer* in 1921 Thomas Wilson highlighted those feelings:

One is sometimes inclined to wonder at the number of people of all kinds one hears, both men who have seen service and civilians express the view that the armistice came anything from a month to three months too soon.

Such sentiments may seem callously indifferent to the further slaughter continued fighting would have entailed but as he says, many felt that the military defeat of the German army on its own territory would have avoided future European problems.

Of course such problems lay far ahead in late 1918. In accordance with the armistice terms the German army immediately withdrew from France, Belgium, Luxembourg and Alsace-Lorraine. On 1 December British troops crossed into Germany and on the 4th reached Cologne and established a zone of occupation covering the entire German west bank of the Rhine. By now, save in the minds of the irredeemably paranoid, the fear of a surprise German counter-attack had finally disappeared.

The immediate effect in Calais was to stop all work on anti-aircraft defences until further orders. Otherwise at Vendroux the German POW's carried on their construction work under guard as previously. In 1918-19 unlike the previous years of Thomas Wilson's service both Christmas Day and New Year's day were dedicated holidays for British forces and on 18 January 1919 the Versailles Peace Conference opened.

Freed from the pressure of hostile operations, and perhaps proud of what they had achieved and their contribution towards victory, the RE officers in Calais started to gather statistics about their work in Calais in February 1919. The statistics for Vendroux are hugely impressive and show that it was not run down until after the Versailles peace treaty was concluded. The figures show that Vendroux was at its height home to 121 officers and 8,823 other ranks. Of these 607 were women, 3,021 were prisoners of war and 2,020 Chinese labourers. In charge of all of these men and women was the RE HQ consisting of just Thomas Wilson plus another officer, and two other ranks who served as their servants at the Château. Further details of life at Vendroux are given in a memo written by Captain Alderson in March 1919 in which he describes the comforts accorded to the 9,000 personnel as follows:

> *bath houses, grounds for sports, various denominational huts, YMCA, YWCA, Cinema, Post Office, and last but not least a Church of England which the Padre created out of an old French Barn by donations of labour and material from everybody who could assist.*

On 17 February 1919 Thomas Wilson went on leave to the UK and was due back on 3 March. He did not return and Colonel Radcliffe, even in peacetime a stickler for compliance with leave, records "Capt. Bracken not having returned from leave to UK telegraphed to his home address and advised HQ Calais base." The entry for the following day reads "Telegram received from Capt. Bracken stating that W.O. had extended his leave and that he would return today."

On the following day Thomas Wilson reported to Colonel Radcliffe at the Calais base. This short extension of leave is unexplained in the War Office paperwork but perhaps Thomas Wilson unlike Colonel Radcliffe was rather more relaxed about his entitlement to leave now that peace was plainly restored. A photograph of his four-year-old son Erik was taken during this period. It shows him wearing Thomas Wilson's uniform which goes down to his ankles. He is supporting himself with a rifle in one hand, saluting with his other and grinning from ear to ear.

Twenty-four years later aged 29, wearing his own uniform as a Lance-Corporal in the Royal Electrical and Mechanical Engineers, he would die in Burma at the hands of the Japanese. Erik, like his father, saw service in France and was evacuated from Dunkirk in 1940. At his death on 3 April 1943 he was serving in Burma with the Royal Scots as a wireless operator when a grenade was thrown into the back of his truck as he communicated with HQ. He is commemorated on both the Brough Church war memorial, that of Appleby Grammar School and in far away Burma where his name along with 20,000 others who have no known grave is listed on the Rangoon Memorial.

On Thomas Wilson's return, Calais was still very much an army town and the band of the Royal Engineers played in the Richelieu Gardens over three days during April 1919 and the Officers Club continued to function nearby. However as the signing of the Versailles Treaty on 28 June approached the numbers of personnel in both Calais and Vendroux was reduced and the facilities were gradually closed up.

After the Treaty was concluded the German prisoners were released and the facilities at Vendroux were dismantled; the materials were sold to the French authorities. However this was evidently a slow process and as late as 17 September 1919 there were sufficient personnel at Vendroux to justify a performance of *The Rivals*. Colonel Radcliffe's diary ends in October 1919 without explanation and seemingly the final pages have gone missing from the file.

General demobilization had commenced on 9 December 1918 and followed a complex and unpopular individual formula rather than the disbandment of entire units. However the Royal Engineers as before and since were given the job of clearing up and resolving the war's many loose ends. In Thomas Wilson's case these were particularly protracted, although unlike many other former civilian officers, there is no suggestion that he attempted to achieve an early release from his commission. He almost certainly considered, as previously, that while he remained of use he must see the job out and his continued absence from his wife and family was, a secondary consideration for him.

His immediate subordinate at Vendroux in late 1919 was temporary Captain McDouall. A mining engineer, born in New Zealand in 1884, he had joined the army on 29 August 1914 as a trooper in the 2nd regiment of King Edward's Horse.[367] During 1915 he moved up the ranks from Trooper to

Lance Corporal, to Corporal and finally to Lance Sergeant before being granted a commission in the Royal Engineers in early 1916. His file shows he left
the army in November 1919 and retained the rank of lieutenant. He complained about this demotion but as he had not held the temporary rank of
Captain for the required period of six months he was ineligible to retain it on
relinquishment under the relevant Army Order.

McDouall's case illustrates a common if undignified scramble for promotion and honours before the BEF in France was finally disbanded. Field
Marshall Haig, left with little else to do, fuelled this jobbery and self-seeking
culture at GHQ in those last days in France. In this Thomas Wilson played no
part probably because of his natural modesty or because he considered it
ungentlemanly. He may also have been confident in his 55th year of his future
professional career without the need for baubles and a higher military title.

As McDouall was discharged ahead of him, Thomas Wilson was the last
officer out of Vendroux on the final day of 1919 and as such he was responsible for the handover to the French. As he travelled home in uniform on New
Year's Day 1920 he had completed a period of service of exactly four years
and four months, just like the conflict period of the Great War itself. By virtue
of the vicissitudes of Army life and through no reluctance of his own he had
matched those of his fellow countrymen lucky enough to survive the entire
conflict. Surely as he crossed the channel for the last time and returned to
civilian life he thanked God for not being among the countless millions of
dead and injured.

20 – A LAND FIT FOR HEROES?

On his arrival at Rampson on New Year's Day 1920 it is easy to imagine him being greeted by a 'Welcome Home' banner made by his children. His arrival, depending as it did on the Anglo-French handover at Vendroux, would have been expected. It was doubtlessly anticipated with high excitement by his younger children, the youngest, Erik, at five, only vaguely knowing his father from brief periods of home leave.

However the celebrations would not have lasted very long. Throughout the war his wife and large family had lived on his capital and investment income as a necessary supplement to his military pay and even that had now ceased. Therefore with a wife and six children to support, he needed to rapidly re-establish his civilian career.

This was particularly so as his domestic expenses had increased in 1918-19 because of the expense of his children's schooling. In the autumn term of 1918 his eldest daughter entered boarding school and his eldest son started to board at Appleby. Dorothy did so in order to continue her education beyond sixteen which Kirkby Stephen Grammar School then only provided for the very few girls destined for university.[368] The place selected for her instead was Polam Hall School in Darlington where she was to spend a year and two terms. Founded as a school for the daughters of Quaker families in 1848, it had been on the Polam site since 1858. Polam Hall had originally been built as a private mansion with extensive grounds to the south of the town in 1794, and it made a most attractive school.[369] In 1919 the school, by then far from exclusively Quaker, was described as "a commodious building standing in 23 acres of ground" giving a "liberal education" in a "home-like character." The non-academic nature of its syllabus was not hidden:

The Departments include:– Conservatoire for Musical Study; Studio for Advanced Art Work; Domestic Economy School; Training Department for Kindergarten Teachers and Nursery Governesses. Special attention is given to the health of the pupils and to their physical culture.[370]

The sixth form fees at Polam included a summer stay in the Swiss Alps, which Dorothy took in the summer of 1919. These decisions about his elder children's education would have been taken or sanctioned by Thomas Wilson in France and communicated home. He had known of Polam since the 1880s when the old Quaker girls school in Kendal had transferred to Polam in 1888.

A strong believer in the benefits of education and aware that his own professional success had depended upon his schooling rather than significant money or connections, he was to ensure that his children (with one exception) remained in education until at least seventeen, regardless of the cost or their abilities. On his return from France, his youngest children Betty and Erik were at school at the local South Stainmore primary school a short walk away. His middle children Mary and Jack were in the local grammar schools of Kirkby Stephen and Appleby and thus obliged to travel daily by rail from Barras Station. The 1920 North Eastern Railway timetable illustrates their journey: departing Barras 8.13 they arrived at Kirkby Stephen in ten minutes but for Jack going on via a different line, there was only five minutes to change trains for Appleby where he would arrive at 8.49, before dashing from station to school. Returning at 4.54 he met his sister on Kirkby Stephen station at 5.15 and they reached Barras at 5.38. To us it seems a long school day and their journey was always prone to delays and cancellations. It is scarcely surprising that Robert, already promisingly clever, boarded at Appleby and so avoided the vagaries of the train service, as soon as he entered the senior school in 1918.

The combination of these complex school arrangements and his own great love and pride in the Stainmore area ruled out the family's return to a house in Newcastle. Also Thomas Wilson would have rapidly realised that the city of Newcastle was a very different place from what it had been in 1915. The Armistice had led to huge lay-offs in the great armaments factories and ship-yards of the Tyne. More generally a combination of unemployment, poverty, a rising Labour Party and assertive Trade Union movement led to serious fears for social unrest and even Bolshevik-inspired revolution breaking out in the larger cities of post-war Britain. Having removed his family from the threat of enemy aerial bombing in 1915 he was not about to expose them to fresh threats in 1920. However, without obvious other possibilities for earning, and solely dependent upon his contacts in Newcastle, he had no choice for himself but to return there and re-open his office at 40 Grey Street. As a result, and for the rest of his life, he would divide his week between Stainmore and Newcastle where he converted one of his rear office rooms into a bedroom. With three whole floors of empty office space it is unsurprising that he chose to utilise some of it in this way. Also after Africa and the Western Front sleeping on a camp bed in the office was probably no hardship. His office was not unsuitable to sleep in, having been originally designed and used as the Queens Head Hotel. As a result all of its rooms had high ceilings, fireplaces and the rear courtyard allowed plenty of light to the rear. Those living in the slums of Newcastle would probably have considered his sleeping quarters quite palatial.

When he first returned there, later in January, his dust-sheeted office must have seemed like a time capsule. Untouched for almost five years, while so many momentous events were occurring elsewhere, the view from his windows of the architectural glories of Grey Street might have suggested that Newcastle was unchanged. However, elsewhere in what was now[371] a city of 275,000, dreadful poverty and desolation were easily found. Henry Mess in his *1928 Survey of Industrial Tyneside* did not hide the contrasts in 1920s Newcastle:

It ranges from an unusual fineness of its principal streets and its parks and open spaces, down to huge stretches of the most dismal squalor.

Much of that squalor had been caused by the post-Armistice dislocation of the local economy, which had long been geared towards munitions manufacture. The Elswick shells, recently needed so much, were now not only superfluous but, in an age of disarmament and 'perpetual peace' guaranteed by the League of Nations, positively reviled.

Mess's *Survey* loftily concluded that the pre-War position of Tyneside was precarious "because so much of the industry was due to the race in armaments which could not continue indefinitely." A further problem for the armaments industry was that little of the plant was re-usable. However mistakes were certainly made: despite the manufacture of military aircraft on Tyneside, no-one seems to have considered conversion to civilian aircraft manufacture. A further economic problem was that in the great race 'for ships and shells' the traditional merchant shipping export market of Tyneside had been neglected and by 1919 largely taken over by foreign competitors.

How clearly Thomas Wilson saw all this in early 1920 is unclear. His pressing concern was to re-open his office. Poverty and unemployment were not on display in Grey Street or his other Newcastle haunts: the Town Hall, Union Club and Institute of Mining Engineers. In these three places and others, he re-established himself with his professional and business contemporaries. Unlike him, age had barred them from a military role in the War and this probably made him more of an object of interest and opened doors which, had he been absent for other reasons, might have proved difficult. In 1920, society was full of military titles and his possession of one certainly did not impede the restoration of his former career at the age of 55. The high rates of unemployment did at least mean that he would have had no difficulty re-staffing his office with clerks. In doing so, he preferred Westmerians and now, additionally, former servicemen.

Away from Newcastle the state was busy tying the ends of his military service. On 26 January 1920, the King initialled "GRI" a minute giving him the permanent rank of Captain and this was gazetted in London in early February. Twelve days later the social column of the *Penrith Observer* carried the following announcement:

> *Captain T W Bracken RE, Stainmore has relinquished his commission on completion of his service and retains the rank of Captain. Captain Bracken served in the Royal Engineers with the 2nd, 3rd and 5th Armies in France and on the Flanders Front 1915 and latterly has been in charge as Division Officer at Viendroux (sic) in the north of France.*

In May he received his medals in a War Office registered packet, which he retained along with the enclosed notices as to the wearing of them. This retentiveness demonstrates that, unlike some, he had no wish to forget the War and its sacrifices. For instance, after his return the Bracken family tea caddy was a 1916 4.5 inch Howitzer shell converted by and purchased from a member of the Chinese Labour Company based at Vendroux.

In June 1920 he became actively involved in raising money for new windows in St. Stephen's Church, Stainmore, which would include the War Memorial Window and the stained glass he had brought back from the ruined churches of France and Belgium.

Travelling back and forth between Stainmore and Newcastle in a regular way that we would refer to as 'weekly commuting' was pretty unusual in the 1920s. Whether he did it enthusiastically is unclear but the situation left him with little choice and Polly, as so often before, amply demonstrated an ability to manage without him. Also his self-employment gave him the flexibility to extend his time in either place as the need arose, so avoiding a tie to Friday evening and Monday morning rail journeys. The 1920 weekday[372] timetable meant that he could leave Newcastle at 3.45, change at Darlington and still arrive at Barras at a civilised 6.24pm.

A combination of nostalgia and a general love of rail travel meant that he apparently did not mind the journeys irrespective of weather and not infrequent disruption of the timetable. Newcastle's Central Station provided as magnificent an opening as any and at its end he had the stunning view from Barras Station which his friend the Reverend Thomas Westgarth (Vicar of Stainmore 1911-1929) encapsulated in verse:

High up on Barras Side –
I stand to view the scene
And ask can they be real,
Or is it just a dream?

For 'tis here John Martin stood
To paint 'The Plains of Heaven'
And sure no grander scene
To mortals ere was given.

Once his routine at Rampson was settled he became an important figure in his local community. In the spring of 1920 he became the first secretary of the Stainmore Parochial Church Council which, along with many others at this time, was established to democratise the Church of England by increasing lay involvement in parish church affairs. He retained the post until his death. He also encouraged Polly to commence weather recording at Rampson. To enable her to do this he created a rain gauge in the garden which she measured daily and used to produce an annual weather report which she wrote for the *Penrith Observer* in early January each year.

The same newspaper records his involvement in numerous local projects from 1920 onwards as well as featuring many letters and articles he wrote for the paper. A frequent contributor to the paper's columns in pre-war days, once it was clear that he would in part be based there, he wasted no time in offering to become the newspaper's Stainmore correspondent.

His first contribution in the 22 June 1920 edition was a relatively mundane report of the Stainmore Church Bazaar organised by the new church council to raise money for the new windows. The event was opened by the daughter of the late Canon Irving whose first incumbency had been Stainmore where he ministered from 1857-1866. In 1865 he had baptised Thomas Wilson before being replaced by John Wharton the following year.

His report of the event also indicates that Mrs Bracken was in charge of stalls and Miss Dorothy Bracken, home from Polam, presided over "competitions and other departments." The evening ended not unusually with a dance but what was unusual was that his first piece was highlighted by the editor in his column 'Facts and Gossip of the Week' in which he commented that "Stainmore has been a kind of ecclesiastical Cinderella in this diocese, its successive vicars never getting much notice... from the powers that be." With the combination of a sympathetic editor and Thomas Wilson's contributions, Stainmore was definitely restored to notice as the twenties progressed. Amusingly, in successive weekly editions the editor advised correspondents and contributors that there was insufficient space to include contributions at all or in whole, but space was evidently made for Thomas Wilson's often loquacious pieces. The strength of their friendship is also shown by the editor variously referring to him, in print, as "an esteemed Stainmore correspondent" or "a well known North Westmorland gentleman."

In November 1920 he wrote his first post-War letter to the editor for publication under the pseudonym "Salient, Stainmore." In it he reminded former servicemen in the area of their entitlement to a Government-sponsored smallholding and the imminent deadline for applications for these. The scheme was a part of Lloyd George's programme to provide 'a land fit for heroes to live in' and was designed to make those ex-servicemen who wanted the land, self-sufficient in food, and provide them with a modest income. As Thomas Wilson pointed out, the take-up rate in both Cumberland and Westmorland had been low and for purely altruistic reasons, as the guise of anonymity surely proves, he wanted to avoid them missing out on their entitlement. It demonstrates his compassionate concern for the welfare of those who had served in the War and the difficult conditions they now faced. He, like many officers who survived the conflict, was far more aware of the home conditions of his men on completion of his service than he had been on enlistment.

By contrast the Durham and Northumberland coalfields enjoyed something of a boom after the signing of the Armistice. During the War they had effectively been nationalised, with the owners' profits guaranteed at a set level and the miners' wage rates agreed by the Government. That benign industrial environment was to continue into 1921. The coal export market also boomed in the absence of foreign competition. The War had been fought in the French and Belgian mining areas and in consequence their coal industry lay in ruins, while the coal exporters of Germany and Russia had been badly affected by the chaos that had enveloped both of those countries. Poland, a new country created at Versailles and possessing considerable coalfields was still finding its feet. This situation left British coal in a dominant position in the European market and wholesale export prices surged as a result.[373]

While they did so, they favoured Thomas Wilson in his efforts to re-establish his career. His long connection with both the coal producers and Newcastle's coal exporters, helped him back to a second successful phase as a civilian engineer. The extent of his professional re-engagement in the coalfields of Durham and Northumberland is confirmed by a lengthy letter he wrote to the editor of the *Penrith Observer* from Newcastle on 18 April 1921. Its context was a strike which had commenced on the final day of Government control[374] of the industry and which was effectively an attempt to force the Government to nationalise the industry and avoid the pay cut which the mine owners had indicated would be necessary. More alarmingly for the Government, the Miners Union was allied with the railwaymen and transport workers in a Triple Alliance and the call was made and answered for a united struggle to force a nationalisation of the mines. With the Union-allied Labour Party committed to a socialist programme of nationalisation, the threat in respect of the mines was seen as just the start and Lloyd George's Government was determined not to concede on nationalisation.

With national paralysis in prospect, the Government declared a state of emergency on 8 April and started to set up a special defence force to support the police in maintaining the law. At the same time rail timetables were slashed to preserve stocks and emergency regulations limited domestic coal consumption. Evidently many accepted this was indeed a national emergency, as within ten days 75,000 had enlisted for the defence force and recruitment was suspended. As the defence force filled with volunteers and in an emergency environment, Thomas Wilson provided his views of the situation on the ground in the local coalfields. He did so, as he had before 1915, anonymously but the editor described him as "a well known North Westmorland gentleman, who is in close touch with the Northumberland and Durham Coal trade, and who wrote to us yesterday from Newcastle" and many of his readers would have easily identified the correspondent.

His views on the strike are balanced, measured and perhaps surprisingly impartial. Long experience had obviously aroused a strong affection for the miners of the north-east and he reserves his condemnation for the national leaders of the Miner's Federation:

> *General observation in Northumberland and Durham and conversations with those on both sides of the table, confirms the conclusion that the root of the strike trouble is not in these areas. If it were not that the situation is so grave, the general attitude locally would be almost ludicrous. There is scarcely a man one has spoken to who is not prepared to agree to SOME reduction, although not to 5s a day, nor anyone on the owners' side that does not admit a less reduction than that originally demanded might be agreed to. Yet nothing is being done to negotiate terms; the pits are idle, and both sides are sitting still, nursing their loss... As far as Durham and Northumberland are concerned the most marked feature of the strike is the entire absence of ill-will; perfect peace prevails at the collieries. As an official remarked to me yesterday, "no one would know there was a strike on, but we are knowing it from the work we are having to do."*
>
> *One's conclusion is that left to themselves, in Northumberland and Durham, there would have been no strike. Terms would have been arranged. There is no feeling of personal grievance prevailing, such as one has noticed in former strikes; it is a case of following the Federation's lead, and that is by no means a homogeneous body. It has its parties and cliques like the Parliament at Westminster.*

He then proceeded to identify the root of the problem as the Federation's demand for a national pool, into which all the profits of British mines would be pooled, upon which those mines making a loss would draw, and from which the miners' wages would be equalised across the nation. Having explained the plan to the reader, he states that many miners were not clear about it at all but felt it their duty to support their leaders' policy. Far from condemning them for slavishness he applauds their reservation:

> *Later, they will no doubt form their own conclusions by results, for the north country miner is essentially a practical person, nor by any means backward in expressing himself if he thinks he has been led badly or misled.*

His real venom is aimed at the rumour-mongers and propagandists who apparently had sought to deter men from joining the emergency defence force by saying that war had broken out again and they would be sent abroad to fight. In this he identifies far more sinister and dangerous agents than trade unionists:

This rumour rather points to some of the underground influences of unrest, foreign and Sinn Fein, which have been so active for some time, as fire raising in farmyards in the Blyth area, attempts on bonded stores, and the burning of Gosforth Aerodrome and elsewhere, have shown, and to whom the strike is a little godsend to be made the most of, to serve other ends, and as a means to incite disturbances.

With these forces at work he was obviously unsurprised that many striking miners had volunteered for the defence force and had nothing but admiration for the state's local display of its forces and weaponry:

The other day four light armoured cars each with its machine gun, parked temporarily in the Bigg Market, Newcastle, and their crews, attracted attention. A fine workmanlike lot they were, as much at home on their job and as business-like as when in France. The military movements in the garrison centre have been noticeable; so have been the men in civilian or other attire in the New Defence Force, to which the mining villages have contributed no small number of men, who found idle time hang heavy on their hands. In spite of clothes, the swing of the march, and the gait and expression, show clearly that it is with many a case of "back to the army again."

In fact it was not. The other branches of the Triple Alliance did not stay out in support of the miners and after thirteen weeks the miners' strike ended in response to the Government granting a £10 million subsidy to ease the drop in wages. In return the miners relinquished their demand for a national pool and, state subsidy apart, the mines remained in private hands.

In November 1921 Thomas Wilson's friend Richard Millican was elected Lord Mayor of Newcastle. He had helped found the Cumberland and Westmorland Society on Tyneside in 1904 (the year he became a city councillor) and had served as its president since 1912. A native of Alston, he was the first Cumbrian Lord Mayor and Thomas Wilson ensured that his election was prominently reported in the *Observer*. Prior to being Lord Mayor he had chaired the council's leading committee, the Watch, and this connection would certainly have eased Thomas Wilson's path back to Town Hall-inspired municipal work, which had formed part of his practice since 1901.

Outside work and without his wife and children to occupy his weekday evenings in Newcastle, he re-joined the committee of the Cumberland and Westmorland Society on Tyneside and was elected vice-president at the 1920 annual meeting – a post he would retain until his death. During his absence, the society had done much for the injured servicemen of the two counties, who were recovering in the city's hospitals, as well as contributing knitted garments and other small comforts to the soldiers serving with regiments associated with Cumberland and Westmorland. In this united war-time environment the society in Newcastle had thrived and in June 1922 Millican hosted the annual conference of the various Cumberland and Westmorland Associations and Societies in Newcastle Town Hall. A dinner in the Mansion House followed the conference. Millican's vice-president, Thomas Wilson, attended both conference and dinner and at the latter listened to and doubtless agreed with the words of the London President:

> *One of the greatest glories of this County Association movement is that in a country torn asunder by partisan and denominational differences it can get people of differing views to come together with their place of birth as a common magnet, actuated and animated only by love and by affection for the fair counties from which they sprang. Local or county patriotism is the righteous and God-given feeling which is the root of true valour, patriotism and civilisation. It is county patriotism which is the foundation and feeder of national patriotism, just as national patriotism is the foundation and feeder of Imperial patriotism.*

County patriotism was certainly of great importance to Thomas Wilson and whatever the full nature of their professional ties, in public, it was the Lord Mayor's link to Cumberland and its sister county which mattered most. Displaying an impressive knowledge of local history and its prominent personalities, he wrote, following the Conference, a short article for the *Observer* published on 13 June 1922:

> *An esteemed Stainmore correspondent writes: at the Conference of the Cumberland and Westmorland Association of Great Britain reference was made to the president of the Tyneside Association being the first*

316

Cumbrian Lord Mayor of Newcastle. ...Some time ago a long and interesting list was given in the 'Observer' of Bishops who had their birthplace in one or other of the two sister counties, and municipal honours have not been wanting. Amongst others who have gone out, in their youth, from the land of lakes and fells and attained distinction, two Lord Mayors recur to memory – one from Appleby, Sir James Whitehead, Lord Mayor of London in 1889. The other Sir Cuthbert Buckle, Brough, also a Lord Mayor in the latter part of the reign of Queen Elizabeth and who by his will dated 28 June 1594, left funds towards providing a school in his native parish.

In articles such as this and others he wrote, he exhibits an impressive and bookish interest in the history of his county. In another piece he wrote for the same paper in February 1926 he comes across as a diligent researcher, quietly locked in his study but with an obvious eagerness to share the fruits of his labours:

Today on looking through some old papers in search of a notice issued jointly by the proprietors of the Tan Hill, Kettle Pot, Barras and North Stainmore coal pits, seventy or eighty years ago, which might supplement the interesting article and notes in your column on the subject, I came across the enclosed, which evidently relates to some of the prospecting mentioned, which was done after the South Durham and Lancashire Union Railway, as it was then called, was built:

"For some time past boring has been prosecuted at Stainmore, and it is most satisfactory to find that there is now every reason for believing that the most valuable veins of kidney ore exist near Barras Station, a locality fixed upon, and maintained as the most likely for the metal, by Mr Pease MP, and those united with him in the arduous and protracted search."

With his knowledge and interest in history he must have read, with regret, the *Observer's* extensive 1920s coverage of the disposal of the local landed estates, together with the great houses, upon which they were centred. The Westmorland world of his boyhood and middle age was fast disappearing, to be replaced by a far more fractured and fractious one. The country estate with which Thomas Wilson had the closest and longest family association was Ingmire. Surprisingly, given Sedbergh's location some way outside the *Observer's* area, the sale of Ingmire Hall and its estate merited an editorial, which if not actually written by him, was almost certainly written at his prompting:

The passing of an Historic Local Estate cannot help but create a feeling of sadness. In the majority of cases, the explanation is that the ever increasing burden of taxation and other outgoings, makes the continuance of the old order impossible. Although the reasons behind Major J H Upton's decision to dispose of his beautiful mansion and other houses of historical interest extending together over 4,430 acres are known only to him, the event marks the severance of some very old ties. Ingmire was long the home of the Otway family but when the main branch passed to an heiress the estate passed to the Uptons an ancient Cornish family. The Otways had been in the area since Richard III and there are complete records of them since Henry VII.

The estate's farms and houses, including Bowersyke and Moss Foot, were sold off in small lots but the Hall and 23 acres of surrounding parkland were purchased by the Liverpool baronet Sir John Harmood Banner.[375] However the hope of preservation this inspired was short-lived. After Banner's death in 1927 Ingmire had several rapid changes of ownership, before being destroyed by fire, possibly deliberately,[376] in July 1928.

Faced with such dramatic and to him unwelcome change, his consolations were his constant faith and his family, and in the academic achievements of his eldest son he took especial pride. Following his return from France he watched on Speech Day as Robert received his school year prize in each of his final three years at school from, respectively, the Provost of Queen's College Oxford, the Bishop of Carlisle, and the Bishop of Hereford. He passed his School Certificate in the First Class and with distinctions awarded in French, Chemistry and Mechanics. The school also awarded him the Lord Lowther Major Scholarship in 1921 and a School Exhibition following his leaving the school in July 1922. Together these awards were worth £70 a year for three years and would have been a significant contribution towards the costs of university.

With their elder brother's brilliant school record setting the standard his younger brothers Jack and Erik probably felt eclipsed from the start. Erik did not overlap with Robert at Appleby but the headmaster thought he compared most unfavourably to his elder and even middle brother and wrote "poor progress" on the general comments section of his school record when he left, aged seventeen, in 1931. In 1943 another headmaster recorded, underneath this comment, his army service record following his death in the Burmese jungle.

The combination of Robert's academic record and his school's ancient connection with Queen's College Oxford would probably have gained him a place there but instead, whether as a result of his father's persuasion or not, he matriculated as a student of Armstrong College, Durham University, in the Michaelmas term of 1922. Armstrong College was adjacent to their former home in Eldon Street, Newcastle and had been co-founded by his father's Institute of Mining and Mechanical Engineers and Durham University in 1871. Robert's university choice certainly gave his father some family company during his weekdays in Newcastle. His course of study was for a BSc. in Applied Science, specialising in Civil Engineering with a view to eventually joining his father's practice in the city. Whether Robert actually lodged in his father's office at 40 Grey Street is unclear but he certainly spent many of his spare hours there and on his father's recommendation was admitted as a student member of the Institution of Civil Engineers in November 1922.

That same autumn, following bazaars, fetes, concerts and private subscriptions, including a substantial one from Thomas Wilson, sufficient money had been raised to proceed with the new windows for St. Stephen's Church, Stainmore. The church council approved the design of a three light war memorial window by Pearce and Cutler of Birmingham and applied to Carlisle for a faculty approving the work, which the Diocesan Chancellor granted in December. On Friday 1 June 1923 the windows were unveiled by Major Ingham of Augill Castle and dedicated by the Bishop of Carlisle, Dr Henry Williams.[377] The *Observer* permitted Thomas Wilson one and a half columns to describe the service and the day's events. His account includes an almost verbatim account of the Bishop's sermon in which the former Oxford academic[378] bravely tackled the subject of the religious meaning of the war. Its reproduction suggests that either Thomas Wilson was a master of shorthand or, rather more likely, the Bishop handed him a copy of it afterwards.

In his account, he accutately describes the war memorial window, placed in the south wall, as:

> *of excellent design and workmanship, and is much above the average for a country church. The two large panels contain the figures of St. Michael and St. George, and the wings are embellished with national and imperial symbols of a very appropriate character.*

As he hints the window was an extremely lavish one but particularly so given it commemorated only two men of the parish who were killed in the war. They were farmer's sons and "most curiously" as Thomas Wilson put it, cousins bearing the same name. One George Alderson of Calva, had died at Passchendaele in October 1917 while serving with the Border Regiment. The other George Alderson had died of wounds at Barras in September 1919, following service with the Loyal North Lancashire Regiment. Although he chose to remain silent about it, another 'curiosity' was that one victim had died in the very house where Thomas Wilson had been born and the other George Alderson had been born in another historic Brunskill property, Calva.

Also unveiled that day was the remodelled and enlarged west end window and it was this which now contained the fragments of stained glass that Thomas Wilson had carried home from France and Belgium. With typical modesty his account leaves his own contribution without attribution:

An interesting feature of this new window is that the central panel is composed of pieces of glass that were picked up by a Stainmore officer during the war at Ploegstaert, Neuve Eglise and Arras. One of the pieces is slightly cracked by the heat from an exploding shell.

In the west window containing the fragments he retrieved, the face of an angel, a flower and trefoil foliage are easily identifiable and as well as being cracked, the glass of one piece has actually bubbled in the heat of the explosion.

After the service and unveiling, refreshments were served in the adjacent school which had been:

tastefully decorated with national emblems and flags of the empire by Miss Mabel Teasdale, assisted by Miss Betty Brunskill Bracken.

At this gathering the Rural Dean of Appleby and Kirkby Stephen, Canon Harris, who had served as an Army Chaplain from 1915-18 spoke of the men's death being "an example of noble courage and a memorial of virtue unto the nation." The lengthy newspaper account ends with an almost lyrical account of his view of the church, seen next day, before he wrote his column:

On Saturday, bathed in the sunshine of a perfect June day, the tasteful interior of this little and remote church seemed in full harmony with its setting, whilst seen from the green velvet of the uplands, spangled with wild pansies, anemones, and buttercups, the dale and valley of the Eden, backed in the distance by the Lakeland mountains, looked at their best.

21 – POLITICS REVIVED

The General Election of December 1918 was the first since December 1910 and was fought on revised constituency boundaries. One of many revisions was the reduction in Westmorland's representation from two MPs to a single member. Colonel Weston, the old Conservative member for South Westmorland was returned for the new seat. Weston had been in Parliament since 1913 when he won South Westmorland in a by election and he was again returned without a contest in November 1922 – which Bonar Law's Conservatives won with a majority of 79.

In December 1923 another General Election occurred and Weston was returned for the third time without a contest. Nationally the election led to the Conservatives losing 91 seats. In late January 1924 the Conservative Government resigned so paving the way for Britain's first socialist government, albeit only in a minority in the Commons. With such a fractured Parliament, nobody expected the new Government led by Ramsay MacDonald to last long and Colonel Weston, unwilling to risk his first fight since 1913, rapidly signalled his intention to stand down. The Association selected a new candidate in April 1924.

The man selected was the Hon. Oliver Stanley, the 28-year-old younger son of the 17th Earl of Derby and a youthful war hero who had won both the Military Cross and the Croix de Guerre in France. His Tory pedigree was almost without equal. His father had been Secretary of State for War from 1916-18; his grandfather Governor General of Canada and a prominent politician under both Disraeli and Salisbury. His great-grandfather had been Prime Minister three times. Although the Stanleys are usually more associated with Lancashire they did have a Westmorland connection, from ownership of the Witherslack estate, which was presented to Oliver Stanley by his father in 1922.

In 1920 Stanley had married Lady Maureen Vane-Tempest-Stewart in Durham Cathedral. She was the first daughter of the 7th Marquess of Londonderry. Born in 1900 she had been brought up amid the splendours of the Londonderry estates of Mount Stewart, County Down and Wynyard Park, County Durham. Her mother, Edith, Marchioness of Londonderry (1878-1959) was one of the great political hostesses of the day and holder of the most lavish parties at Londonderry House, in Park Lane.

By this marriage two great Tory political dynasties were tied and it is scarcely surprising that the Westmorland selection committee were dazzled by this young, glamorous aristocratic couple, with so many great political connections.

As had been anticipated Ramsay MacDonald's government did not last long. A general election was held on 29 October 1924. In Westmorland, Labour fielded its first ever candidate. He was roundly defeated by Oliver Stanley who gained a majority of 10,693: he was to hold onto the seat until 1945. Nationally too the Conservatives did well and Stanley Baldwin became Prime Minister for the second time.

In Newcastle Tory fortunes had ceased to mirror the national outcome and the city and the north-east was gradually becoming a Labour heartland. The Conservatives had won the new seat of Newcastle Central in 1918 after being unrepresented in the city since 1906 but this was to be the high water mark of Tory fortunes there. Labour took the seat in 1922 and then continued to hold it in the general elections of 1923, 1924 and 1929. The Conservatives only regained the seat in the grave economic emergency of 1931, and in this situation Thomas Wilson and his 350 fellow members of the Union Club[379] in Westgate Road were in possession of what was increasingly Newcastle's last Tory redoubt.

Whether it was this obvious political trend in his adopted city, the unwelcome novel existence of a Labour Government, or the danger posed by the long untested Tory loyalty of Westmorland, that stirred him again to activism is unclear. It may well have been a combination of all three that rallied him to the Tory cause for the first time since 1910.

At Rampson, the day before the general election, tragedy struck when Mary Bracken died suddenly of what proved to be encephalitis lethargica, or sleepy sickness, aged just nineteen. Always considered delicate she had not been sent to board at Polam like her elder sister and as her younger sister would from 1928-29, but was kept at home under her mother's care when she left Kirkby Stephen Grammar School in 1921. At home she continued to study and assisted with the daily recording of the rain gauge. Although never strong, her death came as a great shock, particularly to her younger sister who was now reluctant to go to bed, in case she also never woke up. Thomas Wilson and Polly, born in an age where youthful death was common and having experienced their share of it, probably found it easier to come to terms with. Her funeral and burial took place at St. Michael's, Brough on 31 October. Mary alone had written and signed the 1922 and 1923 rainfall reports which the *Observer* then published. In January 1925, her mother put both their names at the bottom of her report for 1924 in a final tribute to her young daughter.

The rainfall for December 1924 and January 1925 was particularly extreme, resulting in significant flooding in both Appleby and Carlisle. Polly recorded the December 1924 rainfall total as 6.42 inches, the second highest December figure since she had begun her records in 1920. It was followed by 2.6 inches, much of it falling as snow, during the first five days of 1925 and 1.3 inches recorded over the 24 hours of 2 January. Curiously though her rainfall total for 1924, 37.40 inches, was the second lowest she recorded. The highest was 50.15 inches for 1927. Over the ten years for which Polly's readings are available the average annual rainfall was a whopping 44 inches recorded in her Rampson garden gauge, 980 feet above sea level. Again over a ten year average, she recorded some rainfall on 247 days per year. Putting these figures in context, the current London annual average is 23.3 inches falling over an average of 153 days.

On one of Stainmore's rare fine days in early September 1925 the Westmorland Conservative Association held a Conservative Festival at Augill Castle. Augill 'Castle', in fact an 1841 mansion in the baronial style, was two miles from Rampson and its owner, Major Ingham, a friend of Thomas Wilson's. For the festival, a platform was erected in the courtyard of the castle for use during the principal event, Oliver Stanley's speech. Other than his speech, there were cake and other stalls and the inevitable tea tent for refreshments. The day's proceedings were extensively reported by the *Penrith Observer's* 'Stainmore correspondent.' The subject of Stanley's speech was the coal industry – perhaps surprisingly, given where he was and the entirely rural nature of his constituency. In it he gave an impressively detailed account of the fortunes of coal mining since the war and the ominous situation it had reached by that summer. Every British mine was losing money and 300,000 miners were out of work. The competition-free days were over. The French and Belgian mines were working again, as were the miners of the Ruhr who had gone back to work after the end of the French occupation of the area. In Oliver Stanley's view, shared by large sections of his party, the days of Government subsidy must end and the only solution was for the miners to accept a cut in their wages. Prime Minister Baldwin had recently defused the difficult situation by ordering a Royal Commission into the matter and, pending its report, a temporary coal subsidy; but the seeds of the following year's General Strike had been sown.

What Stanley did not say and may not have appreciated was that part of the problem was caused by the Conservative government's recent restoration of the gold standard at its pre-1914 level. This led to sterling being seriously over-valued and in consequence British coal being highly uncompetitive in foreign markets. Nonetheless Stanley's speech, as reported by Thomas Wilson, was considered and far from an easy subject for a backbench MP to tackle. It was also, with one exception, very unfamiliar territory for his audience and not even within the speaker's particular experience. As such there must be at least a suspicion that Thomas Wilson had played some part in the genesis of the speech.

In the following month he was heavily involved in the celebrations of the 21st anniversary of the founding of the Cumberland and Westmorland Association in Newcastle or the 'Coming of Age of the Tyneside Association' as the *Observer* headed its report. The main celebration took the form of a Saturday evening dinner for 240 members and guests at the County Hotel in Newcastle. The next day a church service was held at St. Thomas the Martyr, Barras Bridge, to give thanks for the association and its work.

The guest of honour at the dinner was the Lord Mayor of Newcastle; the City Sheriff and Chief Constables of Newcastle, Sunderland and South Shields also attended. The President, now Alderman Millican, was the principal speaker and in his speech he looked back to the foundation meeting held 21 years earlier to the day, on 10 October 1904, when 70 members had enrolled under Canon Rawnsley's chairmanship. Since then, as Millican proudly recounted, the Tyneside membership had grown to 380. The association was second only to London in age, but since 1904 eleven more associations had been established in Great Britain and five overseas. His speech continued:

Few are left who were present that evening 21 years ago but one of them my Vice-President Captain Bracken is here tonight (applause) and much of the development of the Association in its infancy was due to his valuable assistance.

After Millican, Thomas Wilson rose to propose a toast to "our two bonnie counties." In doing so he said:

they are not only agricultural but filled with incomparable beauty and scenery and I am not surprised that Cumbrians and Westmerians who have had to find homes elsewhere are forming associations across our country and Empire.

Another coming of age in 1925 was Robert Bracken's. Just before his birthday in May he sat his Durham University final exam for which he was awarded the only Engineering course distinction of 1925. Overall, based on three years of exams, he gained a first class degree, which was awarded to him in front of his proud parents in the King's Hall of Armstrong College on 1 July 1925. By then he had already commenced his apprenticeship under his father at 40 Grey Street where they now both lodged and worked during the working week.

As Robert joined his father's practice as an apprentice but with a view to eventually taking it over from his father who had turned 60, one of the pillars of his practice, providing engineering skills to the mining and coal export business, was declining out of existence. As Oliver Stanley had foreseen, the Royal Commission reported in March 1926 that 80% of coal produced in Britain was being sold at a loss. Rejecting nationalisation, the report also recommended an end to public subsidy and concluded that the solution lay with the miners, who must accept a pay cut. Armed with these expected conclusions, the Government was determined not to be intimidated by the Miners Federation and had prepared for a mighty struggle. The struggle came quickly when the mine owners published new terms of employment. Depending on local circumstances the cut in pay varied from 10% to 25% and the owners indicated that if this was not accepted by 1 May the miners would be locked out of the pits. In response the TUC announced a general strike in support of the miners beginning on 3 May which lasted for nine days before the TUC called it off, leaving the miners to struggle on alone.

Unlike in 1921 Thomas Wilson did not go into print on the subject of the strike, possibly because the *Observer*'s size was cut to just four pages in response to the emergency. Its editor, although not using the intemperate language of some newspapers who viewed the situation as tantamount to actual revolution, did regard it as a struggle over whether the elected government or the TUC ran Britain.

Given his views in 1921 it seems safe to assume that Thomas Wilson had great sympathy for the ordinary striking miners who were increasingly reduced to near starvation as the strike continued over seven months. It is equally safe to assume that he had nothing but contempt for their leaders who continued the strike even as foreign coal started to be imported for the first time in British history.

In 1926 there was plenty of trouble and bitterness and this was particularly so in the Durham coalfield which was one of the last areas to hold out against a return to work. The mining village of Chopwell, which he had done so much to create in the 1890s, was now known as Little Moscow on account of its militancy.[380] Gateshead magistrates dealt with 50 cases where Chopwell residents had breached the Emergency Powers Act and the village was pilloried in the press as a hotbed of communism. Of course the lurid headlines hid the human tragedy of the strike. Levels of mining employment never recovered and many strikers were victimised and refused re-employment in the mines on any terms.

Henry Mess in his 1928 *Social Survey of Industrial Tyneside* did not hide the dreadful situation in the mining villages:

> *The present situation is deplorable. Many collieries have closed down; the majority of others are working at a loss. Those men who have employment are working longer hours and earning less than for many years past. Many are unemployed and there can be no doubt that there is considerable distress among them.*

In such conditions it is unsurprising that the description of his work in his father's office from 1925-27 that Robert supplied to the ICE when he applied for Associate Membership contains no reference to mining or coal transport work. He describes his practice as that of a "general municipal engineer" and he particularly mentions work on cement testing, steelwork calculations, surveying, ordnance and drainage plans and quantity surveying.

Although work in the coal industry was now over, there is no indication that this seriously affected the profitability of the practice. Large scale unemployment merely fuelled the Corporation of Newcastle's road building and other infrastructure-related job creation schemes. Even the great Tyne Road Bridge of 1925-28 was a case of job creation by the Newcastle and Gateshead Corporations. Although certainly not involved in its genesis Thomas Wilson doubtless monitored progress on what was the largest single-span bridge in Britain[381] and a design possibly inspired by his mentor George Law's 1876 bridge further upriver at Wylam. As the bridge was built out progressively from each bank until it met in the middle, the spectacle of it under construction must have been an amazing one from the streets just south of his Grey Street office.

Another significant aspect of municipal job creation related to publicly funded house building in the city under the 1919 Housing Act. In February 1920, just as Thomas Wilson was re-establishing himself in the city the *Newcastle Daily Chronicle* was heralding the city council's decision to build 520 new homes. According to Mess's Survey by the end of 1927, 4,773 homes had been built in the city with state assistance and there is evidence that Thomas Wilson was concerned in some of the civil engineering aspects of these house building schemes.

At the end of November 1926, just as the miners' strike was ending, Robert Bracken passed the examination for Associate Membership of the ICE and his father ensured that his success was reported in the personal column of the following week's *Observer*. In June of 1927 Robert completed his two year apprenticeship in his father's office and moved to north London to serve as technical assistant in the Engineer & Surveyor's department of Edmonton Urban District Council. The District Engineer, Cuthbert Brown, was an ICE contemporary of Thomas Wilson's and this was almost certainly how he gained the post. Part of the motivation for this move was to broaden his horizons and expose him to different aspects of surveying and engineering. There was though a more personal reason for his being encouraged to move much further away from home: his persistent attachment to Edith Ewbank. Formed during his schooldays, it had survived both university and Robert's professional training. I am told that Edith was not popular with Robert's parents or sisters who had been schooled with her at Kirkby Stephen. His parents almost certainly felt that at 23 he was too young and inexperienced to marry the only girl he had ever shown an interest in: sending him to London might succeed in persuading him of the wisdom of their views.

While in London, almost certainly through the ICE, Robert learnt of an opening in the engineer's department of the Argentine North East Railway and secured the position in November 1927. This was a remarkable echo of his father's career of railway building abroad and all the indications are that his father was delighted by an opportunity for railway construction work, long absent from the British engineering scene. Robert sailed for the Argentine on 2 December 1927 and four days later his proud father engineered the following announcement in the personal column of the *Penrith Observer*:

> *Mr Robert Bracken, Stainmore, sailed on Friday for South America where he has received an important appointment as an engineer. Mr Bracken is the eldest son of Capt. T. W. Bracken engineer of Newcastle and Stainmore. He was educated at Appleby G.S. and Armstrong College where he took his BSc. degree, afterwards serving his articles in his father's office. He was a member of Stainmore Church where he often read the lessons. His genial manner made him a favourite with all and Stainmore's good wishes go with him.*

With his lifelong enthusiasm for railway building, in his 63rd year Thomas Wilson was understandably delighted by this development; but if he thought it would enhance his own practice when Robert returned to England and mean the end of his son's attachment to Edith he was to be doubly disappointed. After a year of active railway construction on the North East Railway, Robert transferred in 1929 to the office of the Divisional Engineer of the Entre Rios Railway at Basavilbaso. This was a promotion carrying far higher pay and he was to share his good fortune with Edith in far away Appleby. She sailed from Southampton on the mail ship Andes on 14 June 1929 and within days of her arrival in Buenos Aires married Robert. Before his marriage, Robert had acquired Argentinean nationality and had informed his father that here, rather than Newcastle, was where his future lay. Indicatively, henceforth the *Observer*'s announcements in relation to Robert were written by him in the Argentine and telegraphed to Penrith. The first came in mid-July 1929:

> *Marriage. Bracken-Ewbank at Buenos Aires, on the 8th inst. Robert Colman Bracken BSc. Via Y Obras, Entre Rios Rlys, Basavilbaso, Argentina eldest son of Captain and Mrs T. W. Bracken, Stainmore, to*

Edith Margaret, youngest daughter of Mr and Mrs T. Ewbank, Rose Cottage, Appleby (By Cable).

The marriage may not have been welcome at Rampson but the manner of it, abroad and in the absence of the entire family, made it worse. In addition the news that Robert was not just turning his back on his father's Newcastle practice but also England came as a bitter blow. The promise of his brilliant academic career was now to be focussed on Argentina.

Since boyhood Thomas Wilson had been quite used to the idea of force of circumstances leading to relocation abroad but in Robert's case this was entirely unnecessary. Also what he had hoped would be a career-enhancing few years abroad like his own years in Lagos, had unexpectedly become a permanent estrangement. He was never to see his son again.

In May 1930 when the marriage led to the birth of a daughter, Sheila (Celia in Argentina), that event was similarly announced by telegram to the *Observer*:

Births – Bracken – at a Nursing Home, Buenos Aires, on the 8th instant to Mr and Mrs R. C. Bracken a daughter (By Cable)."

She was Thomas Wilson's first grand-daughter and the only grandchild born in his lifetime but he was never to see her. For such an enthusiastic family man, his estrangement from his eldest son must have been a heavy blow. His own unusual upbringing at Barras had been the result of a similar estrangement between his parents and paternal grandparents and now the situation was being repeated 65 years later.

His office in Newcastle must now have seemed bereft and his plans for a father to son engineering practice, perhaps even the beginning of an engineering dynasty, lay in ruins. His second son had determined on a farming career amid the beauty of his father's native county and following the career of so many of his ancestors. His youngest son was just fifteen and bringing home unpromising school reports.

There is no evidence that these disappointments depressed or interfered with his work, his journalism and his other interests and pursuits at Stainmore and Newcastle. As in the War, he just kept soldiering on whatever unwelcome things life threw at him and according to one of his obituaries he "always looked on the bright side of life" and "it was always a pleasure to converse with him."

In 1928 women joined the electorate on equal terms to men when all women aged 21 or over gained the vote (in 1918 when women first voted the franchise was restricted to those aged 30 or over). In consequence, Thomas Wilson was involved in the establishment of the Brough and Stainmore Women Unionists to bring women into active membership of the party and his wife was one of its first members. In September the new Conservative group was addressed by Lady Maureen Stanley. Evidently it was felt the new women members were not yet ready to manage their own meetings and Thomas Wilson presided over their meeting with Lady Maureen that evening in the South Stainmore School.

In the *Observer*'s 1931 view "Lady Maureen is one of the best lady speakers who has ever appeared in Westmorland." However aside from her speechmaking abilities and being their MP's wife, Lady Maureen was a highly glamorous and popular figure. A tenacious supporter of her husband's career, she traversed the county's often treacherous roads in her car to attend innumerable party social events. In many ways like a character in an Evelyn Waugh novel, she had entertained the Prince of Wales at Witherslack Hall and in 1929, on a break from Westmorland, travelled to Hollywood to advise Sam Goldwyn on 'the English Style' and met several film stars. On her return she warned the young lady readers of the *Westmorland Gazette* against being seduced by the superficial glamour of a film career.

Oliver Stanley, when not in London, was almost as assiduous in courting his constituents as his wife was and this included Stainmore, which was evidently not considered a remote corner of the county. As part of his 1929 general election campaign he addressed a Stainmore meeting in which he shared the platform with Thomas Wilson. In an indication of local priorities he was welcomed and described as "a gentleman and a sportsman." He predictably chose to speak on the subject of agricultural policy. This time facing a Liberal opponent, he ridiculed his recent attempt to distinguish Liberal agriculture policy from that of Labour and joked, "if that is so there must be some chalk which tastes very like cheese."

Stanley won the Westmorland election eight days later with a majority of 3,878 over the Liberals. Nationally this election in which the Liberals won only 59 seats confirmed them as the third party. Less welcome to the Conservatives, Labour had won 27 more seats than them and Stanley Baldwin surrendered Downing Street to a Labour Prime Minister for the second time.

22 – REST AT LAST

A few weeks before the May 1929 general election the vicar of Stainmore, Thomas Westgarth, died after a short illness aged 60. In his *Observer* obituary, written by the Stainmore Correspondent, Thomas Wilson paid a fulsome tribute to his friend. He approvingly emphasised the vicar's interests in archaeology, local history and poetry. On a personal level his great gratitude had sprung from Westgarth's ministering to, befriending, and generally watching over his wife and young family during his long absence in France. Unsurprisingly among the floral tributes listed in his report was one from "Captain and Mrs Bracken and family."

In Newcastle he remained highly active in the Cumberland and Westmorland Association. As Vice-President he would preside over meetings when Richard Millican was absent and he had also acted as the Association's auditor since 1924. As the 1920s drew to a close the Tyneside membership was reaching 400 and new associations were being founded in other cities in Britain and the Empire. A universal feature of their meetings across the world was that they closed by singing *John Peel*. The famous Cumbrian huntsman John Peel (1776-1854) had been born in Caldbeck, Cumberland where for 53 years he maintained, at his own expense, a pack of hounds. His fame dates from 1829, when after a day's hunting with his friend John Woodcock Graves, Graves wrote the words of the song by which Peel is still remembered, in the inn at Caldbeck.

In 1869, the choirmaster of Carlisle Cathedral set the words to music making them even more widely known. 1929 was the song's centenary and in that year's columns of the *Penrith Observer* much printers' ink was used discussing the merits of the centenary and how it should best be marked. An early contributor to the discussion was the vicar of Caldbeck who was trenchantly of the view that neither Peel nor his song were suitable or worthy of commemoration. Written in a tavern and doubtless after much drinking, the vicar suggested that Peel the obsessive huntsman had neglected his Christian duty to pray and worship regularly in his local church and as such was not a suitable role model for commemoration. The vicar's letter with its rather Puritan overtones stirred Thomas Wilson into writing a letter spanning an entire column discussing the merits of Peel the man, the importance of the song and his life-long memories of it being sung. As usual with his *Observer* letters he signed it off under a pseudonym; this time "A Dalesman, Newcastle-upon-Tyne, 22 November 1929."

Despite his life-long regard and respect for the clergy of the Church of England he firmly if politely rebuked the vicar of Caldbeck for his views:

> *Regardless of the views, no doubt honestly held by the present worthy Vicar, who perhaps it would be most correct to regard as the "English brother" who "does not understand." There can be no doubt that throughout our world wide Empire, and beyond it, 'John Peel' lives to-day and... soul and song still "goes marching on." It is essentially a folk song of the dales and fells fitted to the race, for it brings back to them the home and the hills whilst it does not betray the deeper sentiments which lie behind.*

In contrast to the vicar his own view was:

> *That there was much good in John Peel there can be no doubt. His memory would not have worn as it has had it been otherwise. The writer has talked often with one who as a boy was present with his father at Peel's funeral. Himself many miles from his Caldbeck home he was still a typical Cumbrian dalesman of the old kind, and he held John Peel in very high esteem.*

Here he is referring to John Birkett, a co-founder and oldest member of the Cumberland and Westmorland Association on Tyneside. As Peel's funeral took place in 1854, Birkett must have been born in the late 1830s or early 1840s. He then proceeds to describe his own pilgrimage to Peel's grave at Caldbeck :

> *Under the shadow of the fells he loved and hunted and of Caldbeck's fine old church, Peel has his own modest yet striking, and singularly appropriate tombstone. I first saw it a few years ago when an unexpected chance took me there. The well-worn 'trod' to Peel's grave was a surprise. It made search unnecessary and told its own tale of remembrance.*

His own memories of the song being sung extended from the Barras of his boyhood, to West Africa, and to France and the Western Front:

In one's early days one has heard 'John Peel' sung in the cow-house to the sound of the milk streaming into the milking can. He has been hummed in the tropical bush with the hum of the mosquitoes. He was heard in the winters of 1915-1918.

In his view Peel had a fitting memorial in the song but the author of its words, John Woodcock Graves, who had emigrated to Van Diemen's Land in 1831 and settled in Hobart where he had died in 1886, was at risk of being lost to history. By 1929 word had reached England that Graves's Tasmanian grave was in poor condition and Thomas Wilson thought him far more in need of a memorial, going so far as to suggest a design:

What could be more appropriate to the memory of the author, keen hunter himself, than the figure of a fox, life size in bronze, in the act of stealing away on first hearing the distant hounds. On a low base of Tasmanian stone, in dimensions within the limits of the grave space, such a monument could be most striking.

The issue of a memorial gravestone was discussed and agreed to at the next year's annual conference of the 'Affiliated Associations and Societies of Cumberland and Westmorland in Great Britain and Overseas.' The 1930 annual conference was held in Newcastle for the first time since 1922. Once again the conference was given a civic welcome by the Lord Mayor and the conference was held at the Town Hall on Whit Monday. The conference's principal decision was to erect a memorial to Graves in Queenborough Cemetery, Sandy Bay, Hobart, where he was buried. Thomas Wilson had anticipated just such an outcome in his 1929 *Observer* letter:

The Cumberland and Westmorland Associations which have sprung up in recent years in the towns of England and Scotland and in the Colonies, and taken 'John Peel' as their song can do much, and I might suggest that the matter of a memorial or memorials is brought to their notices with a view to its discussion at the next conference.

Just as the meetings of the Tyneside Association were a permanent fixture of his life in Newcastle, so the Westmorland Conservative Association and St.

Stephen's, Stainmore, continued to take up a large part of his non-working time in Westmorland. His wife too, even when he was absent, taking advantage of both her children's maturity and the increasing empowerment of women, got more involved herself. From reports in the *Observer* she attended the Women Conservatives' Garden Fete at Appleby Castle in July 1930 and ran a stall in the marquee. In September she was at a Conservative Social in the Brough Memorial Hall, along with Oliver Stanley and Lady Maureen. In April 1927, on its foundation, she had become the first Secretary of the Stainmore Women's Institute and later was elected Vice-President. Evidently the WI concerned itself with higher things than jam and cake baking. Its first meeting consisted of a lecture by the vicar on "the interesting Roman finds which had been made in the parish of Stainmore."

In November 1930 came the news that the vacant living of Stainmore had been offered by the Bishop of Carlisle to the Reverend Charles Holland of Kenninghall, Norfolk and had been accepted. He was instituted and inducted by the Bishop of Barrow-in-Furness, the Archdeacon of Carlisle and the Vicar of Brough in January 1931. Four days later in a particularly wordy piece, extending to half a column, Thomas Wilson described to the *Observer's* readers the then hardly novel formulae of the Prayer Book rite: the reading of the mandate, the laying of hands on the key to the church door, the tolling of the bell to signify possession and the procession with prayers at the font, prayer desk, lessons desk, pulpit and altar. He then went on to describe the events of the social evening which followed and exhibited that although always modest for himself he was not so modest about his own children:

> *The social evening which followed included a theatrical sketch in which Miss Betty Bracken took part. The vicar in speaking after supper referred to his leaving the flat lands of Norfolk and of his being gladly once again in a parish of hills, dales and moors. Music and games followed, before God Save the King ended the evening.*

The early 1930s brought a very severe recession to Britain and by June 1931 unemployment reached 2.7 million. This level of unemployment and the benefit paid to the unemployed resulted in a severe deficit in the public finances and a run on sterling. The combination of these factors caused the implosion of the Labour Government in August 1931. It was succeeded by a National Government containing members of the three main parties and with

Ramsay MacDonald remaining as Prime Minister. However he had succeeded in splitting his party and only twelve Labour MPs stuck with him. In this environment the Conservatives were the main gainers of the spoils of office and one Tory beneficiary was Oliver Stanley who joined the new government as Under Secretary for Home Affairs.

Stanley's new ministerial duties meant that he could not, as expected, open the new Stainmore Parish Hall in early September 1931. Thomas Wilson had contributed both his skills towards its design drawings and financially towards the £600 cost. In the *Observer* edition of Tuesday 8 September 1931, he contributed two thirds of a column to describing the opening. In Stanley's place, the opening ceremony was performed by the conservative peer Lord Hothfield. Hothfield was a descendant of the Cliffords, the ancient Earls of Cumberland, with substantial land and shooting interests on Stainmore. His father had been Lord Lieutenant of Westmorland from 1881 to his death in 1926 when he left his son both Appleby and Skipton Castles, Hothfield Place in Kent, a house in Mayfair and 40,000 acres of land.

It is perhaps surprising that national politics should feature at such an event but his story of the evening includes an account of a letter from Oliver Stanley apologising for his absence which Lord Hothfield had read out, as well as Hothfield's comments on the new National Government as "a jolly fine thing and they all must pull together to put the financial position right."

In the following month the National Government sought its own mandate and candidates tied to the National cause won 554 seats out of a total of 615 in the general election. Oliver Stanley along with 60 other National candidates was returned unopposed. Only 52 non-National Labour candidates were elected and in November the openly partisan *Penrith Observer* trumpeted the 'Rout of the Socialist Party.' As the *Observer's* editor obviously appreciated, MacDonald's conduct had led to destruction of the Labour Party's chances of governing and the remnant National Labour Party in government was merely a prisoner of the Conservatives.

In 1932 unemployment reached its peak of three million of the insured population and in Newcastle as it did so, at the annual meeting of the Cumberland and Westmorland Association, the Chairman in his opening remarks referred to "these hard times of industrial depression." If those conditions eroded the profitability of Thomas Wilson's business there was no outward sign that this was so. His sister's grandchildren remember him at this time as a popular great uncle, for always having half a crown in his pocket for them. At the Tyneside annual meeting he was re-elected Vice-President and auditor and according to the *Observer* report of the meeting "informed the members that it was 38 years ago this week that the first public announcement regarding the formation of the Association appeared in the Press." This mis-reporting by ten years, prompted a letter from him to the *Observer's* editor a week later:

> *The progress made by these Associations throughout the country, and now in parts far away beyond the seas as well is, indeed remarkable. But either by lingual or typographical slip the date of the Tyneside Society's formation is given as 38 years ago. This should be 28 years ago, when some preliminary references first appeared in your columns in April followed by others during the summer, and the foundation of the Society in October 1904, shortly after the formation of the first of these Societies in London.*

He signed himself 'B' of Newcastle-upon-Tyne and the letter shows that he had lost none of his appetite for precision in reporting. It also demonstrates either a most impressive memory or that he was a hoarder of press cuttings.

Although his health was now failing, this did not entirely curtail his social life. His name appeared in the *Observer* a month later when the wedding of the daughter of Major Ingham of Augill Castle was reported. The wedding at St. Michael's, Brough, was conducted by the Archdeacon of Carlisle and the reception in a marquee on the castle terrace is reported over four columns, with a full list of guests and wedding presents. Lady Maureen Stanley, in the absence of her husband, proposed the health of the bride and groom – a London doctor who had served with the Royal Army Medical Corps during the British occupation of the Rhineland. The writer's gushing and breathless style "A brilliant society gathering composed of people prominent in the society of Cumberland and Westmorland..." confirms that he was not the author of the piece. As well as he and Polly, the Stainmore contingent comprised Reverend Holland and the local landowners the Dalston-Ewbankes. The Brackens' present to the couple is listed as an antique silver basting spoon.

Indifferent as ever to his own health, he did not curtail his travelling between Stainmore and Newcastle as autumn turned to winter. Exposure to the often fierce December weather prevalent in both locations was exactly what his weakened lungs did not require. Despite medical advice he refused to change his routine and had been in Newcastle as usual when he failed to return to Rampson as expected on the evening of Friday 9 December 1932. Although failing to return was not unprecedented, not writing to explain his delay was so, and Polly contacted the Newcastle police late that evening from the nearest telephone.

Early on the Saturday morning the police forced their way into 40 Grey Street and found him dead in the sleeping quarters of his office. He was lying on the floor adjacent to his camp bed. As a sudden unexplained death, an inquest was required and Polly, who had travelled to Newcastle before learning of his death, was obliged to identify his body in the presence of the City Coroner, Sir Alfred Appleby.[382] Her evidence to him at the hastily convened inquest was widely reported in both the Newcastle and Westmorland newspapers:

> It was explained by Mrs Polly Bracken the widow, that her husband was in the habit of sleeping at his office during the week and returning to Stainmore at week-ends. His chest was affected by war service and since the war he had suffered from bronchial asthma. Recently he had suffered from blood pressure.

The police evidence was that they had found him between his camp bed and the fireplace and after he was found the police surgeon had attended the scene prior to removal of the body. He provided the coroner with the credible theory as to what had happened just before his death:

> The theory that the deceased got up during the night to light a fire, and collapsed, was advanced by Dr Blench, the Newcastle Police surgeon, at the inquest in the city on Saturday.

Dr Blench also stated, in the absence of a post-mortem, that all the indications were consistent with death by heart failure within twelve hours of his discovery. Unsurprisingly Sir Alfred agreed and recorded a verdict of "death from natural causes." On the death certificate he recorded the cause as chronic bronchitis and heart failure. Although his death came most unexpectedly to his wife and children and he doubtless would not have wished to inflict the trauma of a coroner's inquest on Polly, three years earlier he had written highly approvingly of his hero John Peel having "kept on till the end came."

Thomas Wilson, after a lifetime of not giving in to adversity, was unsurprisingly not attracted to retirement or to a less active life. Now he had achieved an end equivalent to Peel's in the saddle: in his office, after completing his last week's work.

Taken back to his beloved Westmorland, his funeral took place at St. Michael's in Brough, three days after the inquest and in the afternoon of the day that the *Penrith Observer* had announced his death under the prominent headline, "Tragic Death of Captain Bracken, Stainmore. Collapse in Newcastle Office." He was buried next to his daughter Mary and to the sound of the tolling of his ancestor John Brunskill's great sixteenth century bell.

Shocked by his sudden death at 67, his family must have been comforted by the obituaries which appeared in Newcastle, the *Observer*, and in the other Westmorland local, *The Herald*, published on the following Saturday. They are silent on Africa and his other professional achievements – perhaps because their best source Robert was in Argentina. They mention his war service in France with the Royal Engineers but without much elaboration. Of them all, unsurprisingly the *Observer's* tribute to its correspondent was the most comprehensive and deserves selective quotation:

> *Captain Bracken… was a popular figure on Stainmore, where his engaging manner, and willingness to take part in anything useful to the district he made his home, had gained for him a host of friends.*
>
> *The deceased gentleman… took an active part in the locality. He was widely read and ungrudgingly placed his experience at the disposal of his neighbours.*
>
> *Despite his age in 1915, he took a commission with the Royal Engineers and saw service in France…*
>
> *He was a staunch Conservative…*
>
> *For many years he had acted as voluntary correspondent to the Penrith Observer and often contributed "letters to the Editor" on subjects of both local and general interest. In his writing he displayed originality and clarity of thought.*

As a mark of his popularity and possibly due to his funeral having taken many of his friends unaware, on Sunday evening 18 December a memorial service was held for him at St. Stephen's, Stainmore. His friend the Vicar of Stainmore, Charles Holland, spoke the tribute. His words were quoted in a newspaper report of the service under the headline "A Christian and a Gentleman." Again quoting selectively from his words as reported:

So long as there is a church and a Christian community on South Stainmore, so long will the name and memory of Captain Bracken be honoured, respected and loved.

I think it may truly be said that Captain Bracken more than any man in connection with the history of this church, has left his mark upon it. I most sincerely believe that to him this church was very truly the House of God.

Such was the beauty and humility of his nature that nothing displeased him more than that public mention should be made of anything that he did for the church.

There has gone from our midst one of the finest types, all too few at the present day, of what one looks for in a Christian and a gentleman.

Absent from both funeral and memorial service was his eldest son Robert. News of his father's death had been telegraphed to Argentina and on 19 December Robert, his wife and young daughter boarded the *Asturias* in Buenos Aires. They arrived at Southampton just prior to the year's end. For Polly one happy result of her husband's death was that she saw her son for the first time in over five years and her two-year-old grandchild for the first time.

At some point following his arrival at Rampson, Robert travelled to Newcastle. He cleared his father's office, disposed of the lease of the upper floors of 40 Grey Street and severed the family's long connection with the city. In April 1933 having settled his father's business affairs, he returned to Argentina and to further work on its railways.

In a further tribute, all of the various professional Institutes and Associations in which Thomas Wilson had so fully involved himself, marked and recorded his death in the early months of 1933.

Perhaps appropriately, given that his concern with matters spiritual was never absent from his temporal concerns and considerations, his final obituary appeared in the Carlisle diocesan magazine in January 1933. It is by far the most personal and heartfelt tribute from its experienced clerical author. In a more secular age, parts of it seem remarkable for a layman:

The loss of Captain Bracken to the Church on Stainmore is colossal. He was one of England's gentlemen. From long experience in the Ministry in many different parts of England and among many different types and classes of people it has never before been my privilege to meet or work with a more congenial colleague than Captain Bracken. A more modest or more courteous gentleman it would be impossible to meet.

His long experience from personal knowledge of the work of Church missions in Africa was always of great interest to those of us who were interested in such work.

It will be difficult, as the years go by, not to mourn his loss more and more as we realise it more fully, but I feel quite sure that the most fitting memorial we could offer him... would be a greater zeal and love for Church and Master he loved and served so well.

People of Captain Bracken's type are all too few in the Church today, but the old saying is still very true that "God buries His workman but carries on his work." Let us then thank God for Captain Bracken's life and pray that his work of love and care for his Church may be carried on from generation to generation.

At Brough he rests anonymously, in the shadow of the fine old church, in the company of generations of his Brunskill ancestors; in blissful ignorance that both his beloved Westmorland and the British Empire are no more; surrounded by the lush beauty of the 'Plains of Heaven' and the unchanging hills and fells he loved so well.

NOTES

The most frequently used works are abbreviated as follows:

Chatham, 1921 *The Work of the Royal Engineers in the European War*,
R E Chatham, 1921.

Chatham, 1952 *The History of the Corps of Royal Engineers*, Vol. 5,
R E Chatham, 1952

DNB *Oxford Dictionary of National Biography*

Pevsner *The Buildings of England - Northumberland*,
Nikolaus Pevsner, 2001

Other repeated citations are referred to by author only, or by author and abbreviated title, after the first full citation. Citations starting MAF and CO refer to National Archive catalogue numbers.

1 F. W. Garnett, *Westmorland Agriculture 1800-1900*, 1912
2 a person who occupies his own farm and land
3 Graham Smith, *Something to Declare 1000 years of Customs and Excise*, 1980
4 Ibid
5 John Venn, *Alumni Cantabrigiensis*, 1922
6 The Clergy of the Church of England Database 1540-1835, www.theclergydatabase.org.uk
7 B. Nightingale, *The Ejected of 1662 in Cumberland and Westmorland*, 1911
8 1774-1843
9 The township of Brough was divided into two divisions, Church Brough containing the church and castle and Market Brough containing the commercial centre as the name suggests
10 H. L. Clarke & W. N. Weech, *History of Sedbergh School 1525-1925*, 1925
11 1873 Post Office Directory
12 21 September
13 *Letters and Papers of the Reign of Henry VIII, 1537,* catalogued by James Gairdner, vol.1 498, 609
14 Gairdner vol. 2 1339
15 F. W. Garnett
16 MAF 68/264
17 1789-1854
18 Thomas Balston, *John Martin 1789-1854 His Life and Works*, 1947. Refers to Stainmore as a possible location of the painting

341

19 Barras station at 1,115 feet was the highest mainline station in England until the record was taken over by Dent station when the Settle-Carlisle line opened in 1876
20 1788-1864
21 DNB
22 *The Universal British Directory* of 1791
23 Brian Coe, *Guide to Early Photographic Processes*, 1983
24 Henry Lowther Clarke, 1850-1926
25 Richard S. Ferguson, *Cumberland and Westmorland MPs 1660-1867*, 1871
26 Thomas Bracken in 1889, Hannah Bracken in 1895
27 *History Topography and Directory of Westmorland* 1885
28 Lord of the manor of Brough. A descendant of Lady Anne Clifford 1590-1676, only child of George Clifford 3rd Earl of Cumberland
29 *History Topography and Directory of Westmorland* 1885
30 *Cumberland and Westmorland Herald,* 24 December 1932
31 *Kirkby Stephen Grammar School 1566-1966.* Together with short accounts of other endowed schools in the area
32 Moderations – Oxford's first public examination usually taken at the end of the first year
33 *Clergy List* 1864/*Crockford's Clerical Directory* 1878
34 Doctor of Civil Law. Appropriately he also sat as a magistrate
35 Owen Chadwick, *The Victorian Church*, 1970
36 From its foundation in 1341 the College expressly favoured members from the counties of Cumberland and Westmorland
37 Kendal market has been held on a Saturday since the 12th century. Charter of King Richard I
38 A small drink of alcohol
39 Approximately half way between Lowgill and Tebay in the centre of the Lune gorge
40 Its author was the Rev. E. L. Cutts
41 *Kirkby Stephen Grammar School 1566-1966*
42 Owen Chadwick
43 Roy Jenkins, *Gladstone*, 1995
44 *History Topography and Directory of Westmorland* 1885
45 *Kirkby Stephen Grammar School 1566-1966.* That at South Stainmore was built for 80 children. That at North Stainmore for 48 children. *Kelly's Directory of Westmorland* 1914
46 1495-1568. Created first Baron in 1544 for defeating the Scots at Solway Moss and later sacking Dumfries. His armoured effigy is in the Wharton Chapel at Kirkby Stephen. *Historical Kirkby Stephen and North Westmorland,* R. R. Sowerby, 1950
47 *Kirkby Stephen Grammar School 1566-1966*
48 J. D. Chambers & G. E. Mingay, *The Agricultural Revolution 1750-1880*, 1966

49 Import duties on dairy produce, live animals, meat and hams were reduced in 1846 and the remainder abolished in 1860

50 The Stainmore agricultural return for 1870 records 1 acre of wheat, 4 of barley and 20 of oats. MAF 68/264

51 J. D. Chambers & G. E. Mingay

52 A. N. Wilson, *The Victorians*, 2002

53 J. D. Chambers & G. E. Mingay

54 196 feet high

55 W. R. Mitchell & David Joy, *Settle-Carlisle Railway*, 1966

56 Where a further change of train was then required

57 Great Northern Railway

58 London & North Western Railway

59 It opened for passenger use on 1 May 1876

60 60% over budget

61 Frederick Houghton & Herbert Foster, *The Story of the Settle-Carlisle Line*, 1948

62 Ibid

63 The longest Blea Moor is 2,629 yards long

64 The longest Ribblehead or originally called Batty Moss is 440 yards long

65 1822-1880

66 DNB

67 Dawn Robertson, *The Plains of Heaven,* 1989

68 *Cumberland & Westmorland Advertiser,* 21 November 1876

69 1851-1920, Vicar of Wray on Windermere and later vicar of Crosthwaite and rural dean of Keswick. In 1893 he was made a Canon of Carlisle

70 Joseph Pease married Emma Gurney of the Norfolk Quaker banking family. The Gurneys' bank eventually became Barclays

71 1799-1872. MP for South Durham 1832-1841. The first quaker MP and together with his father responsible for the creation of the Stockton & Darlington Railway

72 George Flynn, *The Book of Darlington*, 1987

73 Ibid

74 The name is misleading. The trams were horse drawn until 1903

75 1828-1903, eldest son of Joseph and created 1st baronet in 1882. MP for South Durham and subsequently Barnard Castle

76 Bridge construction began in 1882 and it was opened by the Prince of Wales on 4 March 1890

77 1817-1898. Created 1st baronet on completion of the bridge

78 1840-1907. Created KCMG on completion of the bridge

79 1812-1896

80 After Baker's 1895 Presidency he remained on the council until his death in 1907

81 1799-1881

82 George Flynn
83 Robert Woodhouse, *Darlington a Pictorial History*, 1998
84 'Darlington – 50 years ago', quoted in George Flynn
85 C. P. Shedd, *History of the World's Alliance of YMCAs*, 1955
86 *Newcastle YMCA 150 years*, YMCA, 2005
87 First published in 1866
88 1829-1906. Dale merits an entry in the DNB on account of his pioneering work in applying the principles of arbitration to industrial disputes
89 1847-1900
90 G. Whittle, *The Railways of Consett and North-West Durham, 1971*
91 published 1870
92 John Davies, *Cardiff and the Marquesses of Bute*, 1981
93 1841-1891
94 The Butes' Durham estate was part of the 1737 dowry brought by Alice Clavering of Axwell Park, Winlaton (John Davies, *Cardiff and the Marquesses of Bute*, 1981)
95 G. Whittle
96 A. S. Wilson, *The Consett Iron Company*, M Phil thesis, Durham University, 1973
97 1836-1904
98 George Stephenson was born at Wylam in 1781
99 the location of the nearest North Eastern Railway station
100 Sunday 5 April
101 17 March 1868
102 Cardiff Castle was one of Lord Bute's seats. Alex Johnson, *High Spen a Hundred Years*, 1980
103 *History Topography and Directory of the County Palatine of Durham*, 1894
104 *Reid's Handy Colliery Guide and Directory*, 1891
105 Thomas Woof married Hannah Mary Bracken on 4 May 1893
106 Alex Johnson
107 part of the Chester-le-Street Division
108 A. S. Wilson
109 His brother Hubert had joined in 1877
110 1810-1900. Mayor of Newcastle 1850. President of the ICE in 1882. Inventor of the breech loaded rifle
111 A. N. Wilson
112 1849-1909. Council Member of the ICE 1903-1906
113 Born 27 December 1873
114 99 Westmorland Road
115 Ed. Lawrence Popplewell, 1985
116 Midland Railway. 72 miles of track between Settle and Carlisle. Built 1869-1876
117 Meriel Buxton, *David Livingstone,* 2001

118 *History, Topography and Directory of Westmorland,* 1885
119 1858-1896 son-in-law of Queen Victoria
120 E. L. Langston, *Bishop Taylor Smith,* 1939
121 1834-1905
122 Metropolitan Railway, Crystal Palace Railway, London, Chatham and Dover Railway (to Blackheath Hill)
123 R. E. Faulkner, *Hill, First Bishop in Western Equatorial Africa,* 1895
124 Born 1845, in East Rainton, Durham
125 Not until 1891 was free elementary education up to the age of ten introduced
126 In the 1901 census the Trotter family are living at 'Robney', Middle Rainton (the following entry is for the Rectory) and Thomas Trotter now 69 is described as a 'horsekeeper'; his wife Jane and twelve-year-old son are also listed
127 Robert died in East Rainton on 25 September 1899 aged nineteen of Otitis Media Meningitis. His given occupation is "ticket clerk at a colliery"
128 Polly was aged fifteen when Dora Bracken died
129 His youngest daughter and last survivor of his children
130 Founded in 1878 and now known as the University of Western Ontario
131 Crockford's, 1900
132 Prior to this he had served on several royal commissions. In the year of his elevation, 1895 he was elected president of the Iron and Steel Institute
133 HM Royal Yacht *Britannia* displaces 4,715 tons
134 Then the Gold Coast Colony
135 The first class cabin fare was approximately £30
136 Compiled by F. B. Archer
137 1897-1898 Edition
138 Founded by George Goldie in 1886 and given a Royal Charter to control the area of the River Niger
139 Kristin Mann, *Slavery and the Birth of an African City – Lagos 1760-1900,* 2007
140 Colonial Office Blue Book 1900
141 In 1869 Portugal abolished the slave trade. It was the last European country to do so. Brazil did not follow suit until 1888
142 Now Ghana
143 A West African tribe long associated with shipping
144 R. E. Faulkner
145 Payne, *Principal Events in Yoruba History,* 1893
146 The headquarters of the Nigerian Railway Corporation remain at Ebute-Metta today
147 Frederic Shelford, *Development of West Africa by Railways,* ICE, 1904
148 Lagos Official Hand Book 1897-1898
149 Sir Gilbert T. Carter KCMG

150 1836-1914

151 Dennis Judd, *Radical Joe, a life of Joseph Chamberlain*, 1993

152 Frederic Shelford, *On West African Railways*, African Society, 1902

153 Lagos Official Hand Book 1897-1898

154 *The Engineer* 25 February 1898 has a photograph of the Denton Bridge under construction.

155 *The Yoruba Mission*, CMS, 1906

156 Now Shaki, Nigeria. Near the source of the Ofiki River, the chief tributary of the Ogun, 40 miles from the Benin border

157 Now Benin

158 On 1 January 1900 the shareholders of the Royal Niger Co were bought out and its territories were transferred to the British Government. The new territory was sub-divided into the Protectorates of Northern and Southern Nigeria with the territory of the Niger Coast Protectorate being absorbed by the latter

159 1858-1945

160 Thomas Pakenham

161 Bussa is now covered by Lake Kainji

162 Thomas Pakenham

163 West Indian Regiment

164 Thomas Pakenham

165 Nikki is now in Benin

166 KCMG 1901

167 *The Lagos Weekly Record,* 9 March 1901

168 On 20 August 1897 Sir Ronald Ross discovered malaria parasites while dissecting a mosquito

169 1871-1943, third son of William Shelford and from 1899 in partnership with him as Shelford & Son

170 Although it is evident from his speech prior to departure as reported in the *Consett Chronicle* that he did anticipate some form of annual leave to England

171 Operating between Hamburg and West Africa since 1890

172 Founded in 1873 as an 'Approved Foundation' it was designed to provide a university education at a lower cost than the University's traditional colleges in an attempt to widen the University's social base – probably suggesting that Hill did not have access to substantial family funding in the 1870s. It was not a success. Cavendish College closed in the early 1890s and its buildings became home to Homerton College in 1894

173 Baedeker's 1890 *Guide to Great Britain* refers to there then being 1,500 workers in the town's lace factory

174 1672-1746. Builder of St. George's, Hanover Square, London 1712-1725

175 Hill's income amounts to £528 pa. Thomas Wilson's 1898 pay of £80 per month,

which as already noted was a substantial sum, is £960 pa

176 William MacGregor, 'Lagos, Abeokuta and the Alake,' African Society lecture. July 1904.

177 Steamers for West Africa departed up to eight times a month at this time. Frederic Shelford, 'On West African Railways', African Society lecture, 8 April 1902.

178 Sir A. C. Burns, *History of Nigeria*, 1936

179 64 miles from Lagos

180 Frederic Shelford's lecture 'On West African Railways', April 1902, reproduced in *African Affairs (London) 1902* part 1 page 339–354. At the lecture the photograph was shown by magic lantern slide.

181 Francis Jaekel, *The History of the Nigerian Railway*, 1997, Vol. 2

182 Derived from the Olumo Rock, the town's most famous landmark and a sacred site to the Egba people

183 Francis Jaekel, Vol. 2

184 1795-1865. Founder of the Institute. Wood had been colliery manager at Killingworth where he met George Stephenson (1781-1848). They both worked on building "the Bluther" steam engine and Wood accompanied Stephenson on his famous visit to Edward Pease in Darlington in 1821. In 1825 Wood wrote *A Practical Treatise on Railroads* and was one of the judges at the Rainhill steam engine trials in 1829

185 Reproduced by Francis Jaekel in *The History of Nigerian Railway,* Vol. 3

186 Richard Knights had replaced William Gee in 1898 when he resigned due to ill health

187 Frederic Shelford, *Some Features of West African Government Railways*, ICE, 1912

188 Mainly derived from the local Egba and Yoruba tribes

189 1854-1925

190 A. N. Wilson

191 Ibid

192 His replacement was Field Marshal Lord Roberts (1832-1914) whose Chief of Staff was Major-General Kitchener

193 3 February 1900 was National Intercession Day: Hill would have held a prayer service for the troops in South Africa at St. George's church

194 In fact it was merely the start of a guerrilla war which the British Army was to deal with brutally by a policy of farm-burning and internment camps. Not until 31 May 1902 was peace finally established at Vereeniging

195 Oluwole had obtained his Durham BA at Fourah Bay College, Sierra Leone, which was affiliated to Durham University in 1876

196 Frederic Shelford, *Development of West African Railways,* ICE. 1904

197 A northern Nigerian tribe

198 C. J. George who had come out from London to represent the Colonial Secretary at the opening ceremonies

199 The tribal ruler of Lagos

200 The other tribal elders of Lagos who wore white robes

201 1847-1919; Governor of Lagos 1899-1904. Declared Queen Victoria's sovereignty over British New Guinea 1888 for which he was rewarded with the KCMG. Represented the West African Colonies and Protectorates at the coronation of Edward VII in 1902

202 The train journey currently takes approximately two hours and 45 minutes along the same track. Nigerian Railway Corporation

203 The train journey currently takes approximately five hours

204 Sierra Leone, Gold Coast and Lagos

205 Much of the criticism was party political and Chamberlain, having spoken in terms of promoting business and balance sheets (rather than Imperial expansion and state building) when authorising expenditure on the railways, left himself open to this attack

206 KCMG

207 The estimate for the Lagos-Abeokuta section was £391,771. The actual expenditure was £460,120. By modern standards, a 17% over-run on a government project seems quite modest

208 Hers was number 189 of 500

209 *Post Office London Directory* 1882

210 Saturday 26 March 1904

211 Pevsner

212 Ward's *Directory of Newcastle* 1898

213 *The Engineer*, 25 May 1906

214 Ibid

215 DNB

216 Marshall, *Biographical Dictionary of Railway Engineers*, 2003

217 W. Howitt, *Visits to Remarkable Places*, 1842

218 Shield & Turner, *Guide Book to Newcastle upon Tyne*, 1846.

219 Numbers 42-50

220 Joan Foster, *Newcastle upon Tyne*, 1995

221 Transactions of The Institution of Mining Engineers, Vol. XXXIX 1909-1910

222 Henry A. Mess, *Industrial Tyneside A Social Survey*, 1928

223 Isle of Wight

224 Pevsner

225 Liberal MP for Carlisle. Speaker 1895-1905

226 James W. Lowther Unionist MP for mid-Cumberland (Penrith) and himself Speaker 1905-1921

227 Dr John Percival 1834-1918. Bishop of Hereford 1895-1918. Formerly headmaster of Rugby 1887-1895. President of Trinity College, Oxford 1879-1887 and headmaster of Clifton College 1862-1878

228 Henry James Tufton, 1st Baron Hothfield, 1844-1926

229 A grandson of the second Earl of Lonsdale & Unionist member for North Cumberland since 1900

230 DNB

231 Lyall Wilkes and Gordon Dodds, *Tyneside Classical*, 1964

232 M. Barke and R. J. Buswell, *Newcastle's Changing Map*, 1992

233 Ian Ayris, *A City of Palaces*, 1997

234 William Bracken (1802-1885) Thomas Wilson's great-uncle

235 Pevsner

236 Joan Foster

237 R. J. Q. Adams, *Balfour The Last Grandee*, 2007

238 Ibid

239 Kerry's subsequent election petition merely served to increased the Liberal majority to five

240 It was not brought into public use until 1 October 1906

241 *The Engineer*, 6 July 1906

242 Joan Foster

243 Ibid

244 CO 520/85

245 Colonial Office Blue Books.

246 The railway bridge was completed in 1916: Sir A. C. Burns

247 712 miles from Lagos, Francis Jaekel

248 Thomas Pakenham, *The Scramble for Africa*, 1991

249 CO 520/85

250 Principal port of the Niger delta

251 Resident Engineer 1908

252 Francis Jaekel, Vol. 1

253 The shipping line's letter inquiring of known next of kin is on the Colonial Office file

254 CO 520/70

255 DNB

256 Francis Jaekel, Vol. 2

257 General Elections were at the time staggered across the constituencies over a period of several weeks rather than everyone voting on the same day

258 Roy Jenkins, *Asquith*, 1964

259 i.e. John Bull, the English working man

260 (1837-1922) Liberal MP for Morpeth 1874-1918

261 Patron Saint of Sweden and 12th century King of Sweden
262 Roy Jenkins
263 Ibid
264 R. Adams, *Bonar Law*, 1999
265 Ibid
266 Richard Holmes, *The Western Front*, 1999
267 Ibid
268 by Sir W. Goscombe John, R.A. 1923
269 Not for themselves but for their country
270 British Field Service Regulations Part 1. 1909
271 Gary Mead, *The Good Soldier. Douglas Haig,* 2007
272 Chatham, 1952
273 Ibid
274 Ibid
275 Initially it was limited to the unmarried and childless widowers but was later extended to include married men of the same age
276 Chatham, 1952
277 Chatham, 1921
278 *The Penrith Observer,* Tuesday 19 April 1921
279 Total casualties from aerial bombing of the UK were 670 killed and 1960 injured. Gregor Dallas, *1918 War and Peace*, 2000
280 Chatham, 1952
281 Richard Holmes
282 Alan Wilkinson, *The Church of England and the First World War*, 1978.
283 *Raymond Asquith: Life and Letters*, ed. John Jolliffe, 1980
284 Malcolm Brown, *The Western Front*, 1993
285 Julian Putkowski and Julian Sykes, *Shot at Dawn*, 1989
286 Jolliffe
287 Now Botswana
288 On 26 January D Company's officer strength increased to three with the arrival of 2nd Lieut. D'Abreu
289 Mary Soames, *Speaking for Themselves*, 1998
290 Martin Gilbert, *Winston S. Churchill,* vol. III 1914-1916
291 26 January 1916
292 Bound by military secrecy Churchill could not disclose his whereabouts to his wife but his reference to it as a 'little town' is something of an exaggeration
293 Martin Gilbert, *Winston S. Churchill*, vol. III 1914-1916
294 Jules-Jean Vynckier, 1855-1941, Curé Ploegsteert, 1908-1936
295 Martin Gilbert, *Winston S. Churchill,* vol. III 1914-1916
296 Ibid. The original of this painting hangs at Chartwell

297 Ibid
298 Mary Soames
299 Ibid
300 Martin Gilbert, *Winston S. Churchill* vol. III 1914-1916
301 Chatham, 1921
302 Chatham, 1952
303 Martin Gilbert, *First World War*, 1994
304 Ibid
305 Robin Prior & Trevor Wilson, *The First World War*, 1999
306 Ibid
307 Ibid
308 Chatham, 1952
309 Klijte, Belgium
310 Down from 241 at the beginning of 1916
311 Martin Gilbert, *First World War*
312 Ibid
313 I am indebted to Mrs P. Worsdale for use of the papers of Private Briggs and to the Trustees of the Imperial War Museum for permitting access to them.
314 Robin Prior & Trevor Wilson
315 Martin Gilbert, *First World War*
316 Major and Mrs Holt's *Battlefield Guide The Western Front – North,* 2007
317 Girardet et al, *Somewhere on the Western Front,* 2003
318 Chatham, 1952
319 Robin Prior & Trevor Wilson
320 Martin Gilbert, *First World War*
321 Girardet et al
322 1/4th Battalion Cameron Highlanders, 51st (Highland) Division
323 *The Bickersteth Diaries,* ed. John Bickersteth, 1995
324 Chatham, 1952
325 Ibid
326 Martin Gilbert, *First World War*
327 Robin Prior & Trevor Wilson
328 Martin Gilbert, *First World War*
329 Girardet et al
330 Chatham, 1952.
331 Robin Prior & Trevor Wilson
332 Martin Gilbert, *First World War*
333 Ypres-Roulers and Ypres-Comines
333 Quoted in *Passchendaele*, Peter Barton, 2007
335 Chatham, 1921

336 Jolliffe
337 Martin Gilbert, *First World War*
338 Barton
339 Ibid
340 Ibid
341 Ibid
342 Martin Gilbert, *First World War*
343 Chatham, 1921
344 Peter Barton
345 Ibid
346 Later he became a colonial governor. Among his governorships was Tasmania 1875
347 Amiens although briefly taken by the Germans in 1914 was not to suffer severe war damage until the German spring offensive of 1918
348 Chatham, 1921
349 Ibid
350 British territory since 1898 when China granted Britain a 99 year lease.
351 now Shandong.
352 Later in the CRE diary, 20/11/17, an exchange rate of 5 francs = £0/3/8, is provided
353 1850-1942, 3rd son of Queen Victoria and an uncle of George V
354 Martin Gilbert, *First World War*
355 22 December 1917
356 Martin Gilbert, *First World War*
357 Gary Mead
358 Ibid
359 Harold Nicolson, *King George The Fifth*, 1952.
360 Martin Gilbert, *First World War*
361 I am grateful to Mr W. J. Allan for use of the papers of Miss Dalgleish and to the Trustees of the Imperial War Museum for allowing me access to them.
362 Martin Gilbert, *First World War*
363 Harold Nicolson
364 As previously the *London Gazette* struggled to keep up and his promotion was not announced officially until 1 October 1918
365 Martin Gilbert, *First World War*
366 Ibid
367 A special reserve cavalry regiment
368 *Kirkby Stephen Grammar School 1566-1966*
369 George Flynn
370 The 1919 *Guide to Darlington*
371 1921 Census

372 Monday-Saturday

373 Henry Mess

374 31 March 1921

375 1847-1927, Accountant and steel maker, 1st baronet. Died at Ingmire Hall 24 February 1927

376 A £500 reward was offered for information leading to a conviction for the suspected incendiarism. *Penrith Observer*, 15 January 1929

377 1872-1961, Bishop of Carlisle 1920-1946

378 Principal of St. Edmund Hall, Oxford 1913-1920

379 *Whitakers Almanack* 1920.

380 *Coal Mining in County Durham,* 1993, Durham County Council

381 Pevsner

382 HM Coroner for the City and County of Newcastle-upon-Tyne 1906-51

INDEX

'TWB' is used as an abbreviation for Thomas Wilson Bracken.

Military names and ranks are given as they appear in the source documents. They may therefore be abbreviated or not reflect the full career of the individual.

Similarly civil honours and titles are given as referred to in the source documents: where an individual is generally known by one name (eg Disraeli), alternative names (eg Beaconsfield) are not indexed.